Hieronymus Bosch

Masterpieces of Art

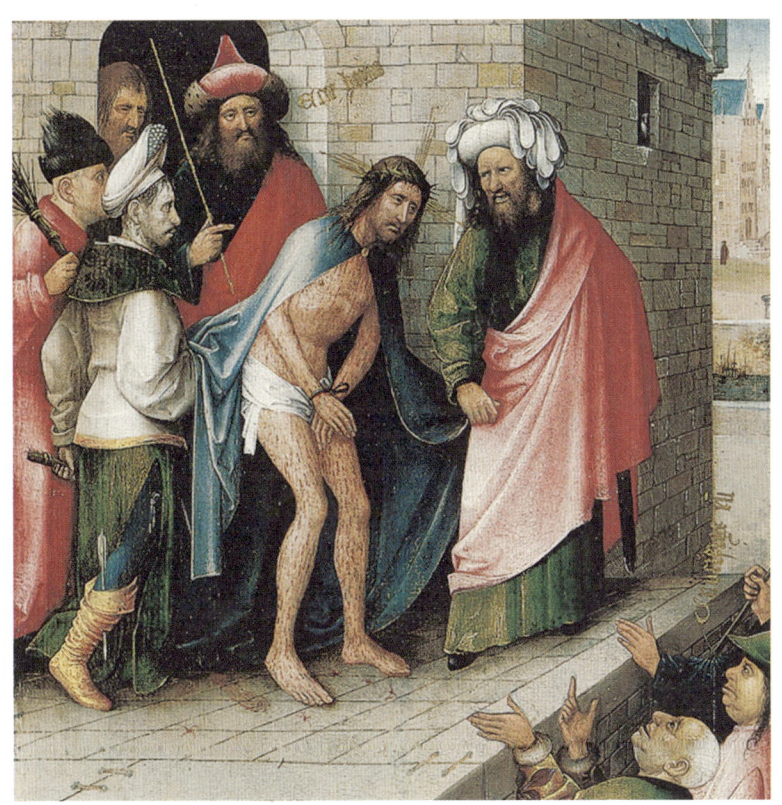

Publisher and Creative Director: Nick Wells
Commissioning Editor: Polly Prior
Senior Project Editor: Catherine Taylor
Picture Research: Jérémie Lebaudy
Art Director & Layout Design: Mike Spender
Copy Editor: Anna Groves
Proofreader: Dawn Laker
Indexer: Helen Snaith

FLAME TREE PUBLISHING
6 Melbray Mews
Fulham, London SW6 3NS
United Kingdom

www.flametreepublishing.com

First published 2016

25
3 5 7 9 10 8 6 4

Front cover: *The Garden of Earthly Delights: Allegory of Luxury*
Courtesy of Bridgeman Images/Prado, Madrid, Spain

Back cover: *The Temptation of St Anthony* (left panel detail)
Courtesy of Bridgeman Images/National Museum of Ancient Art, Lisbon, Portugal

Image credits: Courtesy **akg-images**/Erich Lessing: 9, 91. Courtesy **Artothek** and the following: 54–55 Christie's Images Ltd; 42 Hans Hinz. Courtesy **Bridgeman Images** and the following: 6, 116 Ashmolean Museum, University of Oxford, UK; 7 Bibliotheque Municipale, Arras, France; 76, 77, 96, 97 Groeningemuseum, Bruges, Belgium/© Lukas - Art in Flanders VZW; 119, 120, 121 Louvre (Cabinet de dessins), Paris, France; 10 & 98c & 99, 53 Monasterio de El Escorial, Spain; 11 & 64–65 Musee d'Art et d'Histoire, Saint-Germain-en-Laye, France; 48, 49 Musee des Beaux-Arts, Valenciennes, France; 118 Musees Royaux des Beaux-Arts de Belgique, Brussels, Belgium; 17 & 38 Musees Royaux des Beaux-Arts de Belgique, Brussels, Belgium/De Agostini Picture Library; 13 & 41 Museo Lazaro Galdiano, Madrid, Spain; 57 Museu de Arte, Sao Paulo, Brazil/De Agostini Picture Library/G. Dagli Orti; 8 & 52, 56 Museum Boijmans van Beuningen, Rotterdam, The Netherlands; 40 Museum voor Schone Kunsten, Ghent, Belgium/© Lukas - Art in Flanders VZW/Photo: Hugo Maertens; 37 National Gallery, London, UK; 14 & 70–71 & 93, 31, 92 & 94, 95 National Museum of Ancient Art, Lisbon, Portugal; 4 & 39 Palacio Real de Madrid, Spain; 15 & 16 & 67, 20 & 84 & 85, 21 & 78 & 79, 66 Palazzo Ducale, Venice, Italy/Cameraphoto Arte Venezia; 12 & 87 Prado, Madrid, Spain; 22 & 45, 24 & 106, 25 & 29 & 86, 32 & 50 & 51, 34–35 & 58–59, 72–74, 88, 89, 101, 104, 105, 107–115 Prado, Madrid, Spain; 18 & 75 Prado, Madrid, Spain/Index; 23 & 68–69 San Diego Museum of Art, USA/Gift of Anne R. and Amy Putnam; 122 The Israel Museum, Jerusalem, Israel/Vera & Arturo Schwarz Collection of Dada and Surrealist Art; 3 & 81, 80 & 82, 83 Upton House, Warwickshire, UK/National Trust Photographic Library. Courtesy **Getty Images** and the following: 90 DeAgostini/G. NIMATALLAH; 1 & 47, 19 & 46, 43 Fine Art Images/Heritage Images/Hulton Fine Art Collection; Courtesy **www.metmuseum.org**/John Stewart Kennedy Fund, 1913 36; Courtesy **National Gallery of Art, Washington**/Samuel H. Kress Collection: 61r & 63; Courtesy Wikimedia Commons: 26 & 117, 27 & 102–03 & 125, 28 & 61l & 62, 30 & 124, 33, 44, 60, 123.

ISBN: 978-1-83562-286-5

Printed in China I Created, Developed & Produced in the United Kingdom

Hieronymus Bosch

Masterpieces of Art

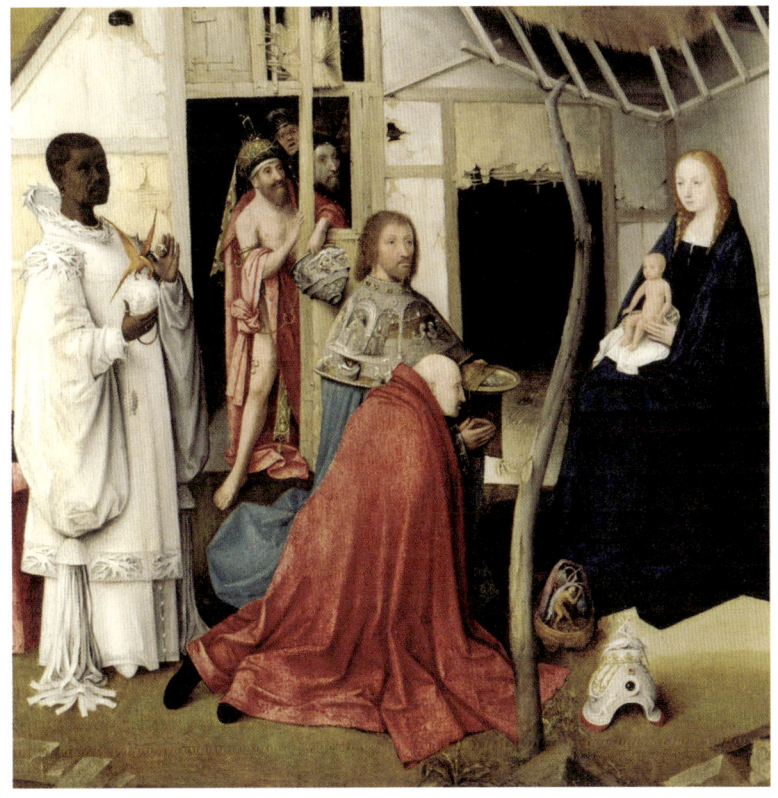

Rosalind Ormiston

FLAME TREE
PUBLISHING

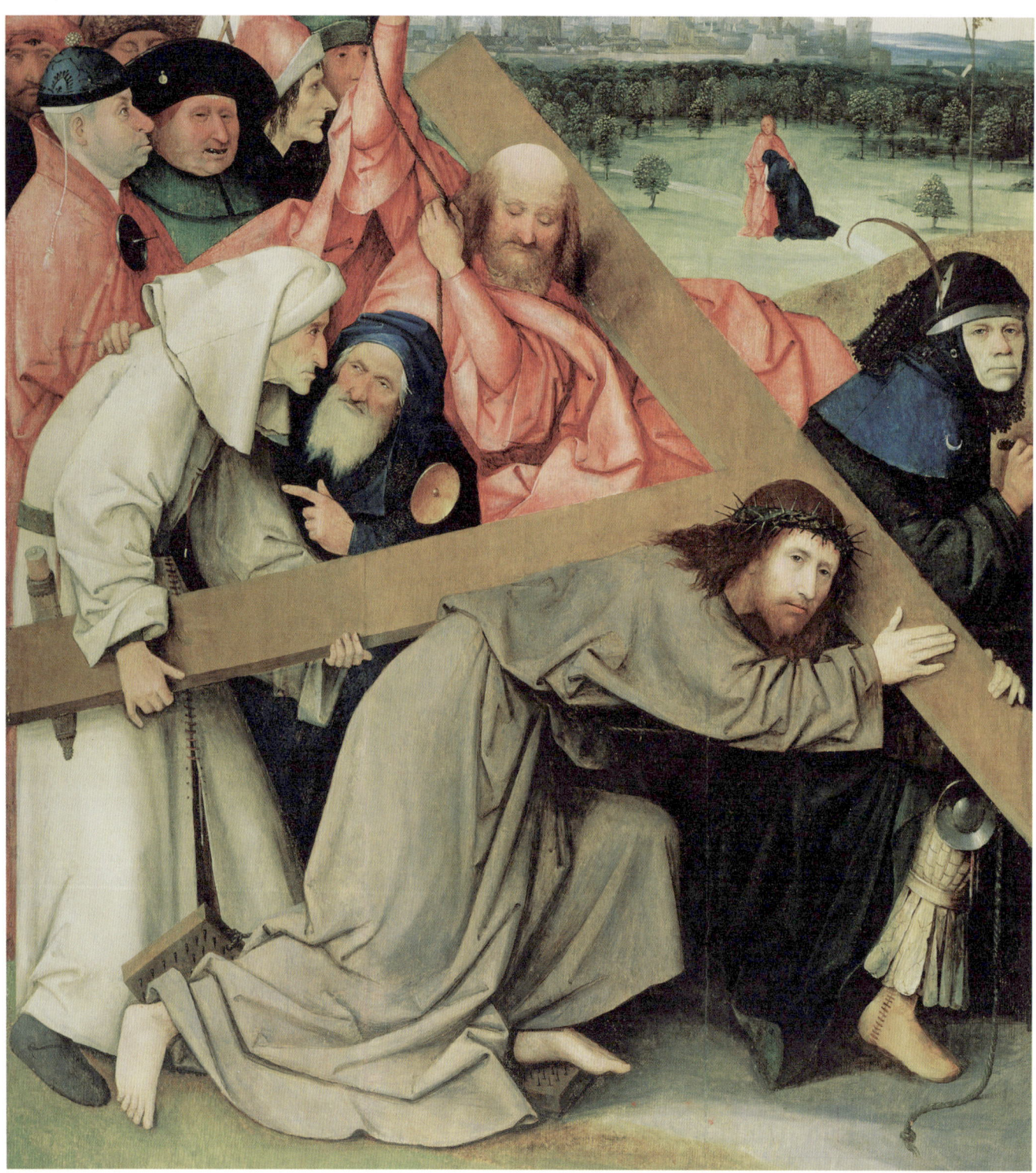

Contents

The World According to Hieronymus Bosch

The Early-Netherlandish artist Hieronymus Bosch (*c.* 1450/55–1516) stands out for his fantastical, wondrous art full of strange creatures both grotesque and heavenly. Twenty-five paintings and 19 drawings by the painter and draughtsman are all that remain of the heritage of one of the Netherlands' most progressive and elusive artists.

The Devil's Painter

More than half of the works ascribed to the artist are religious representations. They are traditional in Christian content and symbolism, following the deep-rooted beliefs of the Roman Catholic Church in the fifteenth century. The artist's depictions, such as *Adoration of the Magi*, *c.* 1470–75 (*see* page 36), *The Last Judgement*, *c.* 1486 (*see* pages 76–77) and *Ecce Homo*, *c.* 1500 (*see* page 47), are pillars of biblical narrative and Christian worship. And yet it is Bosch's marvellously hellish monsters, which appear in some works, that have led to his reputation as 'the devil's painter'. He was a masterful painter of many small, fabulously shocking, details.

Birthplace

Known today as Hieronymus Bosch (Jheronimus Bosch in the Netherlands), he was born Jheronimus Anthonissen van Aken in 's-Hertogenbosch, Noord Brabant, a large market town, later a cathedral city, not far from the Belgian and German borders. A watercolour drawing, *Panoramic View of 's-Hertogenbosch*, *c.* 1530, by the Flemish topographical artist Anthonis van den Wyngaerde (*fl.* 1510–72), shows the prosperous walled city from an elevated point to the south-west (*see* below). Canals and waterways thread through the city's density of houses, and the Gothic church of Sint Jan (Saint John) dominates the skyline.

Bosch died in 's-Hertogenbosch on 9 August 1516, aged around 60 to 65, possibly a victim of the pleurisy epidemic that gripped the city in 1515–16. A drawing in charcoal and red chalk on paper, *Portrait of Hieronymus Bosch*, *c.* 1550 (*see* right), is perhaps the earliest extant portrayal of the painter. It is attributed to Valenciennes-born artist Jacques le Boucq (1520–73), who may

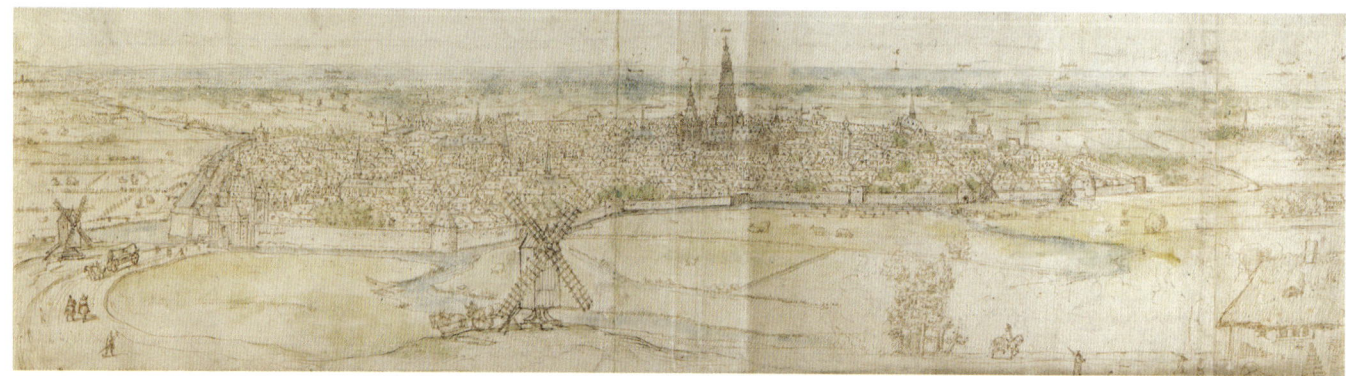

have copied it from a late (now lost) self-portrait by Bosch. If it is a genuine likeness, it suggests that Bosch had earnest, calm features and even ventures to give some idea of his mode of dress.

A Professional Signature

Hieronymus took the name 'Bosch' from the town where he was born, and where he is thought to have lived all his life. In the medieval era, artists were often associated by name with their birthplace, such as Lucas van Leyden (1489/94–1533); or place of work, such as the Master of Alkmaar (died 1540); or by a familiar alias alongside their birth name, such as Jan Mostaert (1475–1555), also known as the Master of Oultremont. Bosch began his career as a professional artist using his family name 'van Aken', and became known as Bosch around 1490–1500. His works were undated, but he signed some in Gothic letters 'Jheronimus Bosch'. Highly skilled copies of his works, once considered originals due to the inclusion of this signature, have been revealed by recent research to be not by his hand. That Bosch chose Gothic lettering suggests he associated himself with the late medieval period, rather than the emerging Classical Renaissance from Italy.

A Celebrated Painter

Limited details are known about the artist. He left no letters or diaries. Any correspondence he may have had with his patrons regarding the prestigious commissions he received has not survived. Official documents and the journals and writings of courtiers and contemporary historians are the few glimpses that cast light into his world. What has been ascertained comes from official papers in the municipal accounts in 's-Hertogenbosch, in addition to Bosch's close involvement with the Illustrious Brotherhood of Our Blessed Lady, an elite religious group in his home city. A record of his funeral conducted by the Illustrious Brotherhood refers to him as *seer vermaerde scilder* ('celebrated painter'), which shows the esteem in which he was held.

Bosch's Family

Hieronymus Bosch's family were originally from Aachen, Germany, hence his family surname of Aken, or Aeken. He was born into a

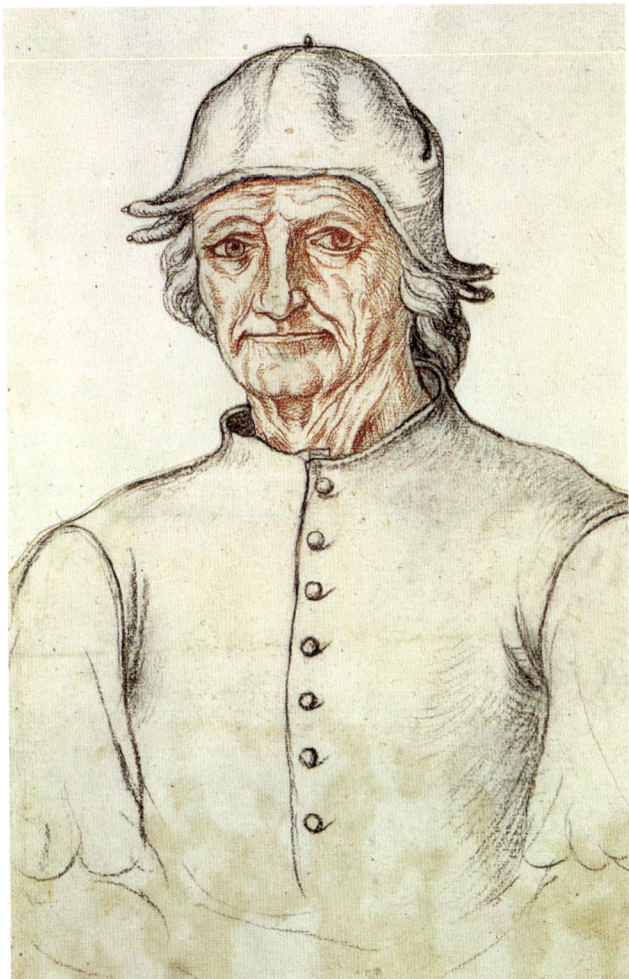

household of painters and craftsmen with a busy and prosperous workshop. Three generations of his family – his grandfather, Jan van Aken (died 1454), his father Anthonius van Aken (c. 1420–78) and three of his uncles – were successful painters. Bosch's elder brother Goossen (c. 1444–98) inherited the workshop when their father died. Their nephew Anthonius Goossenz (c. 1478–1516) was an artist too. Bosch's grandfather was mentioned in the archives of the cathedral-church records of 's-Hertogenbosch from 1430, and he or one of Bosch's uncles may have painted a Crucifixion fresco there, around 1444. The family workshop, which specialized in fresco painting and wood gilding, was on the east side of Markt Square, the main square in 's-Hertogenbosch, from 1462–1523. Bosch lived there until his socially rewarding marriage to the slightly older Aleid van de Meervenne in 1480. The marriage brought prestige, wealth and an estate as well as influential contacts, but it produced no children. At the time of

his marriage, Bosch moved into his new wife's home on the more expensive north side of the Markt Square, whilst continuing to work in the family workshop scarcely a hundred yards away.

Historical Rule in the Time of Bosch

When Bosch was born, *c.* 1450, the Netherlands were ruled by the Burgundian dynasty (*c.* 1000–1482). His birthplace was one of many towns that were formed during an intense period of growth during the eleventh and twelfth centuries, allowing local lords, the landowners, a charter to set up a community. It expanded the population of the Netherlands, led to a growth in new towns and resulted in a very prosperous nation. In 1419, Philip III (reigned 1419–67), known as Philip the Good, Duke of Burgundy, took control of many new territories, including Flanders, and limited the powers of the chartered cities. In 1465, he established the States General in Brussels and a Grand Council to control and unite all the former feudal estates, including Noord-Brabant. The Council had financial and judiciary power throughout the Netherlands. It led to unrest between 1429 and 1470, from territories trying to regain control, but this was eventually supressed.

's-Hertogenbosch

Today, as the capital city of Noord-Brabant, 's-Hertogenbosch (colloquially referred to as Den Bosch) attracts thousands of visitors, who come to see the birthplace of its famous painter-son Hieronymus Bosch. It was founded in 1185 by the noble Hendrik van Brabant, in his ducal domain of Orthen, and was the first Dutch town to receive city status. The 's' of 's-Hertogenbosch stands for 'des' in Des Hertogen Bosch, which translates as 'The Duke's Forest'. The oldest part of the city, initially around nine hectares in size, has the Markt Square at its centre. *The Cloth Market in 's-Hertogenbosch* (*De Lakenmarkt van 's-Hertogenbosch*), *c.* 1530, by an unknown Netherlandish painter (*see* right), shows the central Markt Square, where trade is busy and the covered stalls take up half of the square. The highly coloured bolts of dyed cloth are clearly visible. The painting gives a visual account of the houses in the centre of 's-Hertogenbosch, the citizens, their style of dress and the busy market. His marital home, named Inden Salvatoer, was on the north-east side of the Markt, situated in the middle of the row of houses on the right. His family's home and studio-workshop was on the south-east side of the market place.

Town Expansion

Situated at the convergence of the rivers Dommel and Aa, where the first moats of the city walls were built, 's-Hertogenbosch's series of waterways and canals points towards its status as a trading city, both agricultural and commercial. Its growing economy led to the city's need for fortified second city walls and more land. The waterways, now expanded, were collectively known as the Binnendieze. Houses were built with the Binnendieze at the rear, to facilitate a 'water street' for workshops with trades in brewing, leather, metalwork and cloth and artisan industries. The town had a commercial reputation for organ building and knife manufacture as well as a bell foundry. Today the medieval moat and walls are reminders of this period, including the De Moriaan house on Markt Square, now the oldest stone house in the city, dating from the thirteenth century, and the medieval gatehouse of the convent of Zusters van Orthen. The expanding town had a Latin school run by the Brethren of the Common Life. The Rotterdam-born humanist Desiderius Erasmus (1469–1536) attended the school in the mid-1480s. Records show that 930 monks and nuns, of the Dominican, Franciscan and Carthusian orders, were living in 's-Hertogenbosch by 1500 with around 30 chapels and churches. 's-Hertogenbosch became the third-largest city in Brabant after Antwerp and Brussels. By 1495, the population of the city was 17,280, increasing to 25,000 in the 1500s.

's-Hertogenbosch Society

Bosch's name, alongside those of his sister and two brothers, were first published in 's-Hertogenbosch municipal records in 1474. While the details of his life are limited, much can be learned from the society and city in which he lived, his paintings and his patrons, and the documentation of the Illustrious Brotherhood of Our Blessed Lady, of which he was a loyal member. Local tax returns for Bosch show him in the top 10 per cent of wage-earners in the community, moving towards the top six per cent by the time of his death.

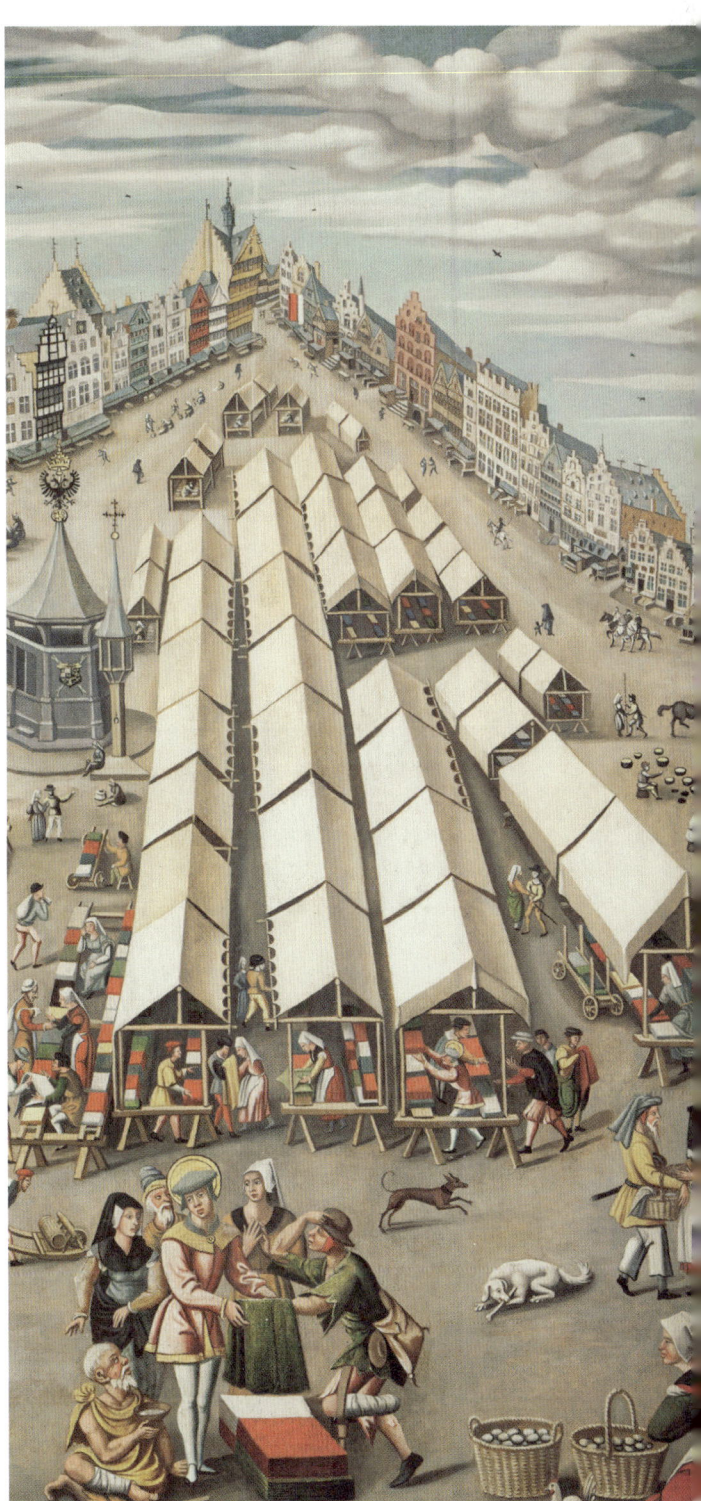

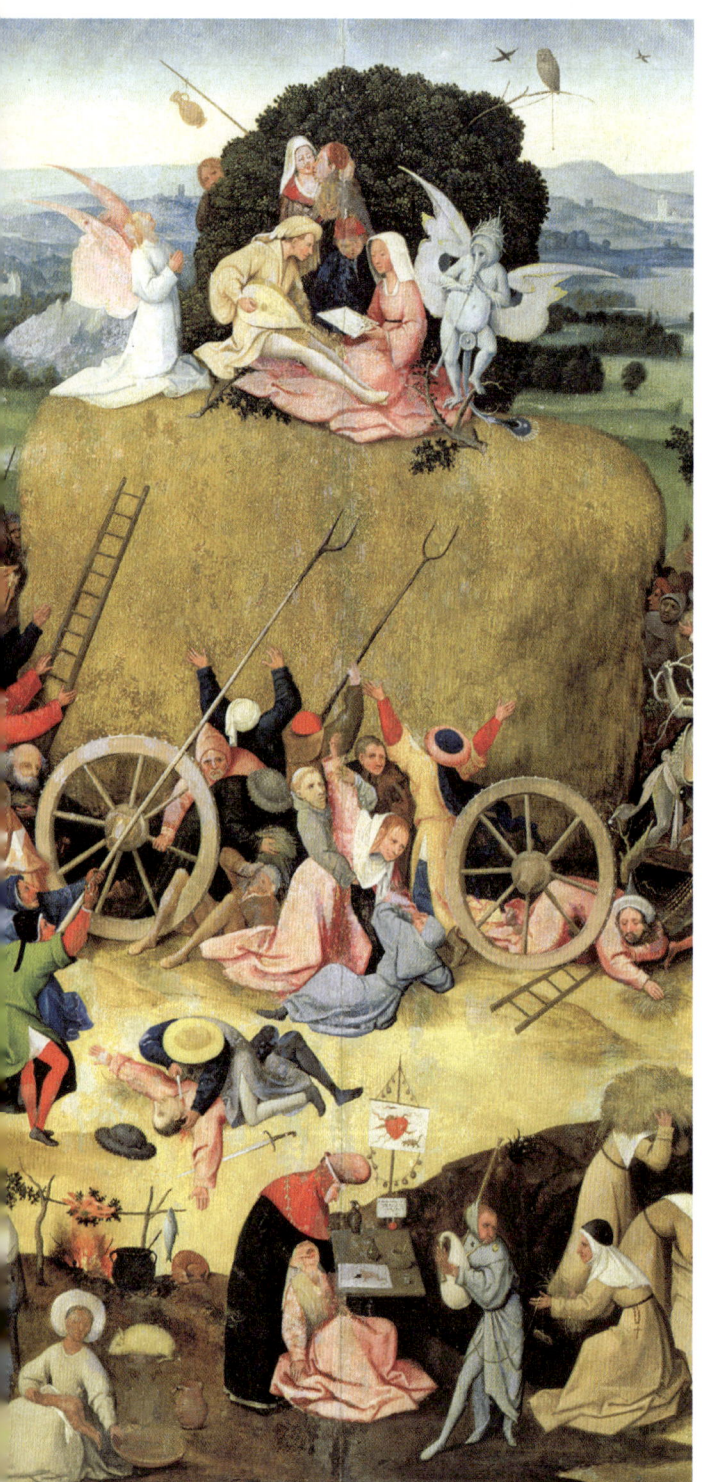

Workshop Practice

The Bosch workshop was well established in 's-Hertogenbosch, although the number of artists and assistants is not known. Recent research has uncovered various 'hands' painting the wooden panel-paintings attributed to Bosch, in addition to his own. It suggests that the painter's family of artists may have been involved in the completion of his larger works, such as the triptych *The Haywain*, 1510–16 (*see* pages 98–101), in addition to superb copies of original works by Bosch, such as *The Seven Deadly Sins and the Four Last Things, c.* 1480 (*see* pages 104–07). It would not be unusual for a popular work, particularly a secular work such as *The Conjuror, c.* 1502–20 (*see* pages 56–57), to be copied for artistic practice or further sales. This is obvious in the artworks painted on panels that were hewn from trees felled close to Bosch's death or after 1516. It follows that Bosch was the instigator of the original content, layout and colour pigments used, and others were possibly employed to help paint them with his direction.

The Artist's Originality

In the artworks attributed to Bosch, it is the different qualities of application that suggest more than one artist painting the work. Different versions of Bosch's art exist, and it is a difficult exercise to ascertain exactly which are the originals and which are copies by his studio or by followers. Research in 2015 revealed that many were not by Bosch, which is disconcerting when so few works remain. One should see the overall concept of a painting by Bosch as distinctive to him, notwithstanding help from his workshop. His extant drawings confirm his individualistic style and originality of content.

Peer Group

Artists in the Netherlands and Europe whose dates of birth or death coincide with Bosch bring to light interesting comparisons. Citations of Bosch and his artist-family are rare and so too are many of his Dutch peer group, such as Geerten Tot Sint Jans (c. 1455/65–85/95), born in Leiden. He took his name from the monastic Order of St John, where he lived as a lay brother and painted murals for the church.

He is acknowledged as the father of Northern Renaissance art. German artist Albrecht Dürer (1471–1528) is documented as visiting the Noordbrabant region and the town of 's-Hertogenbosch in around 1520. One can make comparisons between his art and that of Bosch, although Dürer made no mention of the artist or the workshop. One can even make comparisons with drawings by Leonardo da Vinci (1452–1519), such as a drawing in red chalk titled *Allegory with Wolf and Eagle*, *c.* 1508–16, also known as *Allegory of River Navigation* (Royal Library, Windsor), which relates to Bosch's boat-tree in *The Ship of Fools*, *c.* 1500–10 (*see* page 62), and the ugly, distorted faces in Leonardo's pen-and-ink drawing *A Man Tricked by Gypsies*, *c.* 1493 (Royal Library, Windsor).

Taught to Paint in the Workshop

It is known that Hieronymus was born into a successful family of artists. To have a grandfather, father, uncles and brothers all painters, plus one brother a sculptor, suggests that he was taught to paint by his father or family members, although there is no factual evidence. That he did not sign his earlier works leads to difficulties of attribution. Some extant works, such as *The Conjuror*, are highly skilled copies created during Bosch's lifetime or soon after his death. There are five known copies of *The Conjuror*, also known as *The Magician*. Another work formerly attributed to Bosch is the table-top painting *The Seven Deadly Sins and the Four Last Things*,

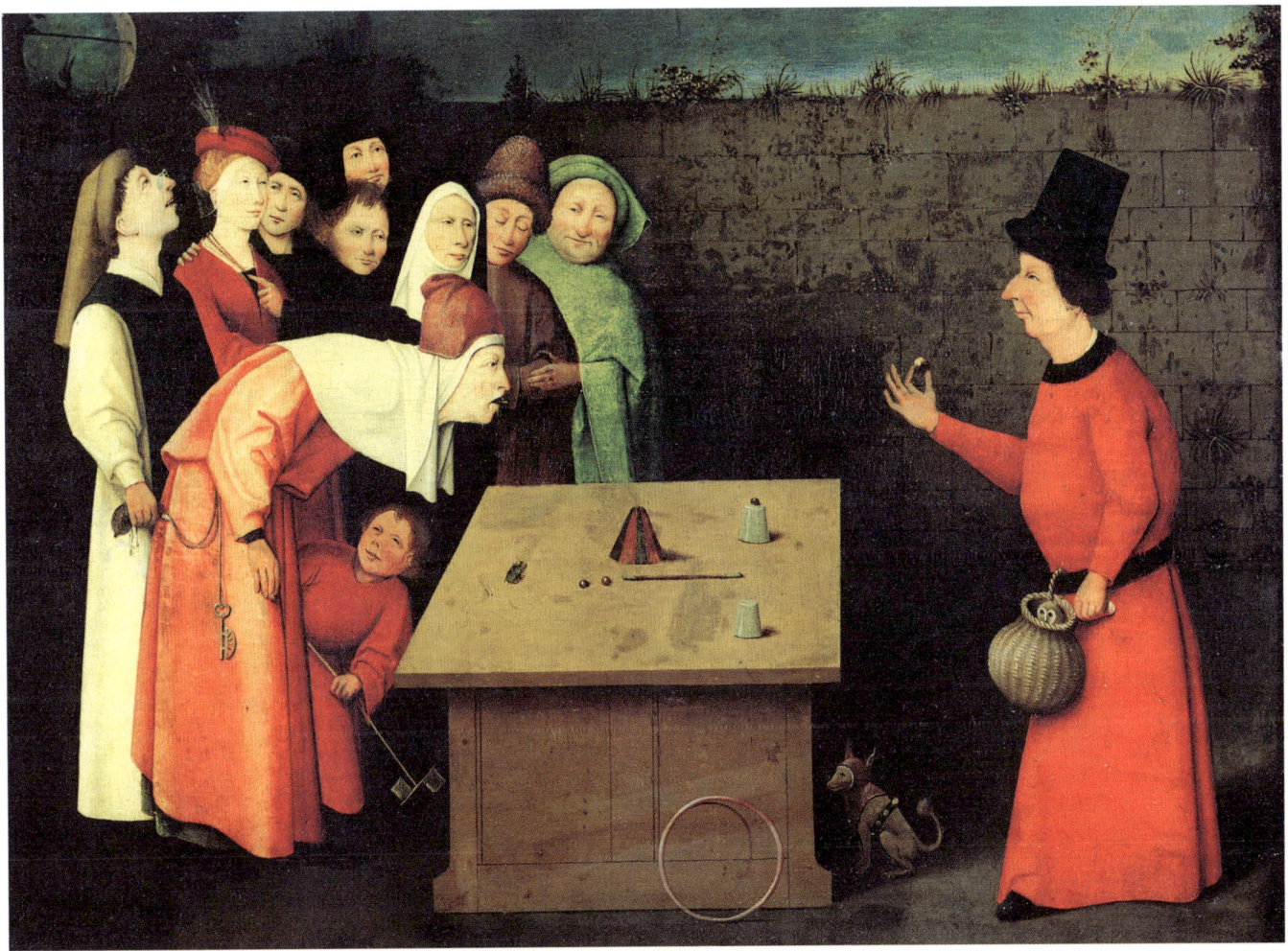

part of the royal collection of Philip II, now in the Prado Museum, Madrid. The king, a fervent admirer of 'El Bosco', may have prayed before this work. Research carried out by the Bosch Research and Conservation Project between 2010–15 confirmed it to be a highly skilled copy.

Fire Engulfs 's-Hertogenbosch

In 1463 over 4,000 homes in 's-Hertogenbosch were destroyed by fire. Bosch quite probably witnessed this catastrophe, and one can see visual indications of this memorable event in his paintings. Houses burning to ash light up his vision of Hell on the right wing of *The Garden of Earthly Delights* triptych, *c.* 1500 (*see* pages 86–89).

A village is engulfed by fire in the central panel of *The Temptation of St Anthony* triptych, *c.* 1501 (*see* pages 94–97), where the destruction of buildings lights up the night sky. The right wing of *The Last Judgement* triptych relates to his vision of a city on fire. In *The Haywain* triptych, the right-hand panel illustrates buildings on fire, a metaphor for Hell. The left wing of a pair of panels *The Hell and the Flood: Hell*, *c.* 1514–16, in the Boijmans Museum, Rotterdam, shows the Fall of the Rebel Angels, cascading through space toward the fiery bowels of Hell. An instantly recognizable medieval symbol for Hell was consummation by fire, which is seen in many of Bosch's panels, but are the buildings he portrayed the memories of what he had witnessed as a young man in his hometown?

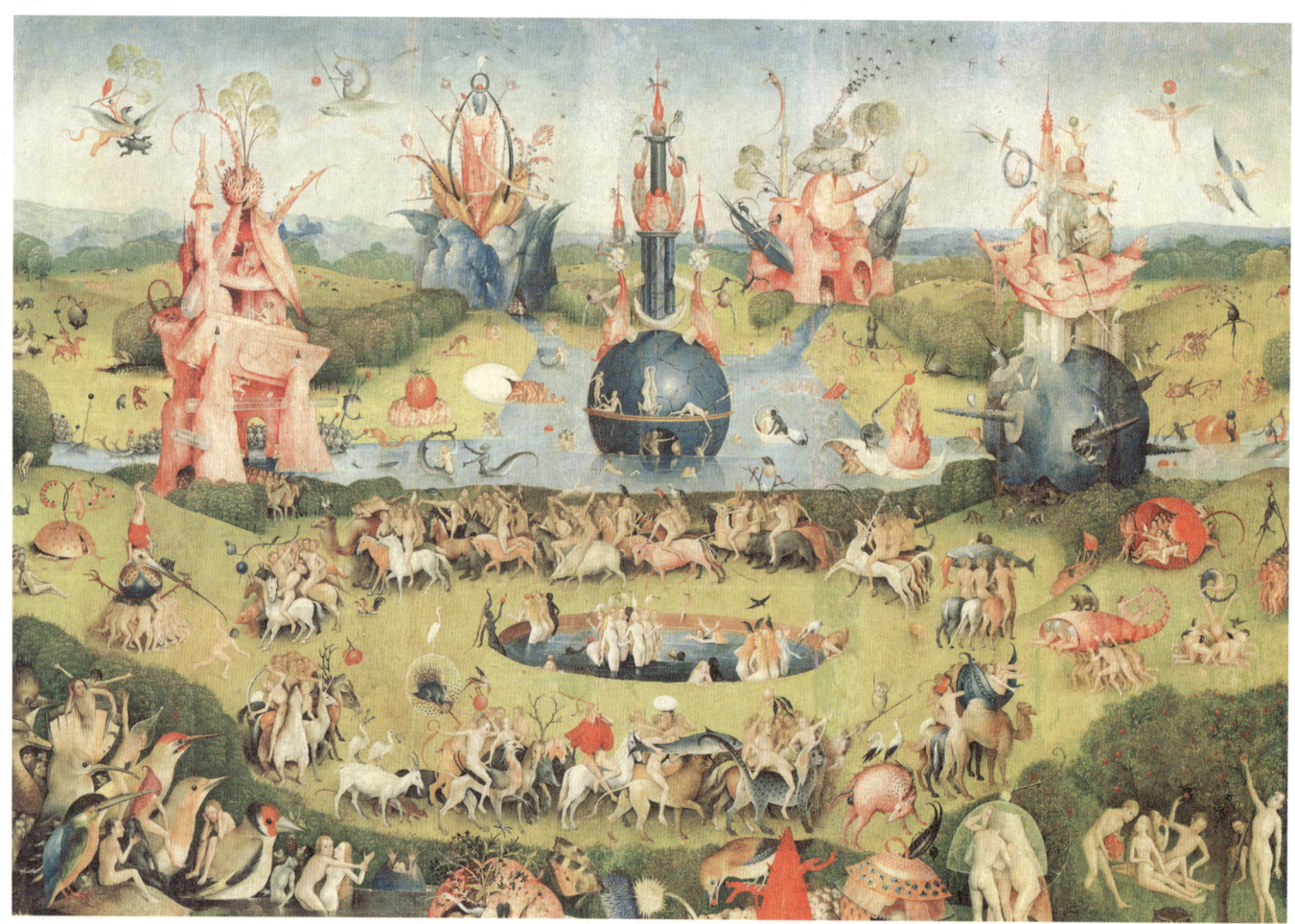

Sint Janskerk

The Romanesque origins of the Church of Saint John the Evangelist (Sint Jan) in s'-Hertogenbosch date to 1220–1366. It was built outside the original city walls. Today only the lower part of the original tower remains, having been replaced by the Gothic building, an architectural style known as Gothic-Brabant, that one can see today. From 1380 to 1559, the new church was built within the expanded city walls. Bosch, living close by, just a street away, would have grown up within the sight and sound of its construction, and watched masons creating the richly intricate decoration of its interior and exterior walls. Much later, in 1561, the church became the seat of a bishopric and thus given cathedral status.

Church Architects

At the time Bosch was nominated for membership of the exclusive Illustrious Brotherhood of Our Blessed Lady, the famous architect Alart du Hamel was building the Brotherhood's new chapel in the new church. The work was continued by Jan Heyns, a lay member of the group. Both architects worked on the new building, knocking down the remains of the Romanesque church, apart from the base of the original tower, to rebuild in the contemporary Gothic style. Heyns died of pleurisy in 1516, the same year as Bosch.

The Illustrious Brotherhood

In 1488 Bosch joined the *Illustere Lieve-Vrouwe-Broederschap* ('Illustrious Brotherhood of Our Blessed Lady'), a closely knit group of clerics, magistrates and notaries, essentially the elite of 's-Hertogenbosch, who engaged in the dedicated worship of the Virgin Mary at the Church of Saint John (Sint Jan). Bosch was a lay, not a religious member. The organization was founded in 1318 by Gerardus van Uden. Its focus was a venerated wooden effigy of the Virgin Mary and infant Christ, kept in the Church of Saint John. The Brotherhood, initially a group of clergy and scholars, had ordinary members and sworn members, and acted as a social network. Its first procession through the streets of 's-Hertogenbosch, to honour the Virgin Mary, was organized in 1367.

A Richly Decorated Chapel

From 1483 the group owned a property in Hinthamerstraat, close to the church, a house that was a gift from a 'brother' named Ghisbertus van der Gates. The present house was rebuilt in the neo-Gothic style in 1846 after its predecessor collapsed in 1839. The house, a museum of the Illustrious Brotherhood, is now a national monument. It stands close to Sint Jan Cathedral, where the Brotherhood installed a confraternity chapel in 1498 (now the Sacrament Chapel), richly decorated with an altar depicting scenes from the life of Mary, by Utrecht-born sculptor Adriaen van Wesel (c. 1417–c. 1490). It was created between 1475–77 and would have cost a large sum of money. It would later include paintings by Hieronymus Bosch.

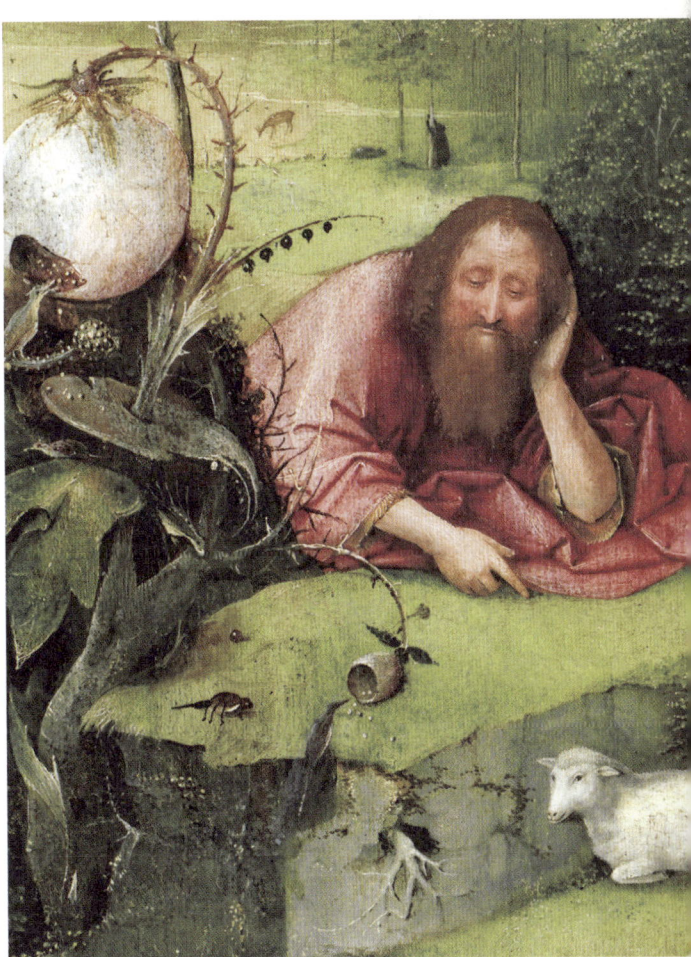

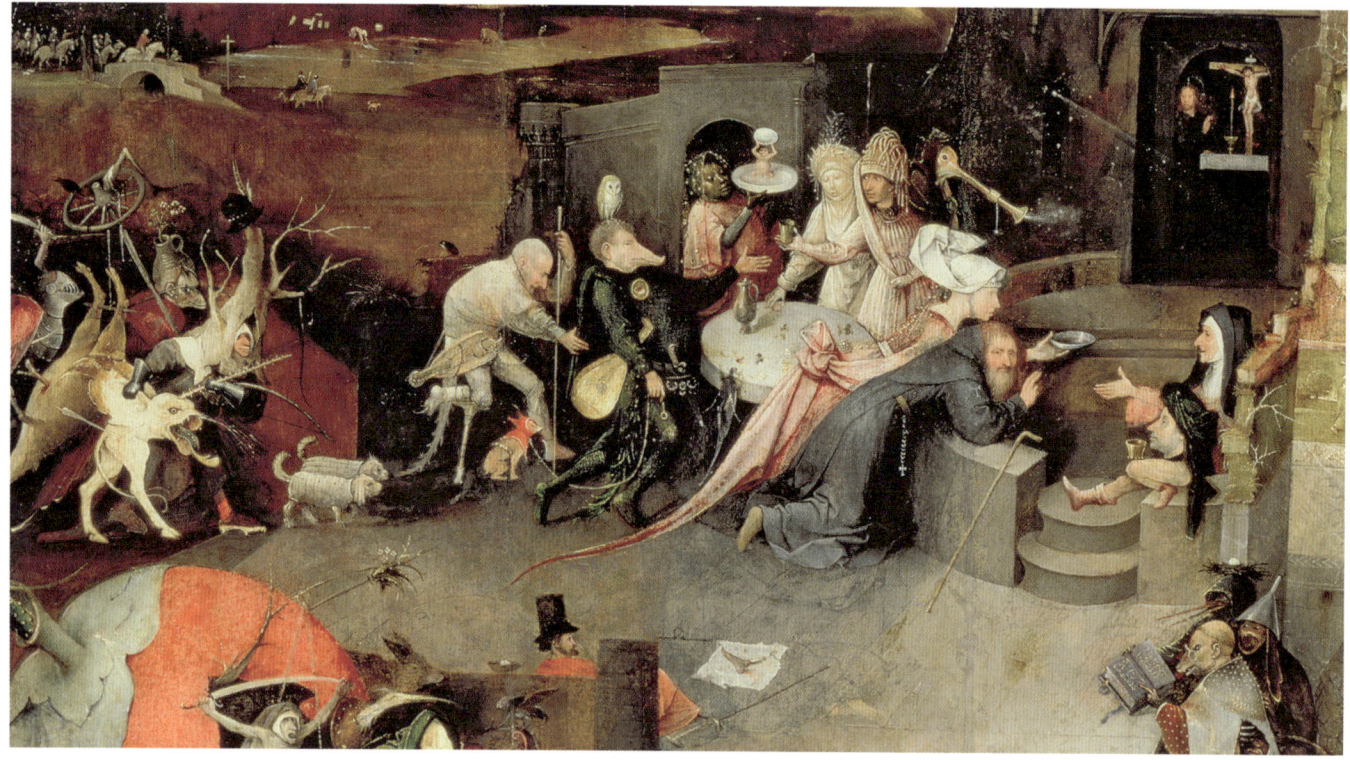

The Swan Brethren

The Brotherhood, funded by donations, contributions and membership fees, was also known as *Zwanenbroedershuis* ('Swan Brethren'), from their emblem and their donation of a swan each year for an annual banquet. The group was open to lay members, men and women living inside and outside the city walls and to nobility and high-status citizens such as Bosch. All contributed to relief of the poor in 's-Hertogenbosch and the continued promotion of the town as a centre of medieval music excellence since. When Bosch joined the exclusive group of 40 members in 1488, he held a 'swan banquet' in his house in July that year for members. One can see a swan brought in as part of a feast in the painting *The Marriage in Cana*, *c.* 1550, originally attributed to Bosch but now dated later and assigned to the work of a follower. Bosch's name 'Jereon Aken' is listed in the archive records. His wife may have been a lay member from the age of 16. Around this time he began signing his work with 'Bosch' as his surname.

In the Brotherhood archives, documentation shows that the fraternity sold 'indulgences', a device of the Roman Catholic Church to raise funds. Purchase of an indulgence was said to limit a person's time in purgatory, or aid their transition to Heaven. It was the sale of indulgences and other corrupt practices of the Catholic Church that led German monk Martin Luther (1483–1546) to begin a Reformation. Bosch would have been aware of this in the years before his death. Indulgences prove the strength of medieval people's belief in both an afterlife and the consequences of their behaviour on Earth contributing to that afterlife in either Heaven or Hell. This belief informs the content of Bosch's extant paintings, which concentrate on the journey towards an afterlife, visualized in *The Haywain* and other works.

Early-Netherlandish Religious Paintings

The majority of commissions for religious paintings in the Netherlands in the fifteenth century – prior to the Reformation – were much like those carried out in Italian cities. It was art destined for chapels, churches and religious communities, or for the nobility and rich merchant class as private devotional works. The iconography was usually based on a major biblical event, such as the Creation, the Garden of Eden, the Annunciation, the Nativity, the Passion of Christ, or the Lives of the Saints. Bosch created paintings on all these subjects, but historians have few details about who commissioned the works or where they were destined to end up. Triptychs such as *The Last Judgement*, *The Hermit Saints*, *c.* 1493 (*see* pages 72–75) and *The Temptation of St Anthony* would look entirely at home in a church. But could *The Garden of Earthly Delights* or *The Haywain*, with explicit scenes of torture or carnal frivolity, be accepted as an altarpiece in a church? There is no reference to either work in a church or chapel. Possibly they were private commissions. At first glance both works, filled with horrific depictions of torture and strange hybrid beast-like animals, seem unrelated to Christian teaching, but a close study of early Christian texts shows how Bosch brilliantly deciphered them, using shock and disgust to convey the full impact of his moralizing message, which would be readily recognized by learned clients.

Noble Patronage

The Duke of Burgundy, Philip the Handsome (1478–1506), may have purchased *The Temptation of St Anthony* as a gift for his father, and an altarpiece depicting *The Last Judgement*, in around 1504. After the death of Bosch in 1516, his art remained a collector's item. Three paintings by Bosch are documented as being in the possession of Cardinal Grimani of Venice in 1521. *Notizia d'opere di disegno* ('A notice of the works of design'), written by Marcantonio Michiel (1484–1552), is one of the most important primary sources on Venetian collections, which recorded panels by Bosch in the collection of Grimani. These are considered to be the four oil-on-wood panels, now known as the *Four Visions of the Hereafter*, 1505–15 (*see* pages 56–59), possibly bequested to the Venetian state on Grimani's death in 1523. Another work, *The Haywain* triptych, was purchased by Philip II of Spain (1527–98) in 1570 for his private collection. An admirer of the artist, he owned several works considered at the time to be by Bosch, or at least good copies. Bosch appealed to noble clients and one imagines they paid a high price for his work.

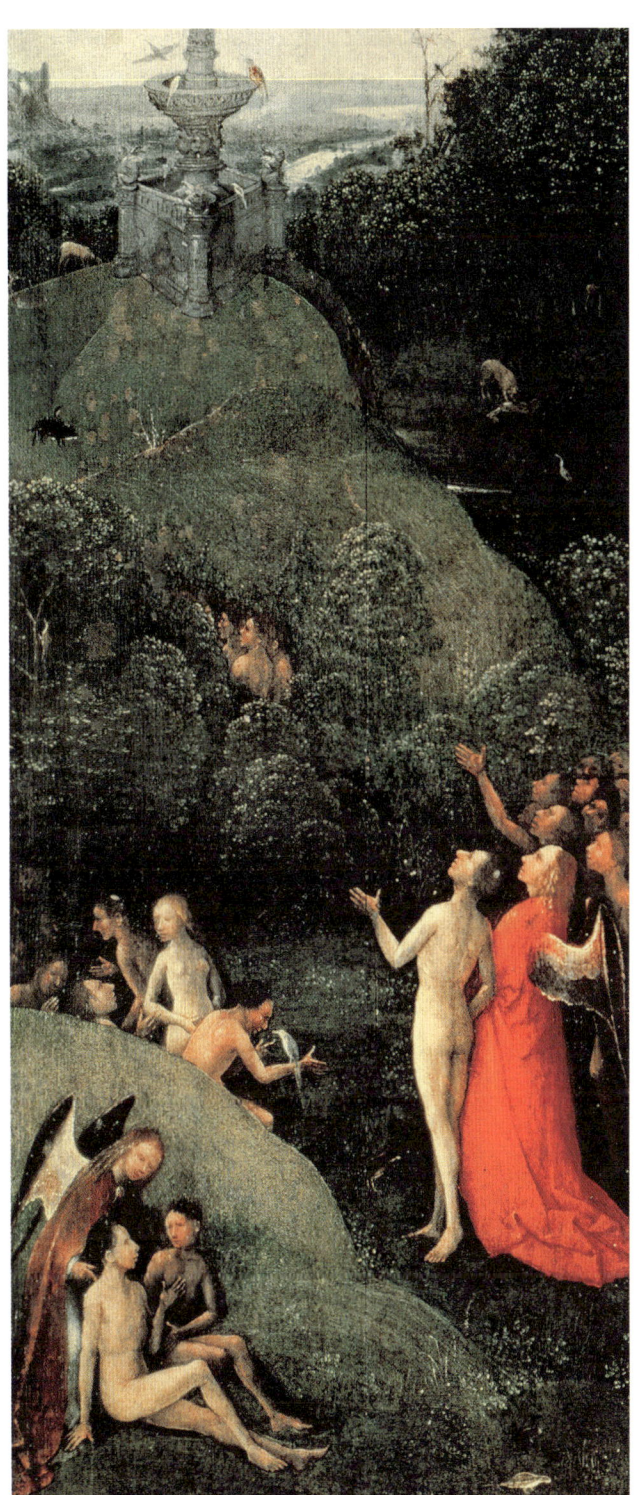

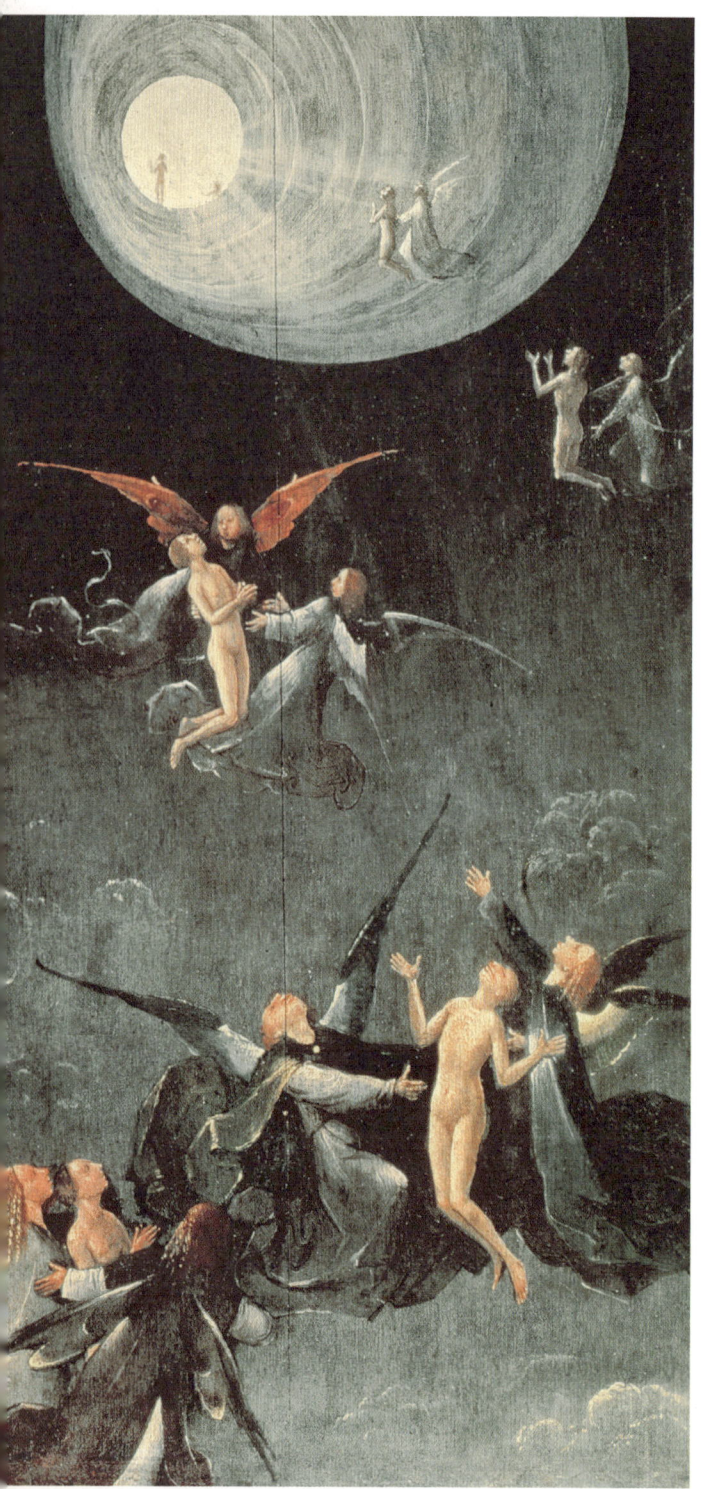

Triptychs

Bosch was engaged in the tradition of the devotional triptych – three-panelled paintings. He painted scenes with conventional figures, places and objects, such as the Three Wise Men at the scene of the Nativity in *The Adoration of the Magi, c.* 1495, made unique with the addition of creatures that represented evil in different guises. The contextual stories added to his comparative vision of the afterlife. The implication was that evil was inherent, even in the Garden of Eden, and the path to Heaven was clear only to those who remained supremely devout.

The Catholic Church was not above Bosch's criticism, even before the German reformer, the monk and scholar Martin Luther, pinned his 95 theses to the door of a chapel in Wittenburg, Germany. Bosch made overtly pointed reference to the greed and worldliness of the Catholic Church. *The Haywain*, a key work in Bosch's oeuvre, had a strong religious message, delivered through comedic and violent symbolism. It was one of the first paintings to depict an everyday scene, instantly recognizable to fifteenth- and early sixteenth-century audiences. It related the everyday to worldliness, greed, materialism; a profound warning, dressed up in a colourful scene, that every traveller was destined for Hell unless they were steadfast in religious faith.

Visions of the Afterlife

Four visualizations of what awaited sinners and the devout were strikingly illustrated by Bosch in an unsigned work: *Four Visions of the Hereafter*, 1505–15. The panels are divided between the option of horrific punishment in *The Fall of the Damned* and *Hell*, or divine reward in *Earthly Paradise* and *Ascent into Heaven*. The original commission for the works and the intended use for them have been lost. Imitation marbling painted on the reverse of each work, originally two in red, two in green, remains on three of the four panels.

Behold Bosch

A small owl, one of Bosch's representations of wisdom and evil, looks down from a window as an observer, on to the scene of Christ presented to the people in *Ecce Homo, c.* 1500.

Ecce Homo ('Behold the Man') is informed by the biblical narrative John 19:4–7. Below the figure of Christ, a group of citizens will decide if Christ should be freed or crucified. Bosch brings Christ's suffering for man into the heart of a contemporary community. Set within a city backdrop, with an alien red flag with white moon flying over castle ramparts, Christ is revealed to the people from an open platform of a building resembling a Dutch city hall. Bosch, closely following the *Ecce Homo* narrative, shows Christ introduced to the crowds by the dispassionate Roman prefect Pontius Pilate, wearing a red pointed hat. Christ, the 'Man of Sorrows', near-naked, wears a flesh-digging 'crown' of thorns, placed there by his jailors to symbolize his title King of the Jews. He sets Christ on a solid stone platform, pushed close to the edge above a baying mob of onlookers, made up of 'chief priests and officers' and Jews, who relish the sight of Christ's flogged, scourged and beaten body spurting blood, his bloodied footprints marking the stone surface. They shout (their words written in gold lettering): 'Crucify Him.' At left, below Christ, and set apart from the main crowd, a group of donors, facing towards the mob, calmly witness the proceedings. One figure, a Dominican monk, calls out (his words in gold): 'Save us O Christ Redeemer.' They were later painted out.

Contemporary Details

Christ Crucified with Donors and Saints (Calvary with Donors), c. 1480–90 (*see* page 32), set on a hill outside the city walls, contains a beautiful Boschian-type landscape. Beyond the crucifix, the eye

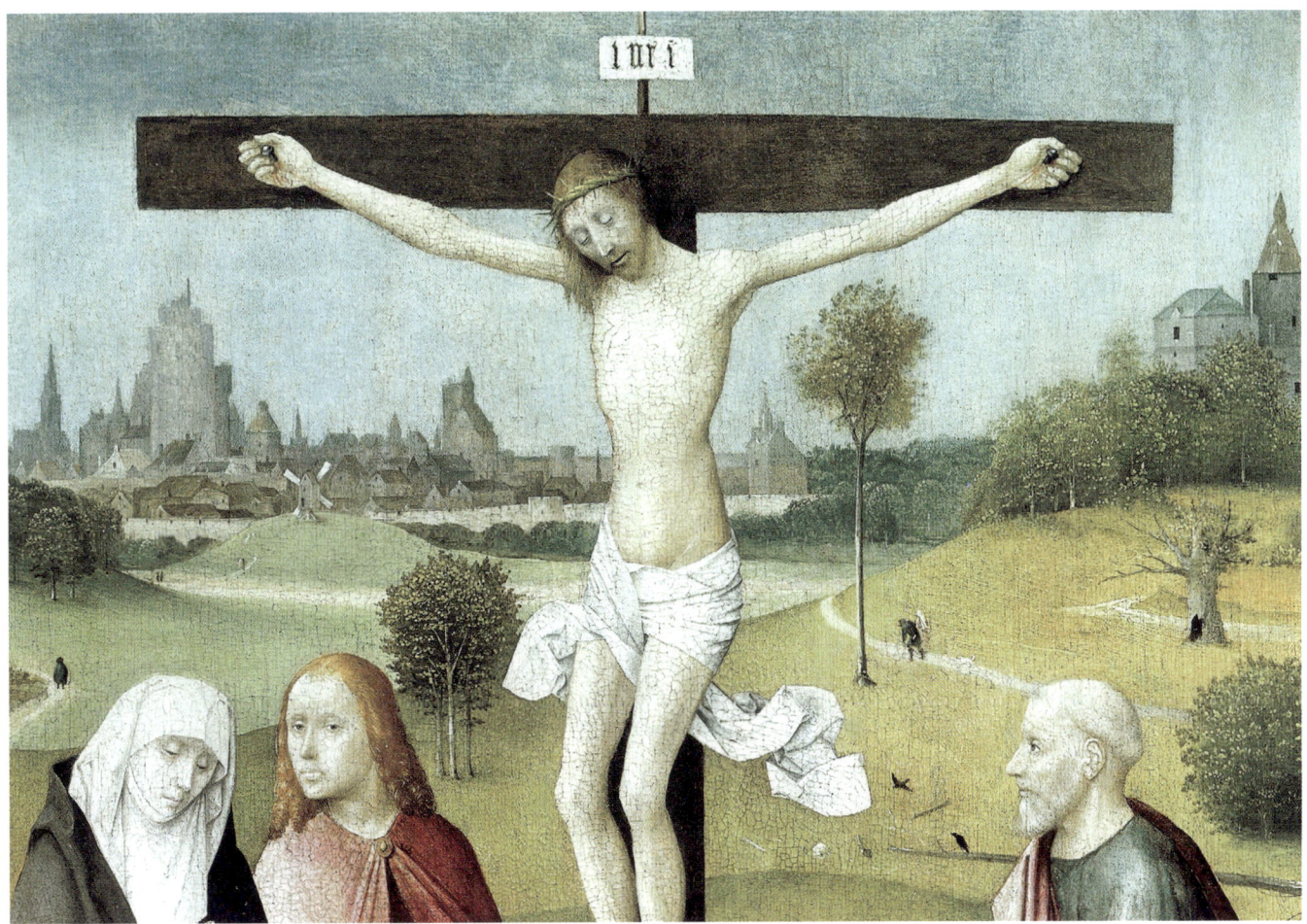

is led not to Calvary, just outside Jerusalem's walls, the scene of the Crucifixion, but a Dutch town. The kneeling donor (name unknown) wears fashionable pink-and-black-striped tights, a jerkin, short black cape and hat, with his sword visible, his noble status evident. He was probably the patron for this commission. St Peter standing behind him was possibly his patron saint. The presence of the Virgin Mary and St John the Evangelist is in line with the Biblical narrative. It was perhaps a personal votive work, or intended for a private chapel. In the form and content of th e work, one can see influences of Flemish art, such as Roger van der Weyden (1400–64).

Storytelling Through Symbols

Arma Christi ('Weapons of Christ') are the 'instruments' or material objects of the Passion of Christ, used during his arrest and trial and the Crucifixion itself. They include the column to which he was tied, the scourges, the crown of thorns, the wooden cross, hammer and nails, and spear. All were visually significant in art of the medieval era when understanding of the written word was not universal and telling of the Gospels in pictorial form was more easily understood. The *arma christi* were first mentioned in the Utrecht Psalter dated to 830.

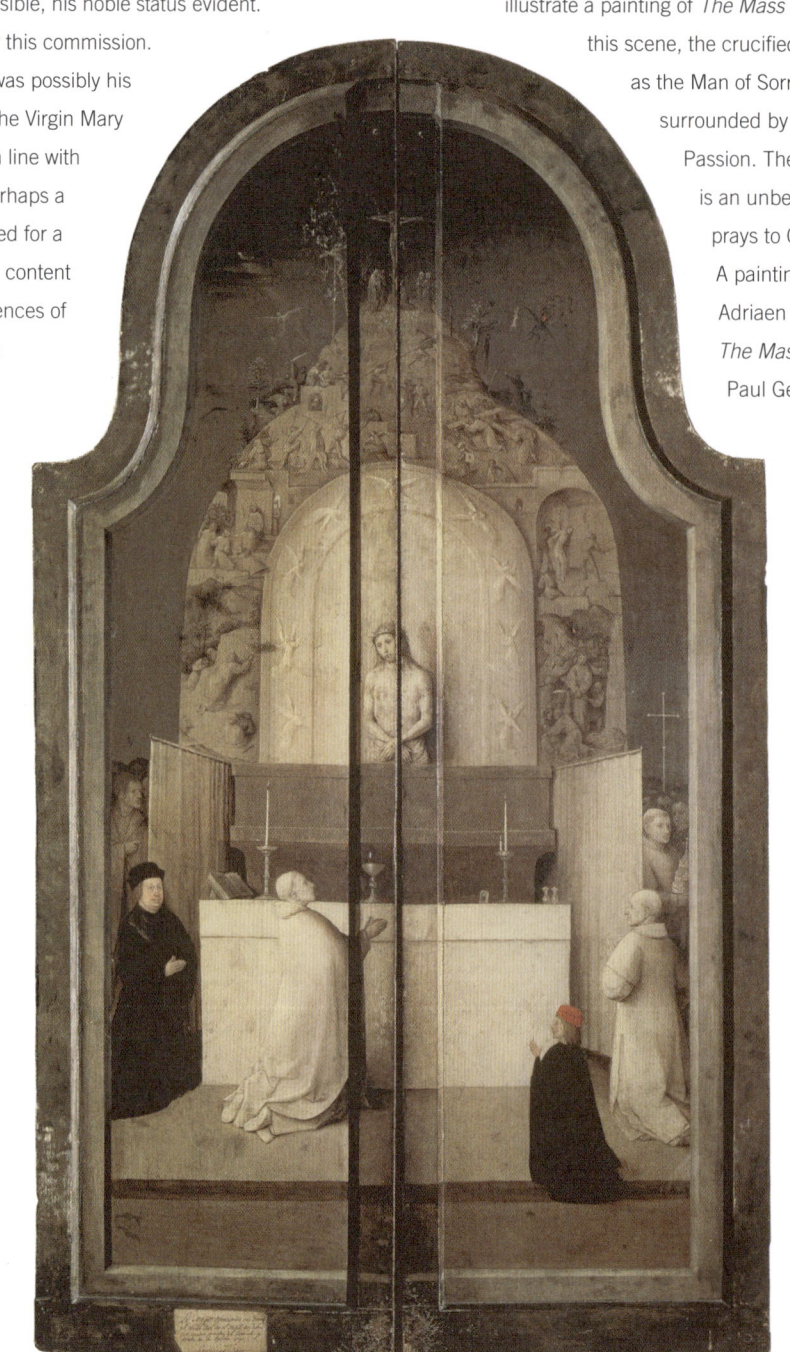

Did the Arma Christi Inspire Bosch?

The outer doors of *The Adoration of the Magi* triptych, *c.* 1485–1510, illustrate a painting of *The Mass of St Gregory*. In depictions of this scene, the crucified Christ appears to St Gregory as the Man of Sorrows on the altar during Mass, surrounded by the weapons used in the Passion. The saint, unsure whether there is an unbeliever in the congregation, prays to Christ to prove his existence. A painting by Netherlandish artist Adriaen Ysenbrandt (*fl.* 1510–51) of *The Mass of St Gregory the Great* (J. Paul Getty Museum) is a traditional depiction. Bosch paints the outer doors in grisaille. He avoids traditional depictions of this biblical narrative featuring the objects as symbols of Christ's Passion, and instead paints complete scenes within the arch above Christ.

Christ Depicted

Bosch depicted Christ on the journey to His Crucifixion in *Christ Mocked* (*The Crowning with Thorns*), 1479–1516 (*see* page 37). At the centre, in a tightly packed frame, Christ, surrounded by four persecutors, looks directly into the eyes of the viewer, acknowledging the spectator's presence. His facial expression is

calm and unemotional, not fearing his accusers. Some weapons are
held in the hands of the grotesque tormentors who press towards him.
Bosch depicts them as menacing men with aggressive physiognomy,
in contrast to the face of Jesus. In the lower left-hand corner, a man
wearing a red head cover wears on his sleeve the badge of the crescent
moon of Islam and the yellow star of the Jews, disdainers of Christianity.
At bottom right, a man reaches up to tear at the clothes of Christ. At
top right, a man carrying a stick wears a dog-like spiked neck collar, a
possible reference to Psalm 22:16 ('For dogs have compassed me: the
assembly of the wicked have enclosed me; they pierced my hands and
feet.') In devotional texts, Christ's tormentors were likened to savage
dogs. At top left, a man with a crossbow bolt held in his headwear holds
the sadistic crown of thorns, held like a halo above Christ's head. A
similar painting, *Christ Carrying the Cross*, *c.* 1515–16, with grotesque
figures surrounding Christ, (Musée des Beaux-Arts, Ghent), originally
thought to be by Hieronymus Bosch, has after recent research been
assigned to a gifted pupil or follower of the artist. Another painting, by
Albrecht Dürer, *Christ Among the Doctors*, 1505–06 (Museo Thyssen
Bornemisza, Madrid), portrays a similarly close composition of figures.

Symbolism and Metaphor in Bosch's Paintings

The depiction of *Christ Mocked (The Crowning of Thorns)* parallels the
Gospel stories, but many components of Bosch's symbolism remain
unclear. In *St Christopher Carrying the Christ Child*, *c.* 1496–1505
(*see* page 40), traditional elements of the narrative parallel the Vulgate
(late fourth-century translation of the Bible in use by the Catholic
Church), which tells that St Christopher carried the holy Infant across
a body of water. As he crosses, the young child becomes heavier,
symbolizing the weight of the world's sins on Christ's shoulders. In
The Golden Legend (a popular depiction of the lives of the saints,
written *c.* 1260 by Italian-born Jacobus de Voragine and published
in Dutch translations from 1478), the young Christ usually carries a
globe to signify the world. Bosch has changed it to a cross, possibly to
pre-empt Christ's death. Other symbols are in place, but many objects
and people are uncharacteristic of the traditional scene. The dead fish
hanging from a tree may represent the dead Christ. Is Bosch creating
complex metaphors for his patrons to unravel?

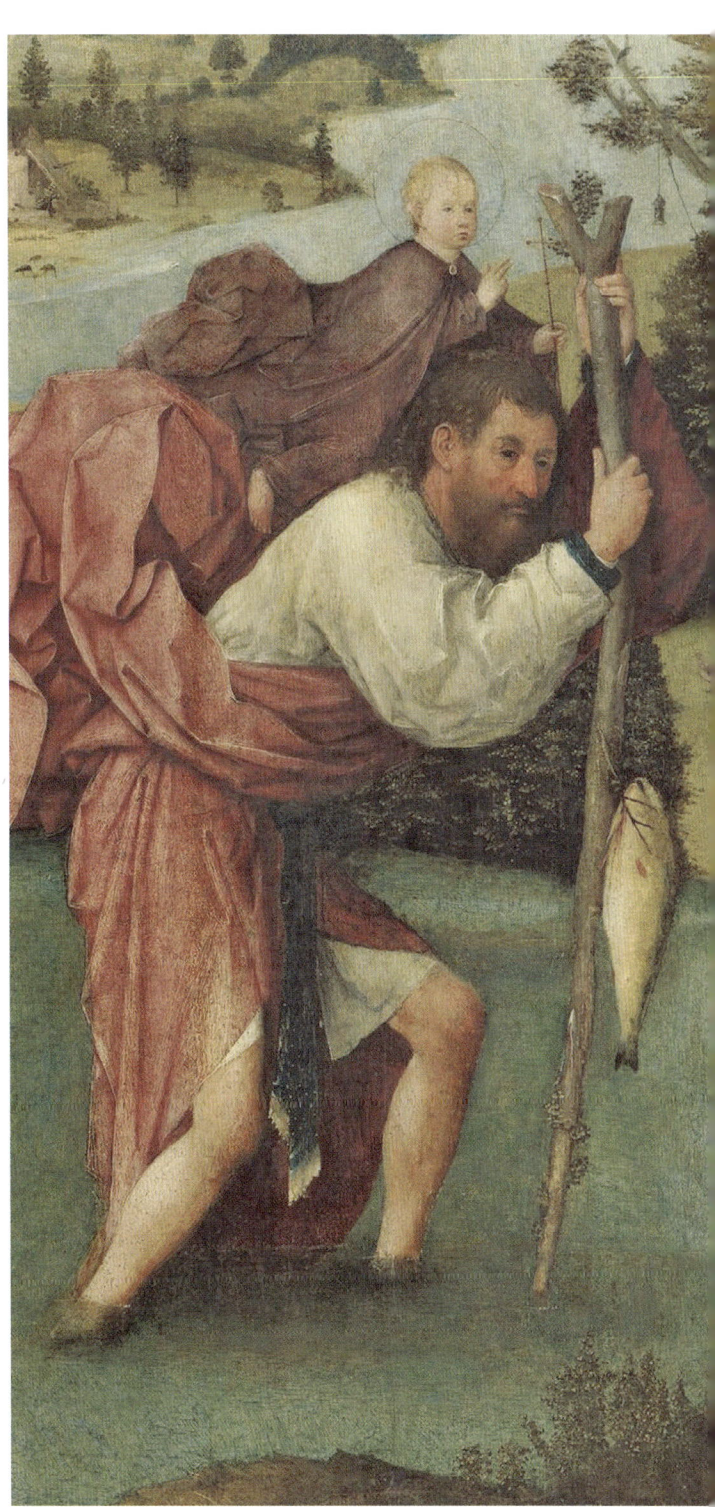

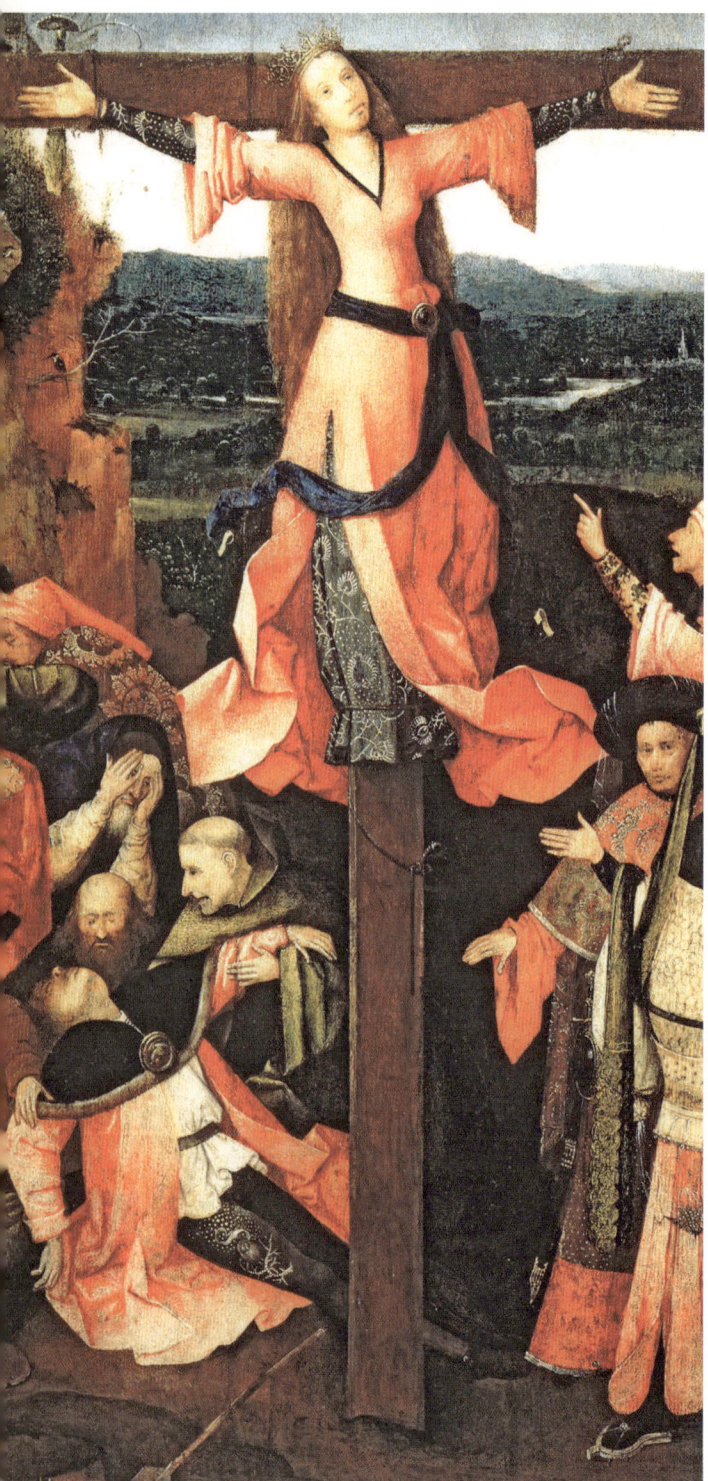

St Julia Crucified

The triptych of *The Crucifixion of St Julia, c.* 1497 (*see* pages 84–85) shows a rare depiction, the crucifixion of a female martyr. Accompanying her portrayal, on the left wing is St Anthony, possibly Bosch's favourite saint, deep in meditation; and on the right wing is an unusual depiction, possibly related to the crucifixion of the saint, a monk escorting a soldier. One can see sunken ships in the far distance, perhaps signifying a desolate material world. Beneath the surface of this triptych, infrared reflectography and infrared photography have revealed a kneeling male donor on each wing panel, overpainted. The exterior doors of the triptych have had their original content removed and the doors are now stripped to the wood. Antonio Maria Zanetti described this work in his *Descrizione di tutte le pubbliche pitture della città di Venezia* ('A Description of All the Paintings in Public Collections in the City and Lagoon Islands of Venice') (*see* page 23).

Research Uncovers a Bearded Female Saint

The legend of St Julia – also known as St Uncumber, St Liberata and St Wilgefortis – emerged in the fourteenth century. With some variations, it told of a young Christian woman, the daughter of a pagan king in Portugal, who wished her to marry a pagan prince. (Much earlier versions call her Julia, a Christian slave belonging to a Syrian merchant.) She refused, wanting to retain her Christian vow of chastity and asked God to make her undesirable to her suitor. She grew a beard. Her father, angered by his daughter's actions, demanded she be crucified. Bosch strikingly conveys the horrified reaction of witnesses to the scene, some well-dressed, others peasants, some fainting with shock, others turning away. Only one man looks on and points his hand toward the proceedings, the girl's father. Her royal status is conveyed by the crowned head, her youthfulness through her long, flowing hair and clothing. On the surface this painting by Bosch shows no visible reference to St Julia's beard, but research with infrared cameras has revealed that a beard was painted on the face, proving that it depicts the martyred saint. The kneeling male donors on the side wings are not known, and the reason for overpainting remains a mystery. Wealthy patrons, particularly in Italy, were often included in paintings as witnesses to a religious event from the Bible, such as the Nativity, or the

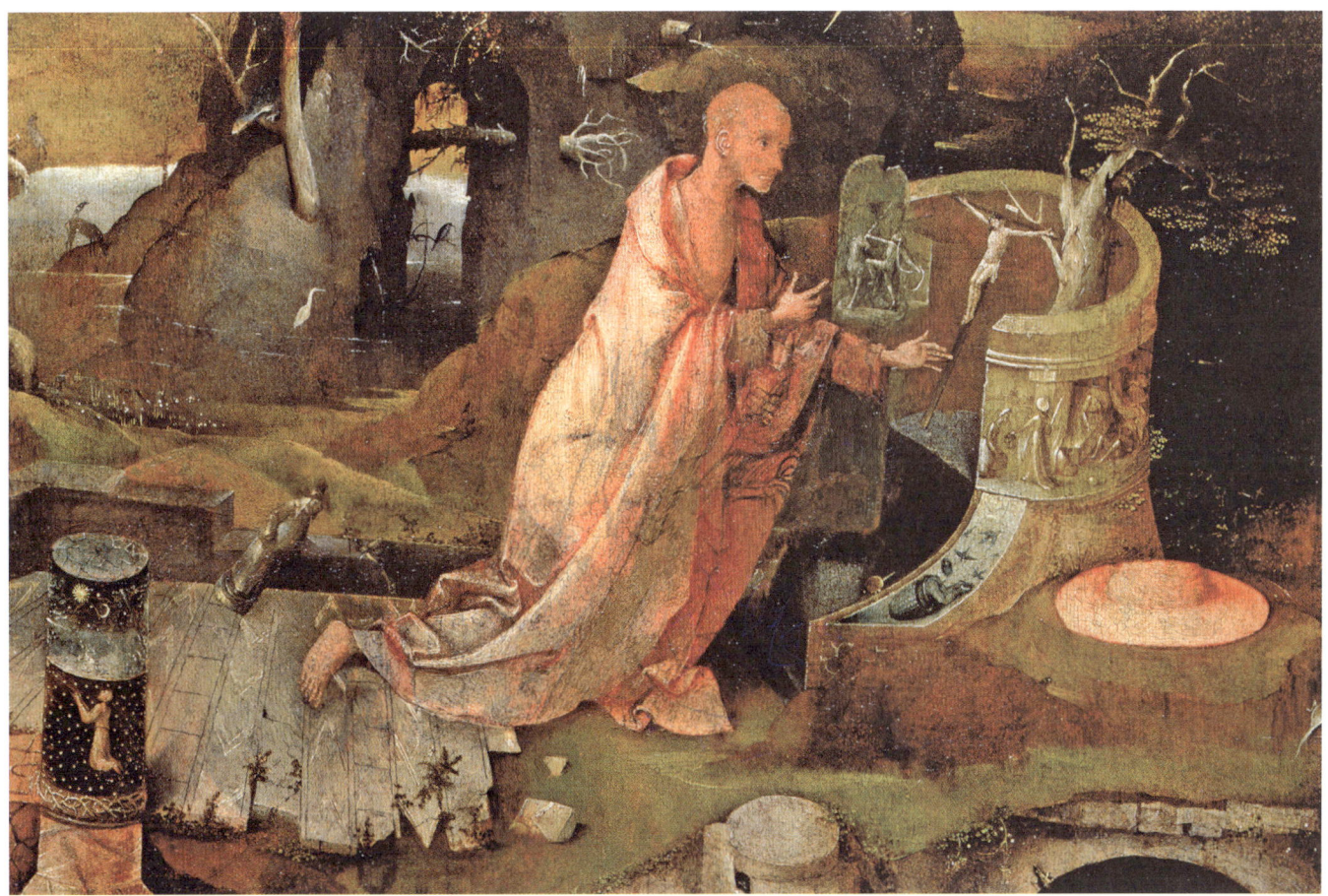

Crucifixion of Christ. The overpainting may relate to a sale of the work, or after 1517 it may relate to the reforming of the Roman Catholic Church.

The Hermit Saints

The Hermit Saints triptych (*see* pages 72–75) places the most famous hermit saints together in one triple-panel painting. St Jerome is at the centre – the panel frame originally included a rounded top – St Anthony is depicted on the left wing in a nightscape, where in the distance flares or fires spit out from the buildings. Close to the saint, strange creatures move across the ground, while a small owl looks out. St Giles is depicted on the right wing. All three saints with their iconographic attributes are visualized in the landscape, at prayer. The paintings from the exterior doors are missing.

Evildoing in Godly Places

Intimations of anti-Catholicism run through Bosch's paintings of Heaven and Hell. In its hellish scene on the right wing of *The Garden of Earthly Delights*, a gorged sow wearing the habit of a Dominican nun tries to seduce an unwilling man into signing his wealth over to the Church. The pig holds a quill in her trotter, a robotic creature before her holds the inkwell. The man, staring directly at the spectator, looks trapped. As we have seen, t he sale of indulgences, a means of pressuring citizens to give part of their income to the Church, in part to fund the construction of the new St Peter's Cathedral in Rome, was eventually undermined when Martin Luther nailed his 95 theses to a door in Wittenburg, in condemnation of the Church's abuse of power.

Heaven and Hell in 's-Hertogenbosch

Many Boschian enthusiasts and historians continue to look for hidden symbolism and metaphors to decipher the iconography in his paintings. An example is the large knife blade with a cutler's mark – a capital 'M' clearly engraved on the blade that is held between two large ears – in the right-wing panel of *The Garden of Earthly Delights* triptych. A second large knife blade is visible below it at centre right, resting on a container. What is the connection between Hell and knives, and could there be an earthly connection to 's-Hertogenbosch? In Bosch's era, a master cutler with this maker's mark was active in the town. Is it his symbol, and if so, why is it given prominence? It opens up possibilities that the triptych represents Bosch's birthplace, as it was a centre for knife-making.

Contemporary Cures?

A comic tale told in medieval times was *The Extraction of the Stone of Folly*, whereby a doctor could cure a man or woman's 'folly' – a colloquial word for stupidity or minor vices – by cutting the 'stone of folly' from a person's head. There is no evidence that this actually happened. In *The Cure of Folly (Cutting the Stone)*, c. 1494–1516 (see page 45), a copy of a Bosch original, a quack doctor operates on a hapless man.

Everyday Evils

Through Bosch's paintings, one glimpses everyday life for the poorer members of society in the late medieval Netherlands. In *The Pedlar (The Wayfarer)*, c. 1494–1516 (see page 44), a pedlar with mismatched shoes travels through the Dutch landscape. The Dutch proverb 'Op een klomp en een slof lopen' translates as 'walking on a wooden shoe and slipper', meaning 'to be poor and needy'. His clothes are ragged and he is weighed down by his belongings. He represents 'Everyman', burdened with the earthly baggage of life. He looks behind him at a dilapidated house, a brothel, which he may have resisted entering or may have just left. The moral of the narrative is that the path to God is narrow and one must be vigilant against temptation. This is one of two depictions of this man. The other is a more colourful version of *Everyman Walking the Path of Life* (see page 106) on the outer wings of *The Haywain*. This depiction embroiders the narrative, showing the evils that can beset a wayfarer. Behind him, another man has been robbed of all his possessions, and a makeshift gallows is visible on the horizon.

Opinions and Sightings of Bosch's Oeuvre

Italian writer Ludovico Guicciardini (1521–89), in his book *Descrittione di tutti I Paesi Bassi, altrimenti detti Germania inferiore* ('Description of the Low Countries'), published in Antwerp in 1567, described Bosch as '… a much admired and marvellous creator of strange and comical images, and uncommonly madcap scenes'. Written half a century after Bosch's death, it is a typical description of the artist that served to highlight the more unusual content of Bosch's art rather than the religious subject matter that informed it. Three works by Bosch on display in Venice were first mentioned by Count Antonio Maria Zanetti (1680–1767), an artist, art critic and art connoisseur, in 1733, in *Descrizione di tutte le pubbliche pitture della città di Venezia* ('A Description of All the Paintings in Public Collections in the City

of Venice'). Zanetti referred to a Bosch triptych of St Jerome with two saints, now known as *The Hermit Saints*. In addition, he described four panels with scenes of 'hybrid animals and scenes of witchcraft', now known as *Four Visions of the Hereafter*, and the triptych of the crucifixion of the female saint St Julia.

Not Universally Understood

The Flemish biographer, artist and poet Karel van Mander (1548–1606), in *Het Schilder-Boeck* ('The Painter Book'), commented rather unfavourably on the art of Bosch, which he must have seen on his travels through the Netherlands. In the book, published by Paschier Wesburch in Haarlem in 1604, Van Mander picked up on the unworldly creatures and devilish people in Bosch's art: 'Who will

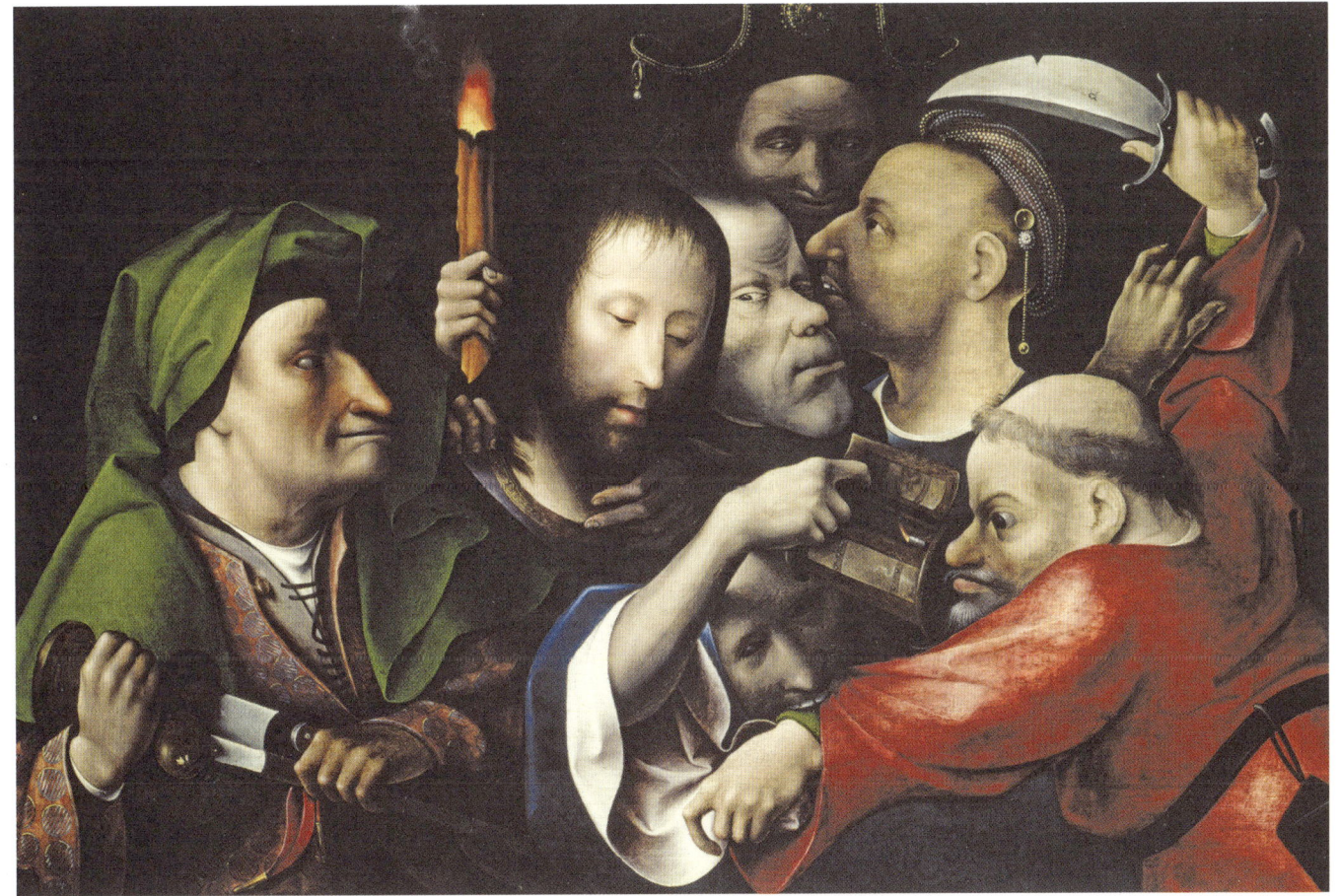

be able to tell of all the weird and strange ideas which were in the mind of Jeronimus Bos, and his expressions of them by his brush? He painted gruesome Pictures.' Van Mander's book was modelled on Italian artist and writer Giorgio Vasari's *Vite de' piu eccellenti pittori, Scultori ed Architettori* ('Lives of the Most Excellent Painters, Sculptors and Architects'), published in 1550 and 1568, which began with Giotto and ended with Michaelangelo. Van Mander covered a wider area of art and artists, from ancient Egypt, Greece and Rome, and from thirteenth- to late sixteenth-century painters. There followed chapters on the Netherlands and Germany, to chronicle the lives of many notable artists.

Respected Collectors

Spanish humanist Don Felipe de Guavera (*c.* 1500–*c.* 1563), a courtier to Philip II of Spain (1527–98), owned six paintings by Bosch. The illegitimate son of courtier and ambassador Don Diego de Guevara (died 1520) was an avid art collector and connoisseur

and owner of *The Arnolfini Marriage*, 1434, by Early-Netherlandish painter Jan van Eyck (1390–1441). The Bosch paintings were possibly bought when Don Diego de Guavera was acting as a court advisor to the King of Spain in the Netherlands. Felipe is credited with writing the first art treatise in Spain, in which he mentions that the quality of Bosch's paintings justified the high price paid for them and guaranteed to be worthwhile investments. In 1560 he wrote *Comentarios de la pintura que excribio Don Felipe de Guevara* ('Commentary on Painting and Antique Painters'), eventually published in 1788, and described certain forgeries as 'pictures to which he [Bosch] would never have thought of putting his hand but which are in reality the work of smoke and the short-sighted fools who smoked them in fireplaces, in order to lend them credibility.' In the treatise he mentions an unnamed, particularly gifted pupil of Bosch, who painted *The Seven Deadly Sins and the Four Last Things*, in the possession of Philip II, citing it as an exceptional piece of art. Felipe wrote the treatise as an educational essay on art to persuade the King to promote the patronage of local artists and improve

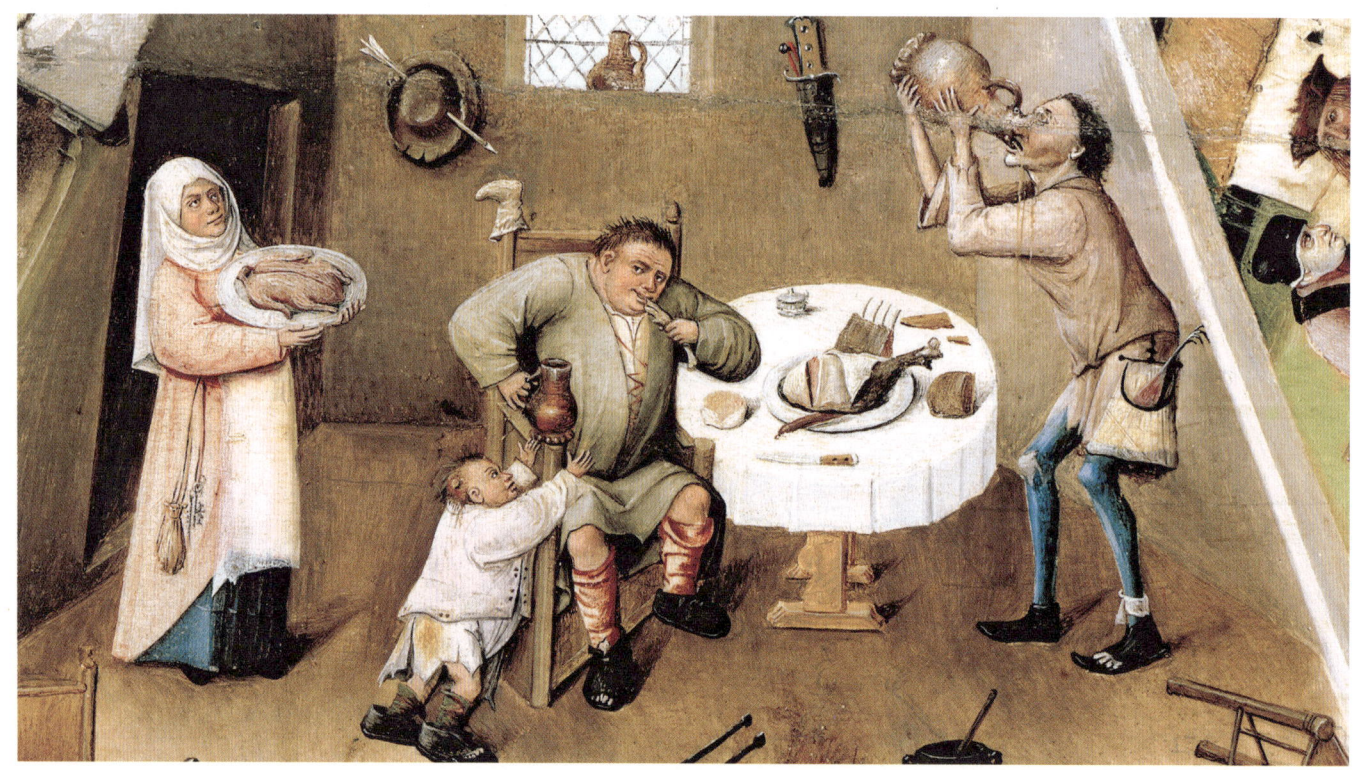

Spanish art. The manuscript, dedicated to the King, was lost on the death of Felipe. It was rediscovered and published in 1788 in Madrid by Antonio Ponz. Felipe wrote that Bosch had a highly gifted student (*discipulo*) who signed his work 'Jheronimus Bosch'. That the student was so accomplished made imitations harder to discover. Today, research and conservation look not only into the paint application but the age of the wooden panels, to ascertain if a work is original. Felipe was aghast at the quantity and poor quality of the myriad of Bosch forgeries in circulation, lamenting the commercial trade in Bosch fakes: 'That which he did with wisdom and decorum, others did and still do, without any discretion and good judgement.' He did not refer to his own collection of paintings by Bosch.

Royal Patrons?

Did the nobility visit Bosch in person? Philip the Fair, regent of the Netherlands from 1494 to 1506, stayed with Hendrik III of Nassau-Breda (1483–1538) in 's-Hertogenbosch in the winter of 1504, travelling to and from Hendrik's wedding to Louise Françoise of Savoie (1485–1511). Seven years after Bosch had completed *The Garden of Earthly Delights,* an eyewitness saw it hanging in Hendrik of Nassau's palace. This suggests that patrons may have visited Bosch personally to see his studio and commission a work. For *The Garden of Earthly Delights* to be displayed as a secular painting, not a religious work, may mean it was a wedding gift.

Hieronymus Cock

To give a face to the Bosch name, one looks to the Antwerp-born engraver and artist, printer and publisher Hieronymus Cock (1518–70). He made commercial prints of Bosch's works in addition to publishing a portrait of him, in 1572, over 50 years after the artist's death. It was published as one of a collection of 22 artists' portraits and biographies (printed in Latin) by humanist Dominicus Lampsonius (1532–99) of Bruges, a poet and painter. In addition, a sixteenth-century portrait etching of Bosch from the Recueil d'Arras, in charcoal and red chalk on paper, now in the Bibliothèque Municipale, Arras, France, was originally thought to be

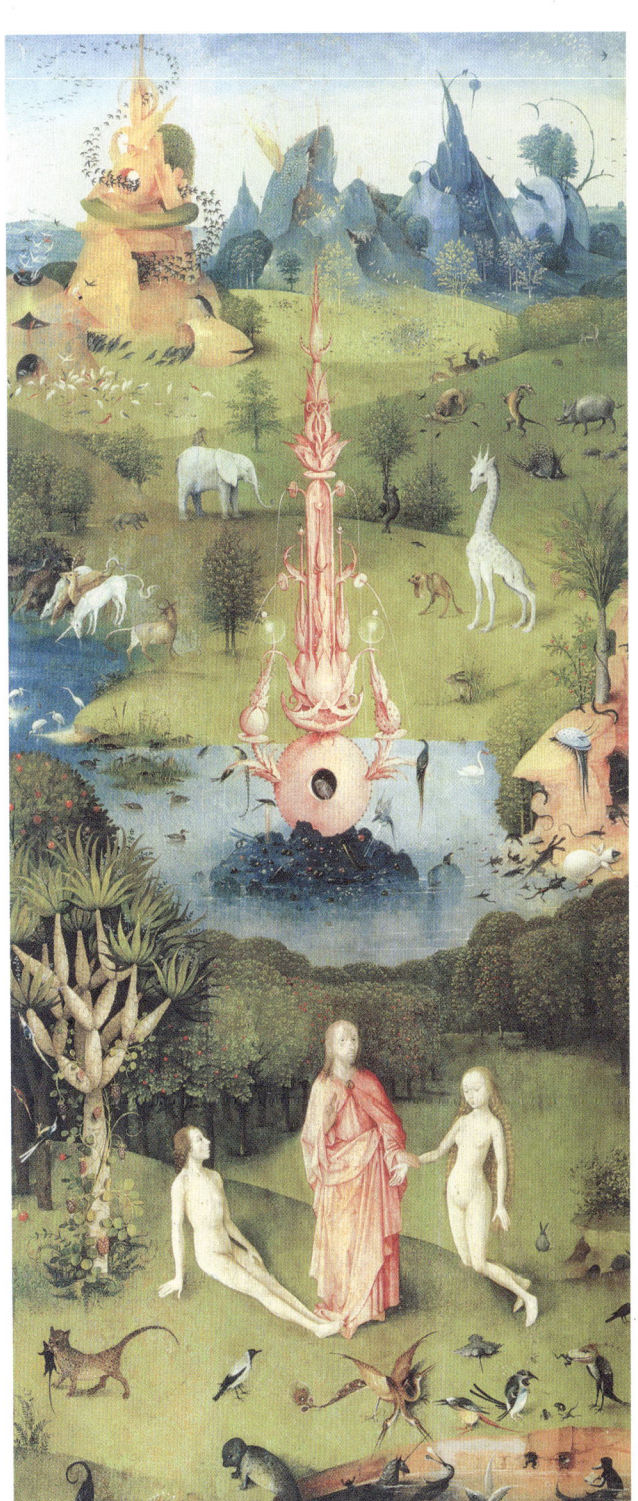

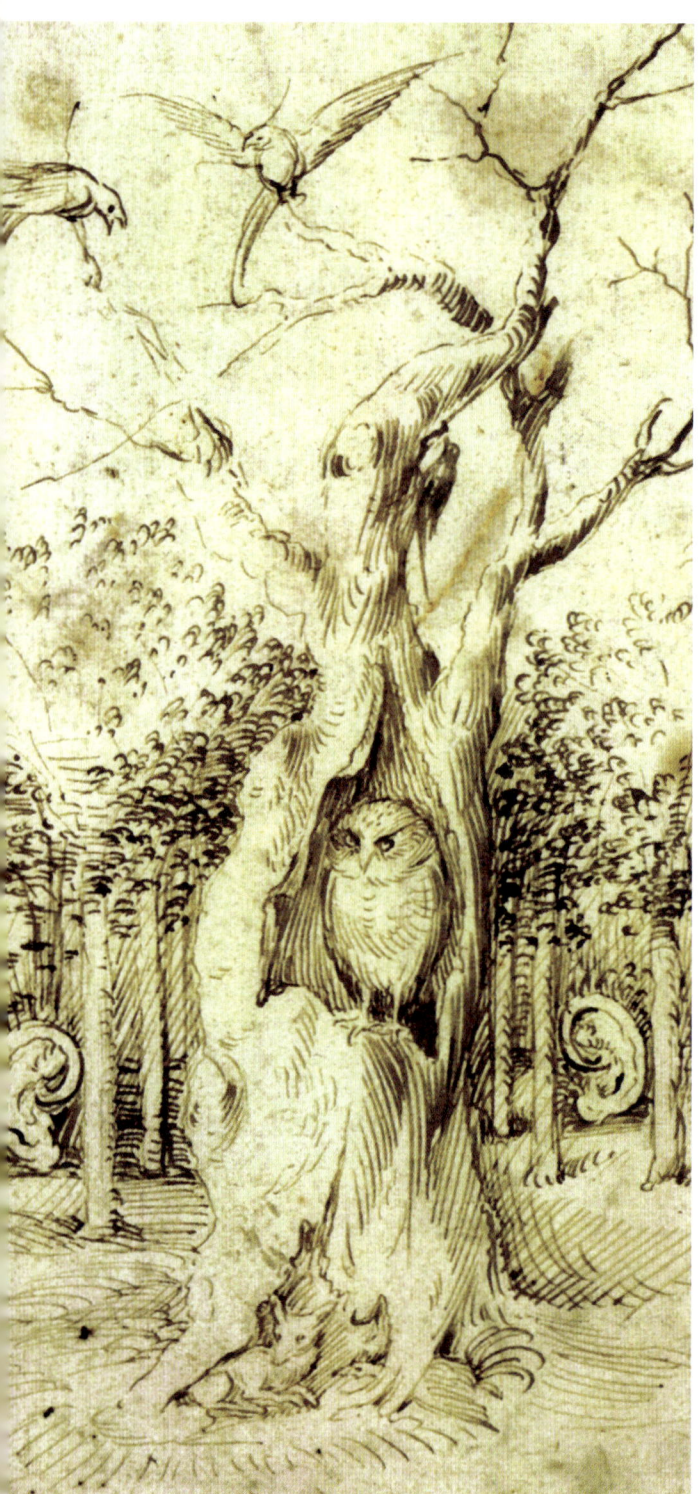

a self-portrait and is possibly taken from an original work (*see* page 7). The image was followed closely in eighteenth-century copies.

Bosch Sources

Written in Latin, *Visio Tnugdali* ('The Vision of Tundale') is a gruesome but engaging tale of the horrendous afterlife waiting for Christian sinners. It was written in around 1149 by an Irish Benedictine monk known as Marcus, living at the Cistercian St James Monastery in Regensberg, Germany. It was a hugely popular narrative, translated into 15 different languages including Dutch, and would have been known to Bosch and the Illustrious Brotherhood. It was printed in 's-Hertogenbosch in 1484, by a publisher from nearby Nijmwegen (Nijmegen). Full of horrific descriptions of torture at the hands of otherworldly beasts and butchers, it is a salutary account of a three-day journey taken by Tundale, an uncharitable usurer, thief and serial sinner. He falls as if dead and his soul is led by an angel through purgatory and Hell to witness the punishments awaiting him if he does not alter his sinning ways. His soul is granted a glimpse of the alternative in Paradise and Heaven, revealing how merciful God is. Reawakening from 'death' and reunited with his soul, he repents and swears to change his ways, to give away all his possessions and preach the word of God. The highly descriptive account of the terrible ordeal of eternal damnation was close to the beliefs of medieval populations and clearly understood.

Owl Imagery

The wondrous creatures of Bosch's art are grounded in real animals, birds and insects, which appear as often as his imaginative creations. Look, for example, at the owls depicted in his works. At least 20 appear in drawings and paintings, such as the three owls in the pen-and-ink drawings *The Wood Has Ears, The Field Has Eyes* (*see* page 117), *The Owl's Nest, c.* 1505–16 (*see* page 125) and in *The Tree-Man, c.* 1505 (*see* page 124). Owls are the onlookers at evil entertainments or dubious events, such as the tiny owl kept in a basket tied on to the belt of *The Conjuror*, or two oversized owls, both staring directly at the spectator, the quiet surveyors of *The Garden of Earthly Delights* in the central panel. In the medieval world, the

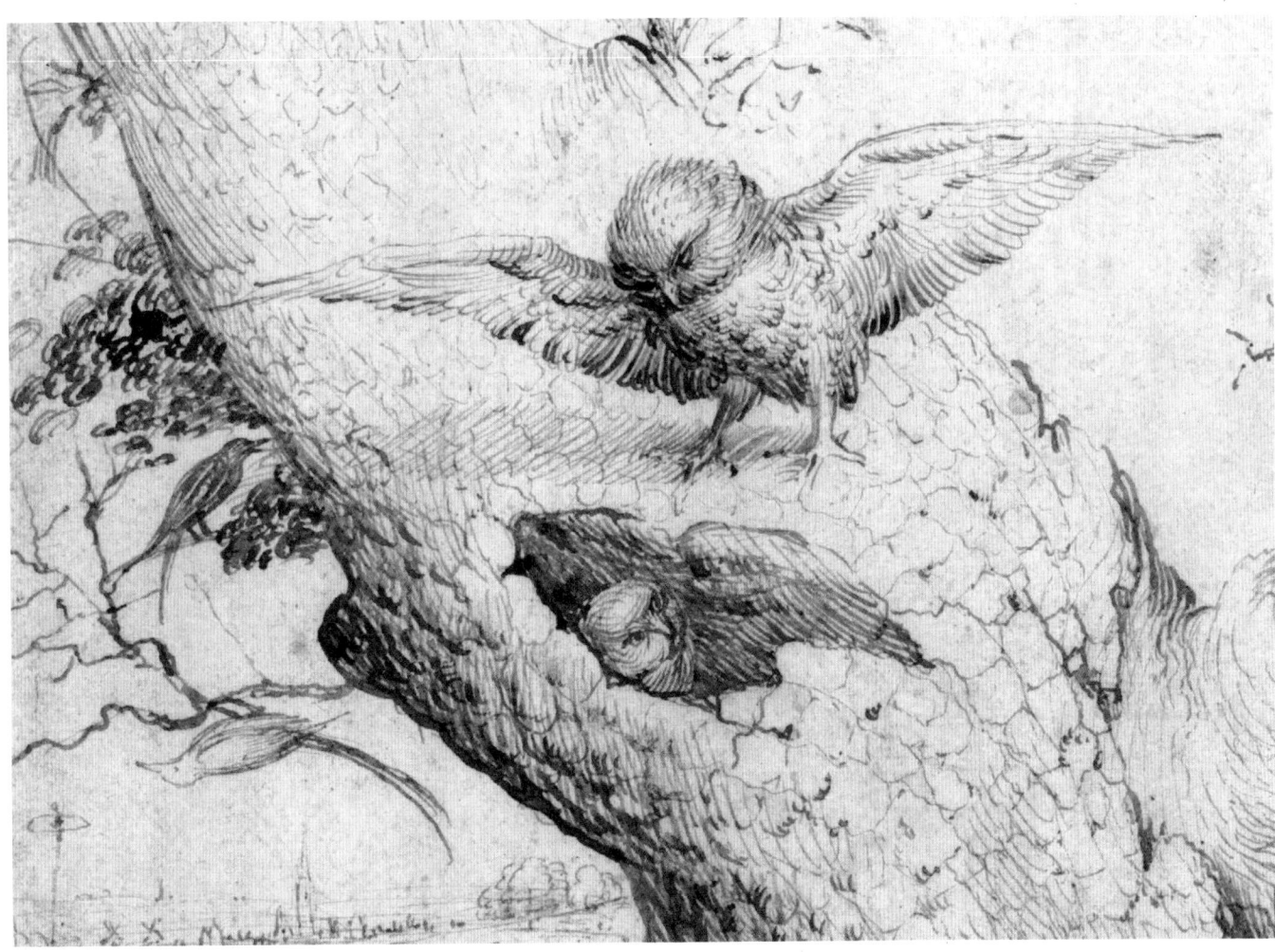

nocturnal owl was associated with the dark side, death, evil and otherworldliness, albeit with a wise head and perceptive mind. There is pleasure in finding them in Bosch's work, often hidden as a small detail, watching and waiting, much like a real owl waiting to pounce on its prey.

An Ancient Allegory

Reference to a 'ship of fools' first appeared in Plato's *Republic* (book vi), an allegory for the 'ship of state', or Athenian democracy, with a captain taller and stronger than others, but deaf and short-sighted with no skills in navigation. The crew argue that they could navigate the ship better than the captain, whilst the boat goes nowhere. In Bosch's era, the tale of a boat or vessel without a pilot or helmsman to steer (a parody of the Catholic Church at that time) was explored in a book of satirical verse titled *Das Narrenschiff* ('The Ship of Fools'). It was the work of the distinguished German poet and humanist Sebastian Brant (1457–1521), born in Strassburg, now Strasbourg, France. The book was published in Basel by his friend Jonas Bergmann in 1494, and became an instant bestseller throughout Europe, with translations in Latin, French, Flemish, Dutch and English. It was popular with every class of people in every country in which there was a translation.

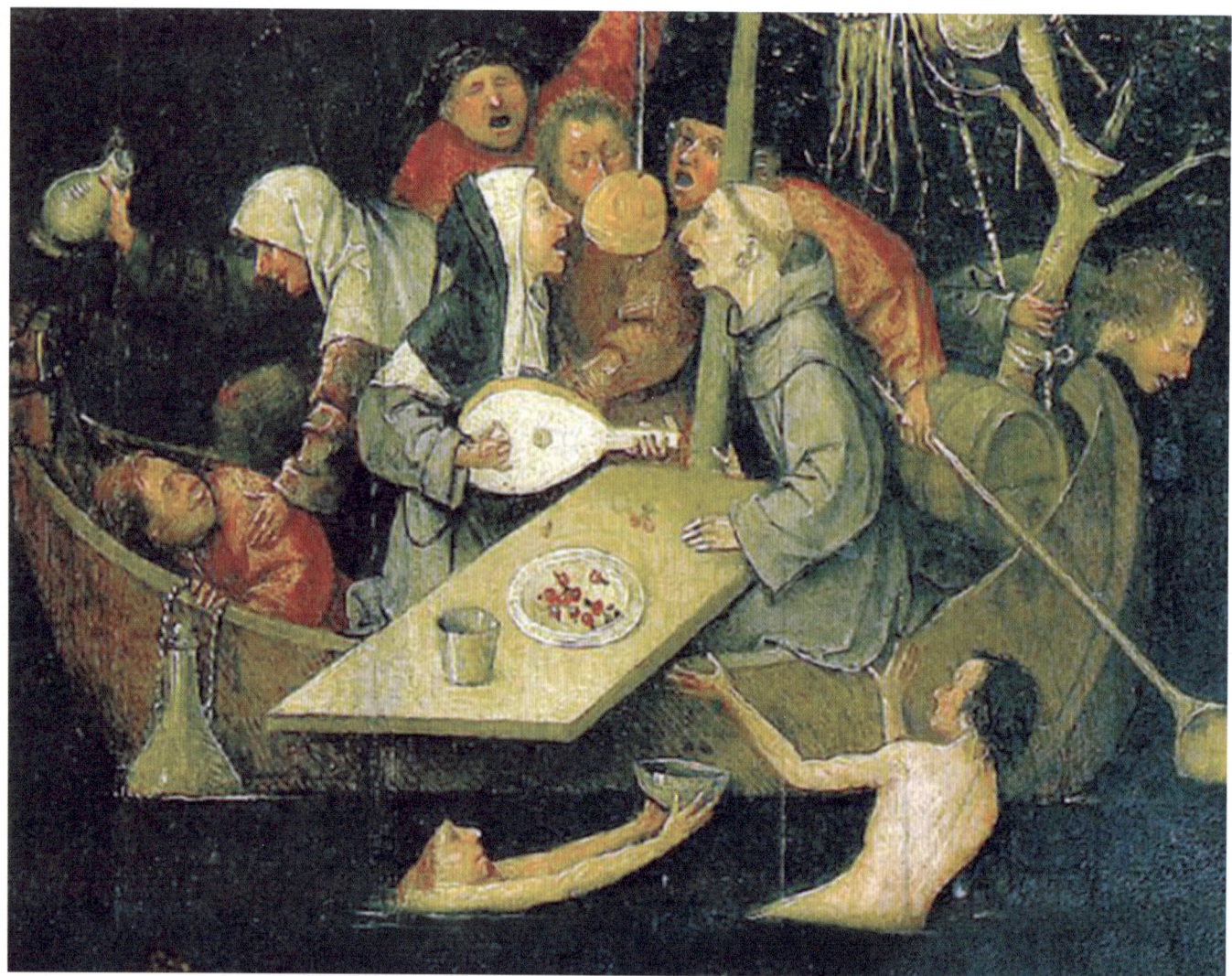

The poem's 113 verses talk about the 110 'fools' on board, with each verse highlighting their follies, from the mockers and scorners, to drunkards, misers and gluttons, adulterers, usurers and gamblers, to churchgoers and false accusers. Contemporary events are part of the text, such as young men who marry older women purely for their money, which was a step-change from traditional poetic verse that normally focused on historical events from Germany's past. Woodcuts, thought to be by Albrecht Dürer, illustrated the text. The boat leaves Basel bound for Narragonia (the land of fools). Without a competent pilot, it sails around, going nowhere whilst the passengers get drunk, sing and argue.

Bosch's Ship

Bosch, a contemporary of Sebastian Brant (also known as Brandt), knew this poem well. He carefully lays out the humorous narrative in his painting *The Ship of Fools*, depicting the main participants carousing and drinking, enjoying life on a fool's journey to nowhere. The painter's focus on religious laity at the centre of the ship is perhaps intended to symbolize the 'Ship of the Church', a widespread term for the Catholic Church in art and literature in the medieval period.

An Abundance of Earthly Delights

Five panel paintings make up this wonderful work, a triptych, large
in size and rich in content. The two outer doors, when closed, show
an ethereal view, painted in monotones, of *The Creation of the
World* (*see* page 90). One looks at the dark outer space around the
world and down on to a city that some historians consider to be
's-Hertogenbosch. It is a calm introduction to what lies within. The
doors open on to visions of the material and spiritual life for mortals
on Earth. From the left panel depicting *The Garden of Eden* (*see* page
88), to the immorality of everyday life in the centre panel (*see* page
87), and the terrifying scene of Hell in the right panel (*see* page 89),
the consequence of material pleasure. The subject matter points to it
being created as an altarpiece. There is no current record of it being
displayed in a church, but it may have been made for a private chapel.

Four Panels from a Lost Polyptych

Four panels at the Palazzo Grimani in Venice, titled *Four Visions of
the Hereafter: Earthly Paradise, The Ascent into Heaven, The Fall of
the Damned and Hell* are considered the wings of a lost polyptych,
dated to around 1505–15.

The most notable of the four is *The Ascent into Heaven (see* page 59).
Here, a remarkable depiction by the artist is possibly based on the
writings of Jan van Ruysbroeck (1293–1381), a Flemish mystic, born
in South Brabant who founded an Augustinian abbey at Groenendael.
He wrote of the soul ascending to Empyrean Heaven guided by a
divine light. In the panel painting, the soul of man ascends from a life
on Earth to his celestial reward in Heaven. Each soul (symbolized by
the body) is lovingly guided by his guardian angel towards a vast cone
of divine light, one of the artist's most wondrous depictions.

St Anthony's Attributes

Bosch painted the life of St Anthony (251–356) in contemporary
landscapes. The hermit monk born in Heracleopolis Magna, Egypt, gave
up his lands and wealth to the poor, to live a solitary life of contemplation
in the desert. He was depicted by Bosch, his followers and painters of

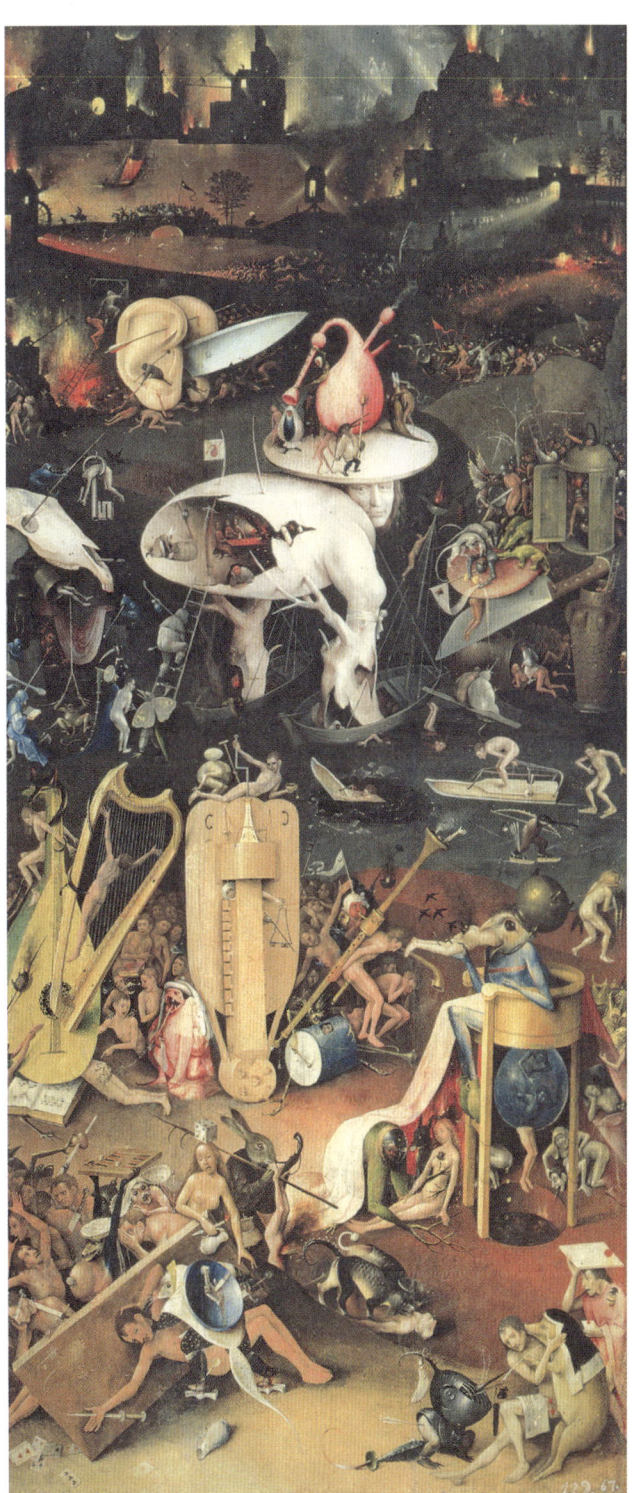

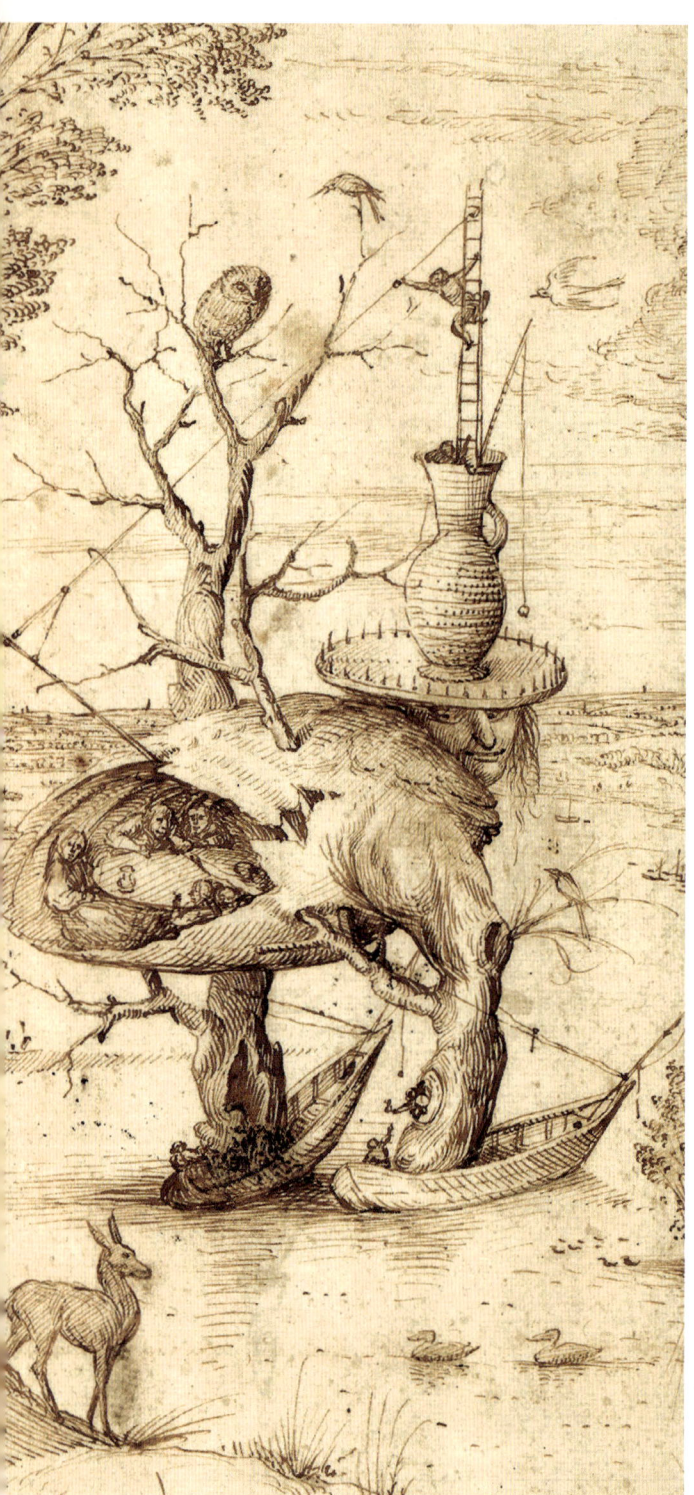

his era many times. St Anthony's attributes appear in Bosch works: the saint's habit emblazoned with the Greek letter *tau* (St Anthony's Cross); a pig or pigs – legend told that he once worked as a swineherd; and a stone, a candle and fire are all associated with him. In the triptych *The Temptation of St Anthony* (*see* page 92), located in Lisbon, Bosch brings together air, fire, water and earth, the four elements of the natural world, to relate episodes from the saint's life on the inner panels, best read from left to right. The left wing (*see* right) reveals supernatural happenings with St Anthony in flight, carried away by devilish winged creatures, praying for God's help. This scene was an immensely popular visual image from the saint's biography. Below St Anthony is a sea of broken ships and on land there is a bewildering scene of disorder. The lower foreground of the left panel depicts the saint, barely walking after his fall, crossing a bridge aided by two monks and an old man.

Drawings

Bosch's few drawings reveal his imaginative mind, translating the actions of a sinful material world into an army of strange creatures. One of the most remarkable is *The Tree-Man*, *c*. 1505. A gnarled, bare tree supports an oversized owl on its upper branches. Its base is a boat with travellers. Propped against or springing from it is an egg-shaped shell, sprouting branches. The heavy roots resemble legs. Most astonishingly, the head of a man (possibly a self-portrait by Bosch) looks back at this 'body' and the spectator. In the far distance a city can be glimpsed. Inside the broken shell, people sit at a table talking. A woman pours wine into a jug for the travellers. This is a preparatory drawing for part of the vision of Hell, the right wing of *The Garden of Earthly Delights*. Bosch drew other strange trees, such as that sprouting from *The Ship of Fools*.

A New Discovery

Bosch drawings are rare, but in 2015 members of the Dutch Bosch Research and Conservation Project (BRCP) were able to identify a drawing in a private art collection. Previously thought to be by an assistant, it has now been confirmed as an original by Bosch. *Infernal Landscape*, date unknown, depicts a hellish scene where gargantuan otherworldly creatures dominate.

Who Painted the Works of Hieronymus Bosch?

As the latest technology is utilized to research the extant paintings believed to be by Bosch, there is concern as to how much of each work can be accurately attributed to the artist. For some works a patchwork of painters' hands has been detected. Today, it is acceptable that conceptual artists conceive an idea and create a template of a work to be created by unknown, paid artists in galleries around the world. The concept remains the ownership of the original artist. This acceptance that an artist does not necessarily paint every spot or mark on a panel or wall can be referred back to the ancient past. For example, in Athens, Greece, sections of the frieze on the Parthenon are the work of many sculptors working to a design, under the direction of the originator of the work. Likewise, it is entirely conceivable that the paintings of Bosch, particularly large triptychs, were painted in part by his family of artists, or painters in the Bosch workshop. It is only today under infrared light and fine microscopes that the different sources are revealed. Of course, changes in content and composition that are revealed by infrared light may show elements painted by others or, in fact, changes that Bosch himself made, so they require expert analysis.

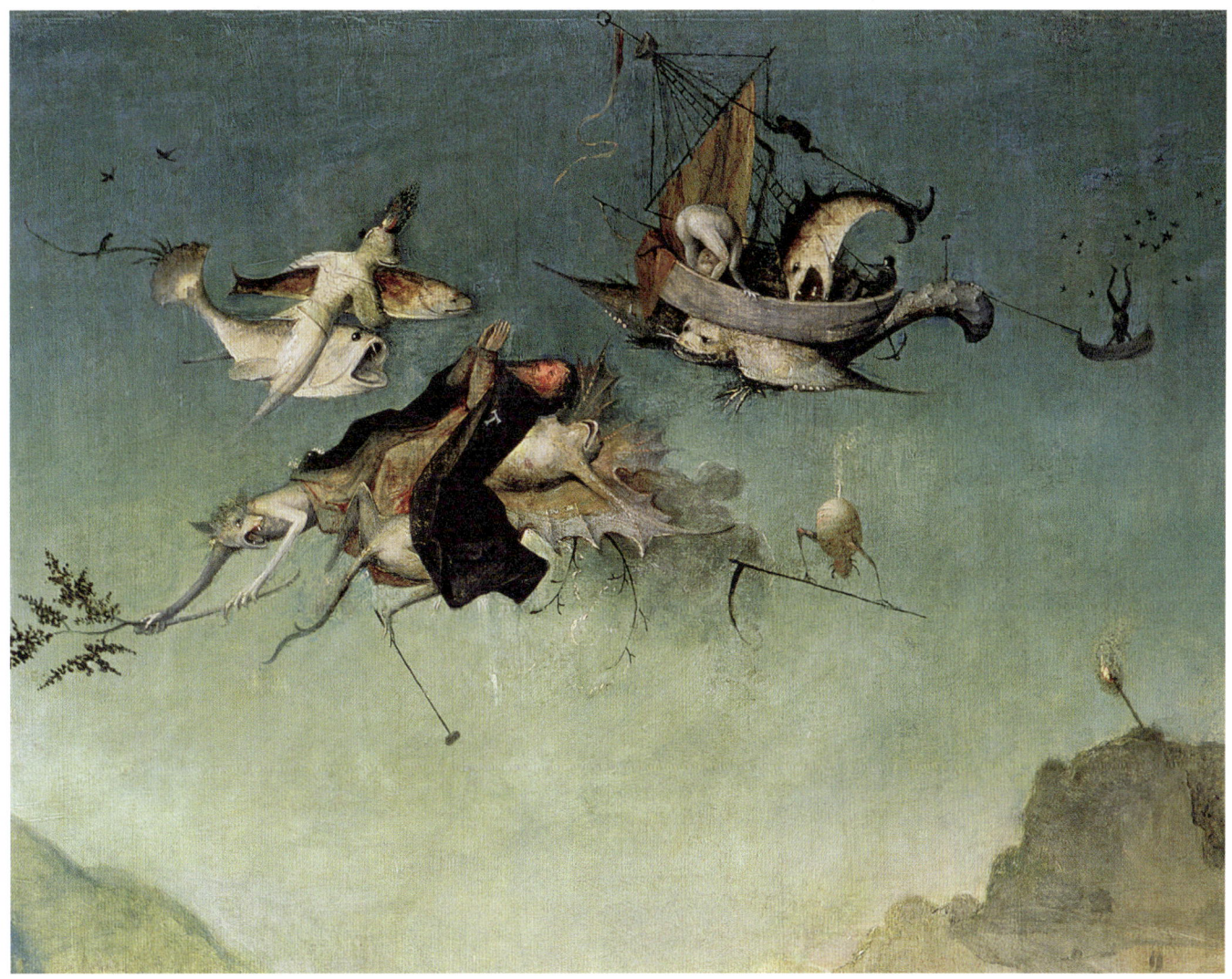

Bosch Uncovered

The 2016 anniversary, marking 500 years since the death of Hieronymus Bosch, has concentrated art researchers' attention on the discovery of exactly which works of his extant oeuvre, are actually by his hand. Whilst some have been proven to be by his workshop or followers, an original work has come to light in the city of Kansas, USA. It is *The Temptation of St Anthony*, 1500–10 (*see* right), a small painting (38.1 x 25.4 cm/15 x 10 in), probably cut from a larger panel, which has been kept in storage at the Nelson-Atkins museum for over 70 years. This panel, always beaut iful but now more interesting as it has been established as a Bosch original, aids further understanding of his work. Its discovery is proof that continuous research will eventually reveal more masterpieces of art, as yet undiscovered.

The Temptation of St Anthony illustrates the saint kneeling by a stream, collecting water in a jug. In front of him, strange small creatures symbolize malevolent temptations in a material world that must be

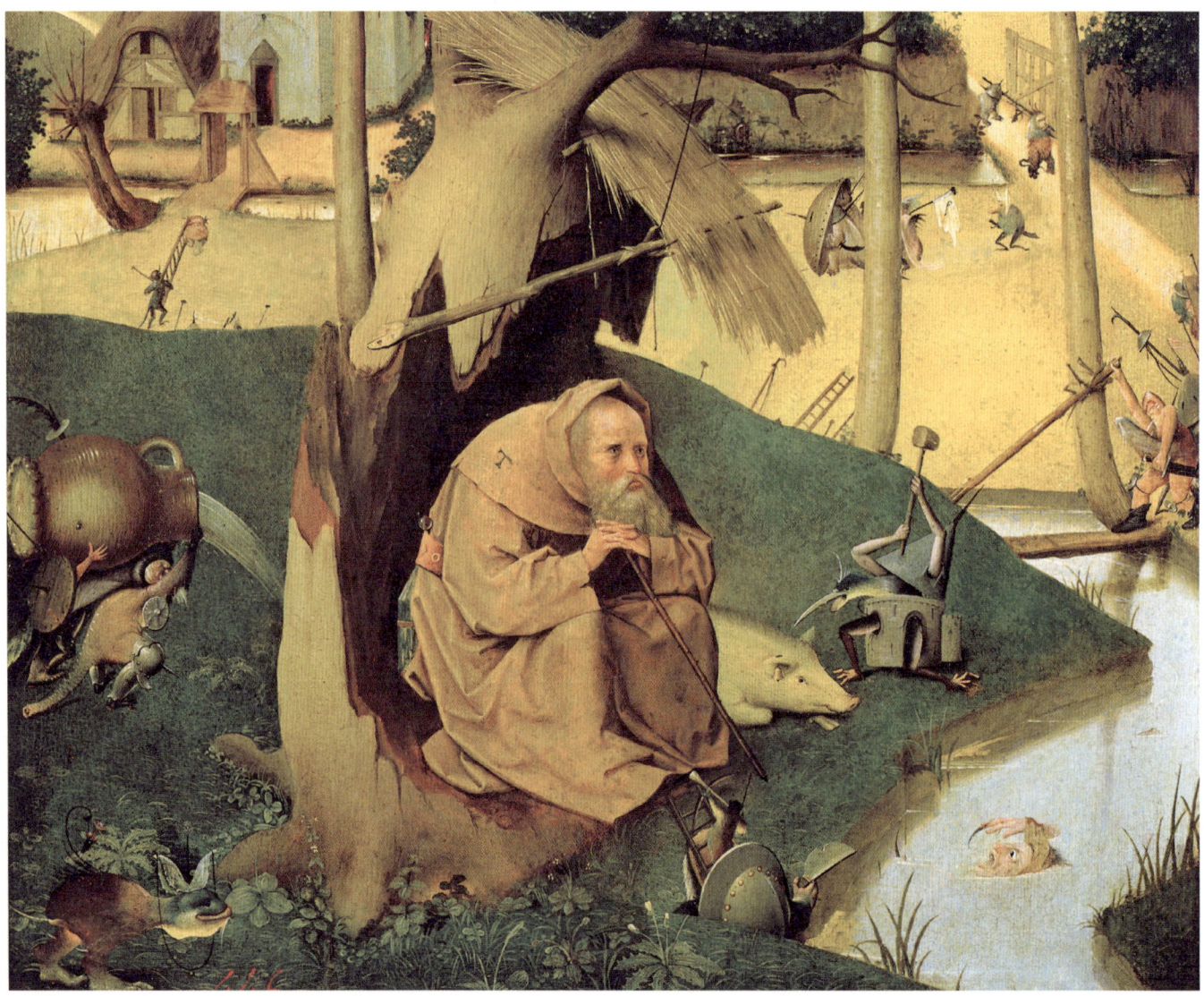

ignored. The small panel concentrates all that Bosch aimed to achieve in his complex portrayals of life on Earth and the hereafter.

Bosch's Legacy

Hieronymus Bosch's untimely death on 9 August 1516 focused attention on other Netherlandish artists working in a Boschian style. The paintings of Antwerp-born Jan Mandijn (*c.* 1500–60) revealed his appreciation of Bosch landscapes and otherworldly content, visible in his *The Temptation of St Anthony, c.* 1550 (Frans Hals Museum, Haarlem). In *Het Schilder-Boeck*, Karel van Mander referred to Mandijn as a follower of Bosch. In addition, amongst others, Brabant-born Pieter Bruegel (1525–69), born nearly a decade after Bosch's death, was a highly gifted painter, who continued what Bosch had begun, using scenes from local life to visualize biblical narratives and folklore in contemporary society. Breugel's *Christ Carrying the Cross*, 1564 (Kunsthistoriches Museum, Vienna), reveals Christ's Passion barely noticed by uncaring local citizens as he drags the Cross towards Calvary. In *The Fall of the Rebel Angels*, 1562 (Royal Museum of Fine Arts, Brussels, Belgium), Breugel's debt to Bosch is significant in the hellish creatures, metaphors for evil, who fall from God's grace. In the modern era, Bosch has been hailed as the 'first Surrealist', his paintings inspiring the 1920s Surrealist art movement.

Hieronymus Bosch Today

In 2016, as the city of 's-Hertogenbosch commemorates the 500th year since the death of Bosch, the son who brought fame to their community, the world's most qualified researchers continue to study his paintings and drawings, aided by ever more sophisticated technology. What has emerged is the difficulty of knowing which works can be wholly attributed to the artist. Works found to be painted on wood hewn from trees after the artist's death make one part of the research straightforward, but it is the smaller details, such as the evidence of more than one artist at work, that may draw the focus from his achievements. Bosch's moral messages stingingly delivered through scenes of everyday life make him a unique talent in Netherlandish art. His few extant drawings show Bosch to be an artist with a singular vision, memorably delivered.

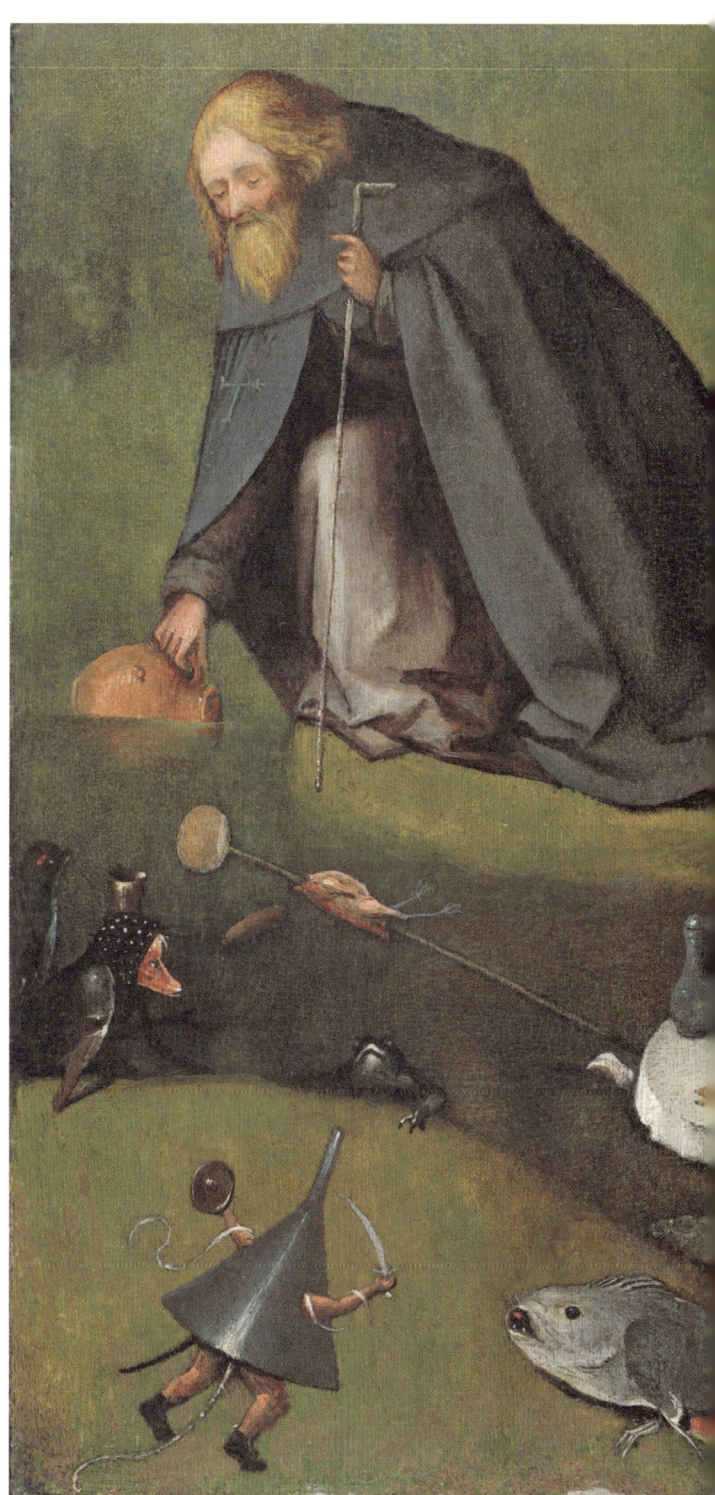

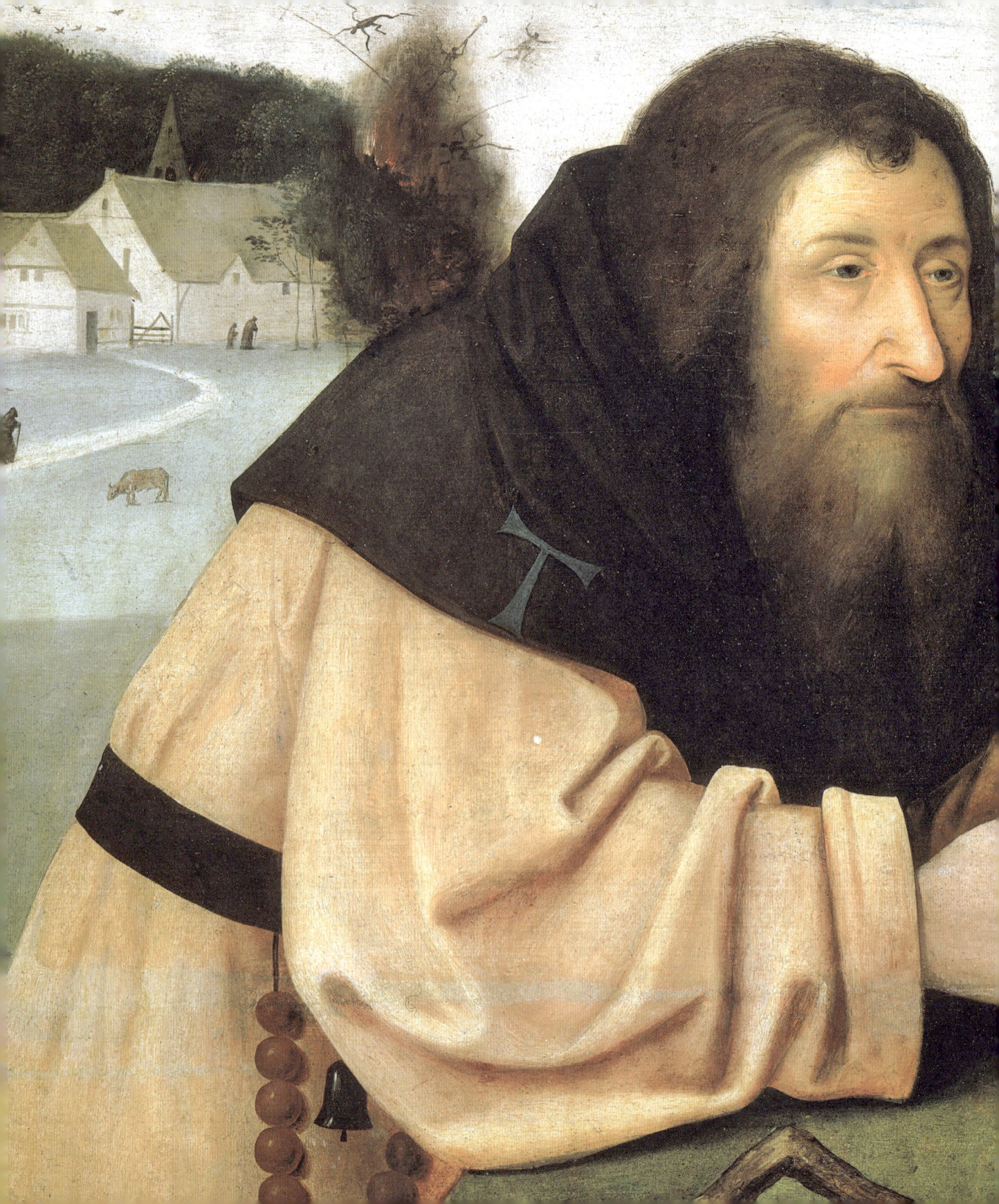

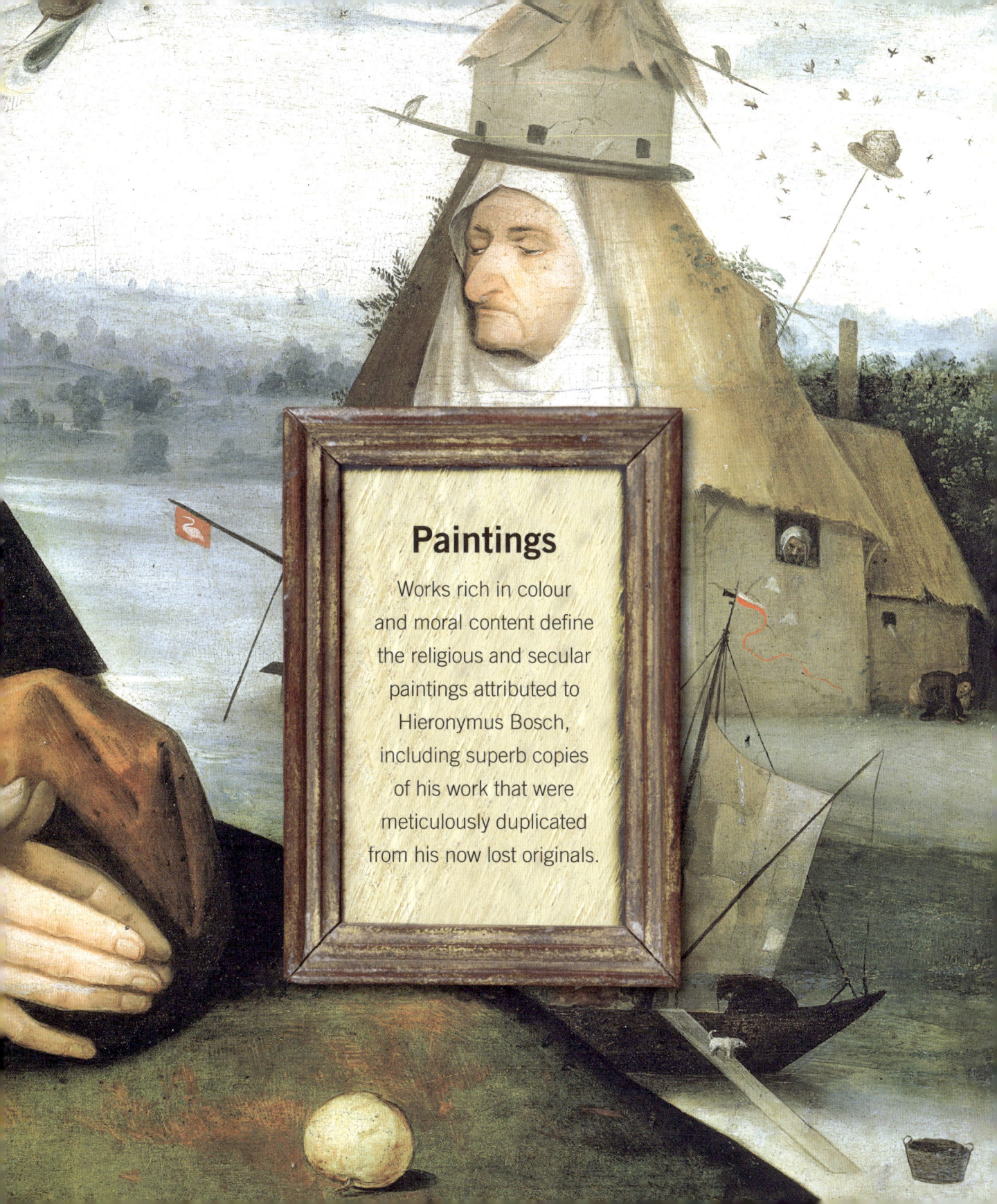

Paintings

Works rich in colour and moral content define the religious and secular paintings attributed to Hieronymus Bosch, including superb copies of his work that were meticulously duplicated from his now lost originals.

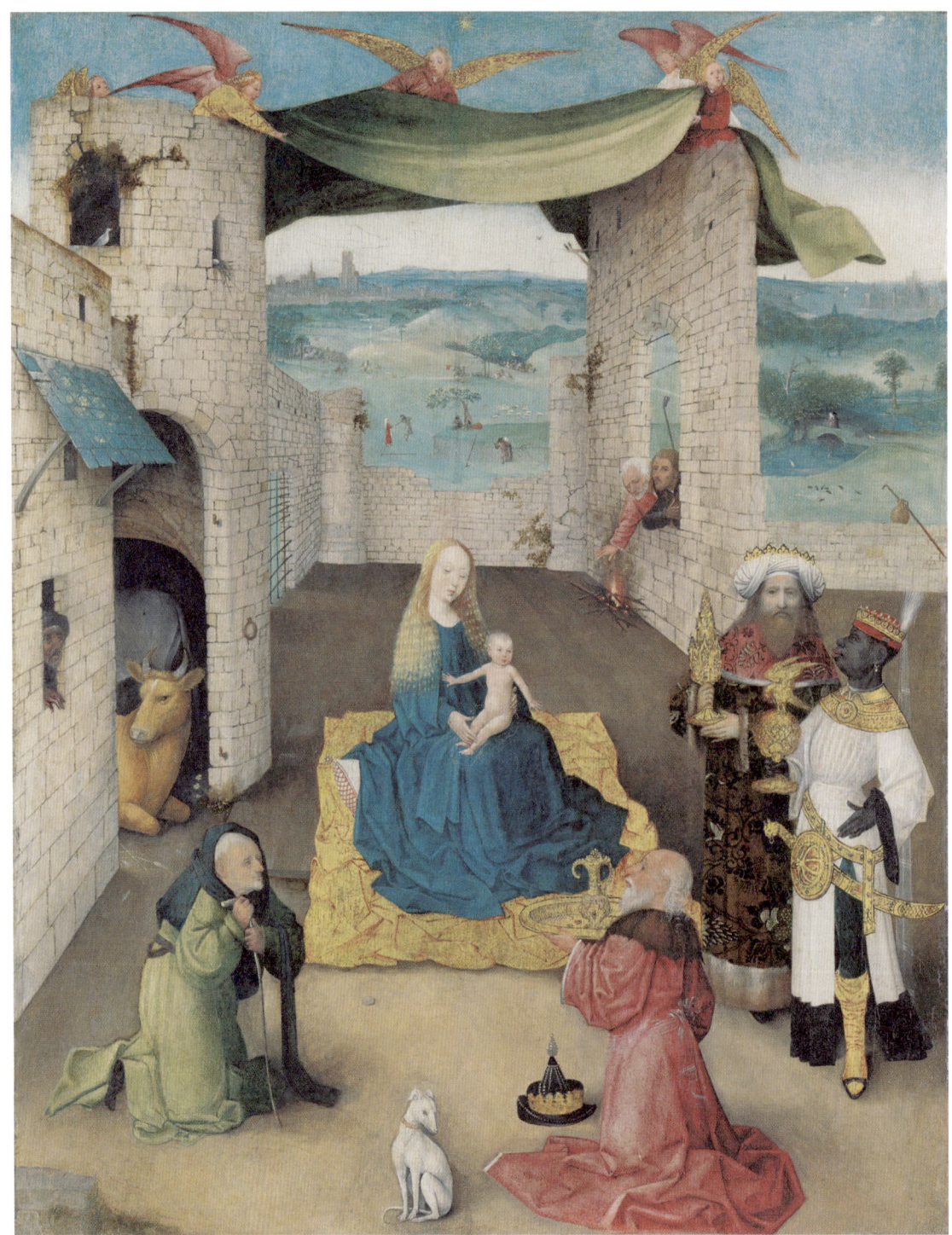

The Adoration of the Magi, *c.* 1470–80
Oil, tempera & gold on panel, 71.1 x 56.5 cm (28 x 22¼ in)
• Metropolitan Museum, New York

Depicting the visitation of the Three Wise Men from the East to acknowledge the newborn Christ Child (Matthew 2:1–12) and his mother the Virgin Mary. The painting is recognized as one of Bosch's earliest works.

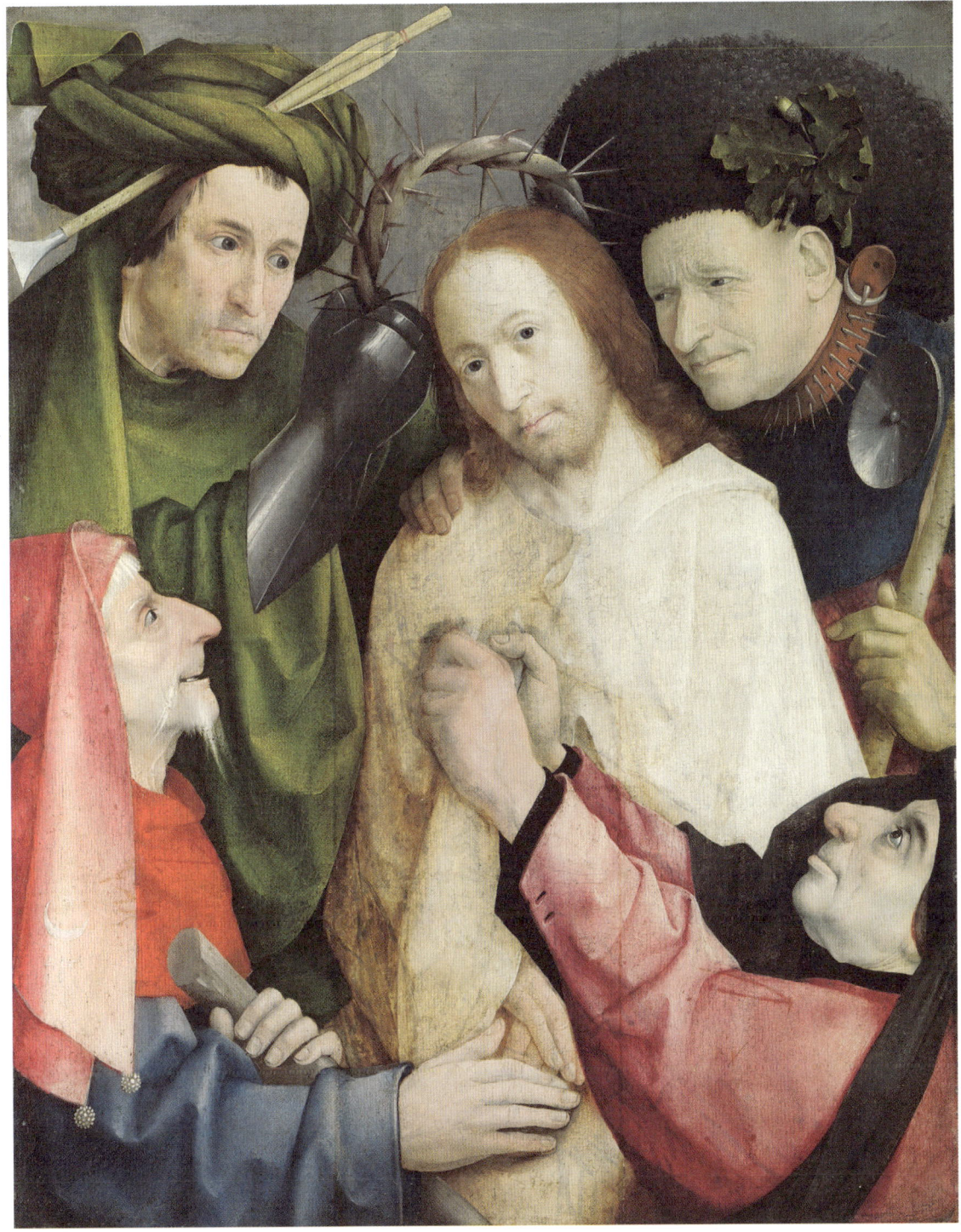

Christ Mocked (The Crowning with Thorns), *c.* 1479–1516
Oil on oak panel, 73.5 x 59.1 cm (29 x 23⅓ in)
• National Gallery, London

A narrative of Christ on his journey to be crucified, in which Bosch portrays the calmness of Christ in contrast to his persecutors who jostle and push near him, carrying the *arma Christi*, the weapons of Christ's Passion.

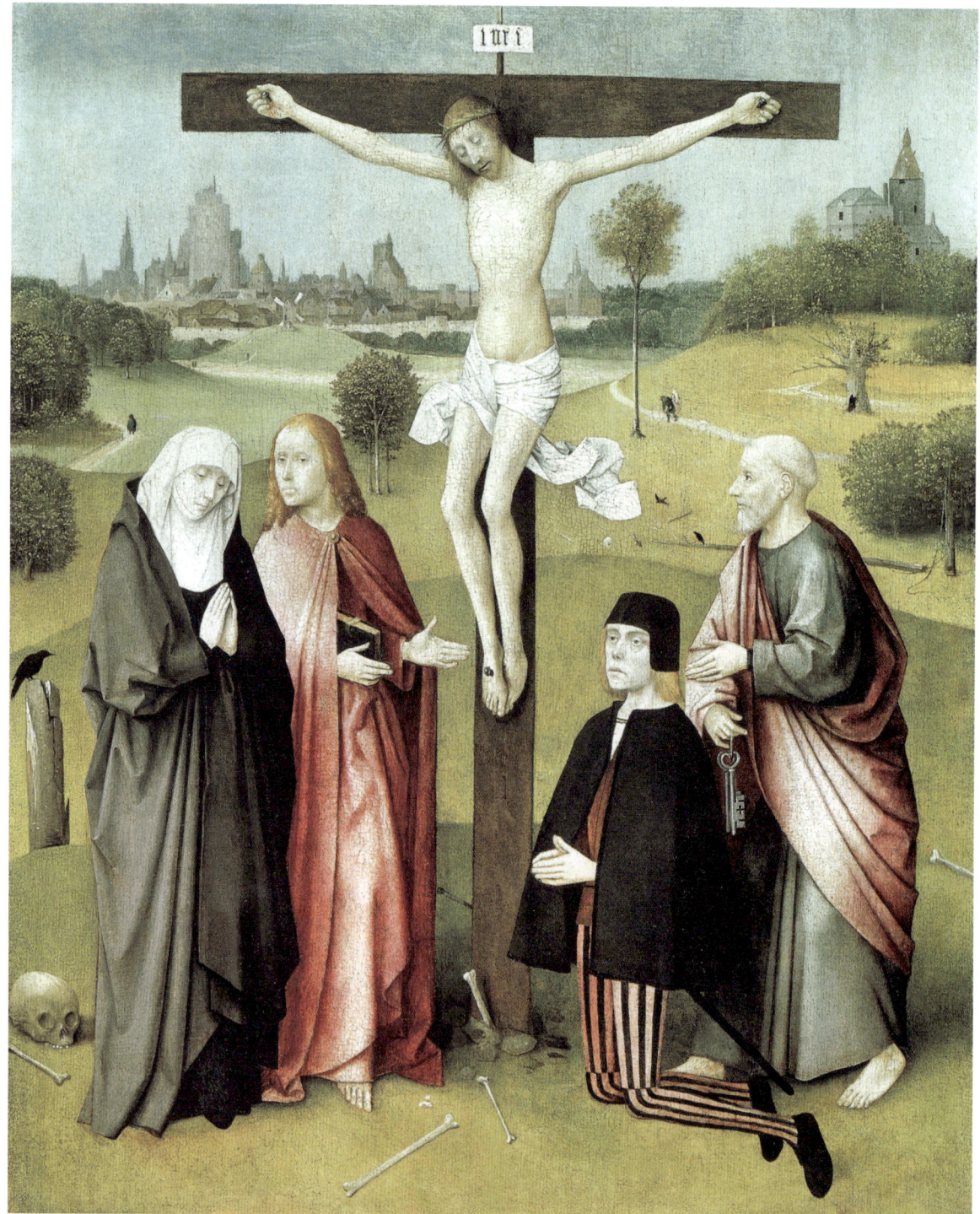

**Christ Crucified with Donors and Saints
(Calvary with Donors), 1480–90**
Tempera on panel, 74.4 x 61 cm (29⅓ x 24 in)
• Musées Royaux des Beaux-Arts de Belgique, Brussels

The crucified Christ is attended by the Virgin Mary standing with John the Evangelist, both mentioned as present in the biblical narrative. The kneeling donor, a noble wearing fashionable contemporary dress, is supported by his patron saint, Peter.

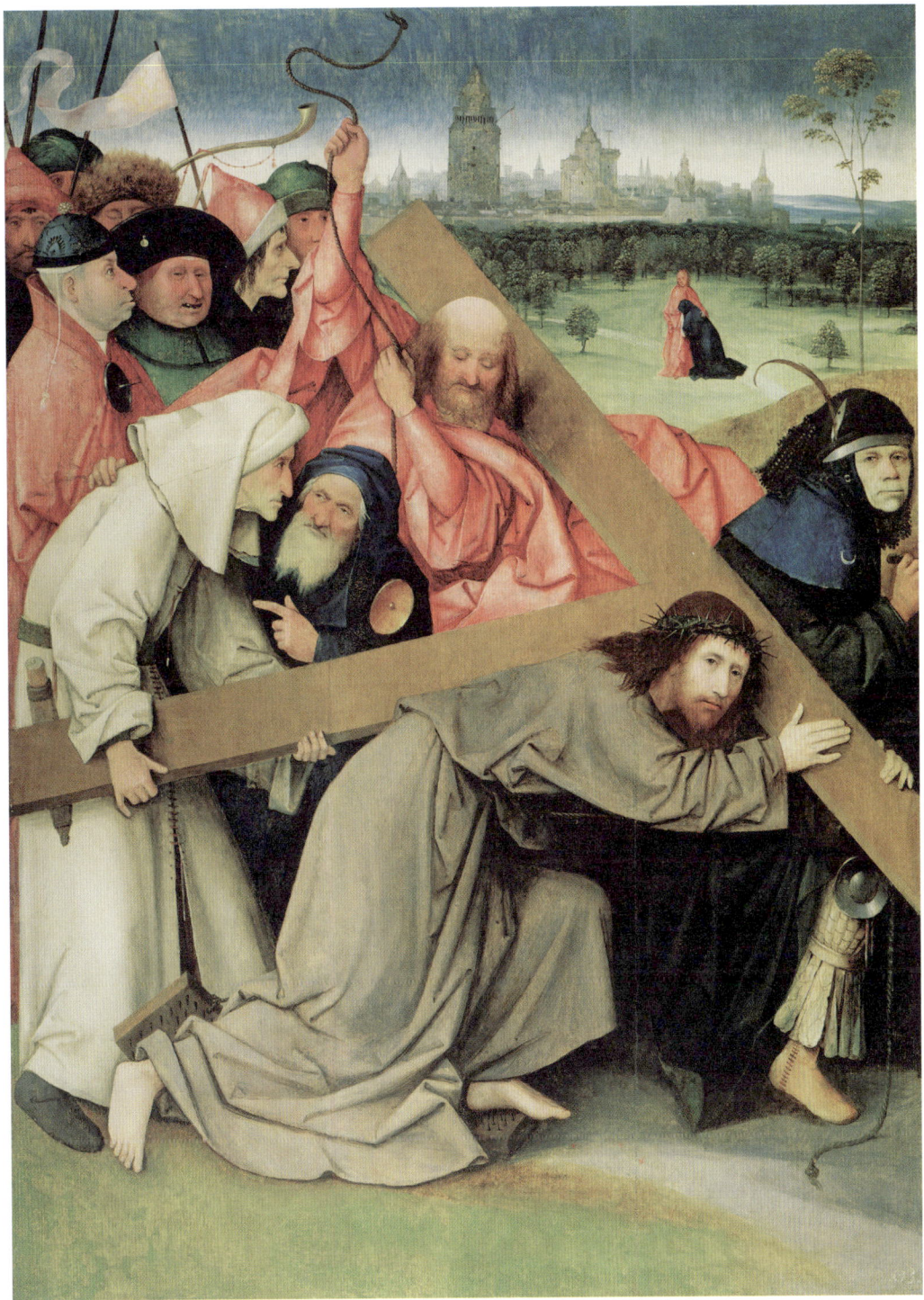

Christ Carrying the Cross, c. 1485
Oil on panel, 57 x 32 cm (22 x 13 in)
• Palacio Real de Madrid, Madrid

Christ burdened with the weight of the Cross looks out to onlookers on his journey to the Crucifixion. His persecutors have tied wooden blocks of nails to his bare feet to increase his suffering.

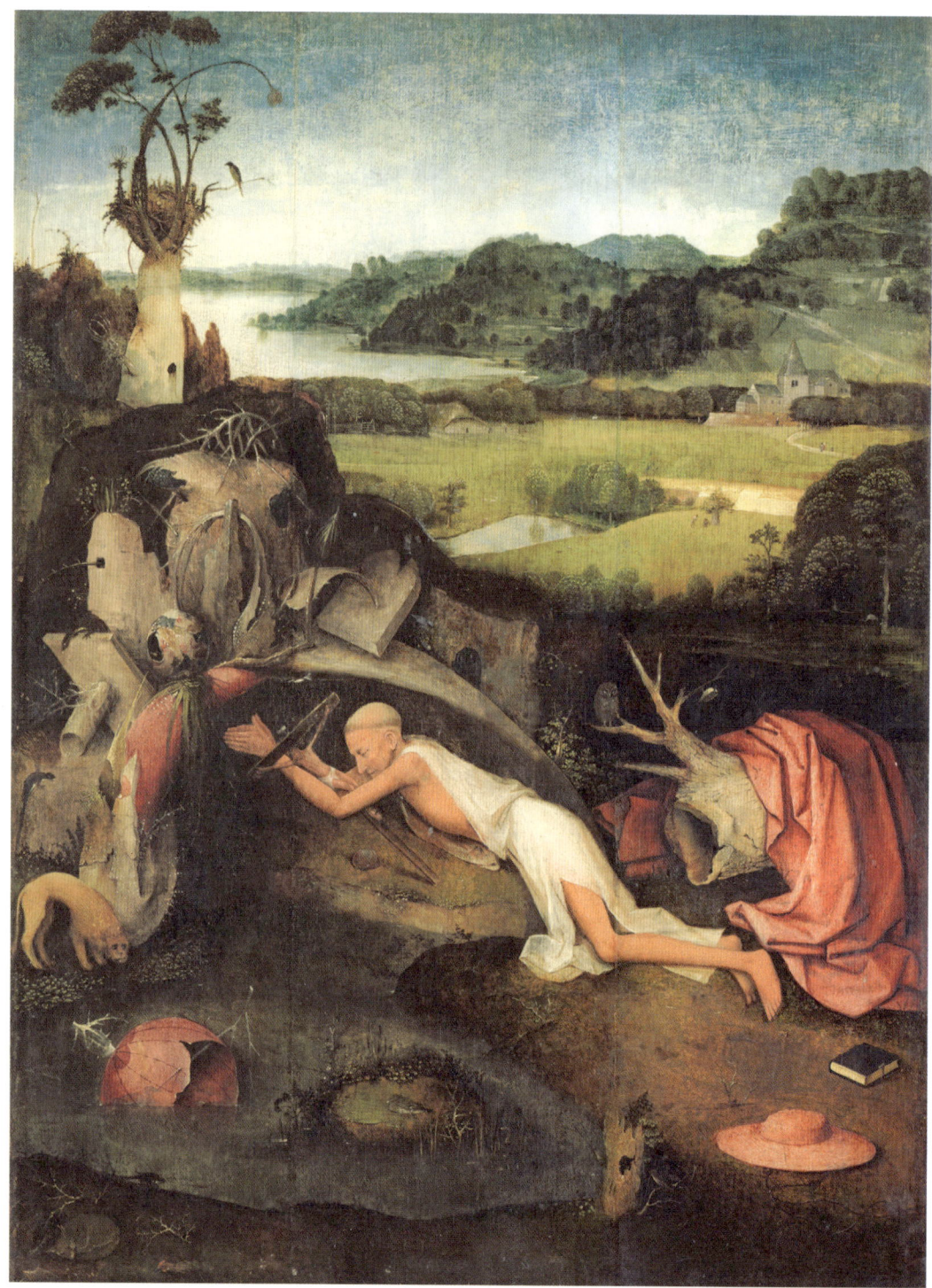

St Jerome at Prayer, *c.* **1485–95**
Oil on panel, 80.1 x 60.6 cm (31½ x 24 in)
• Museum voor Schone Kunsten, Ghent

Holding a crucifix between his outstretched arms, a penitent St Jerome prostrates himself to pray before the image of Christ on the Cross. Within the serene landscape, an owl, symbol of evil, observes the hermit's woodland home.

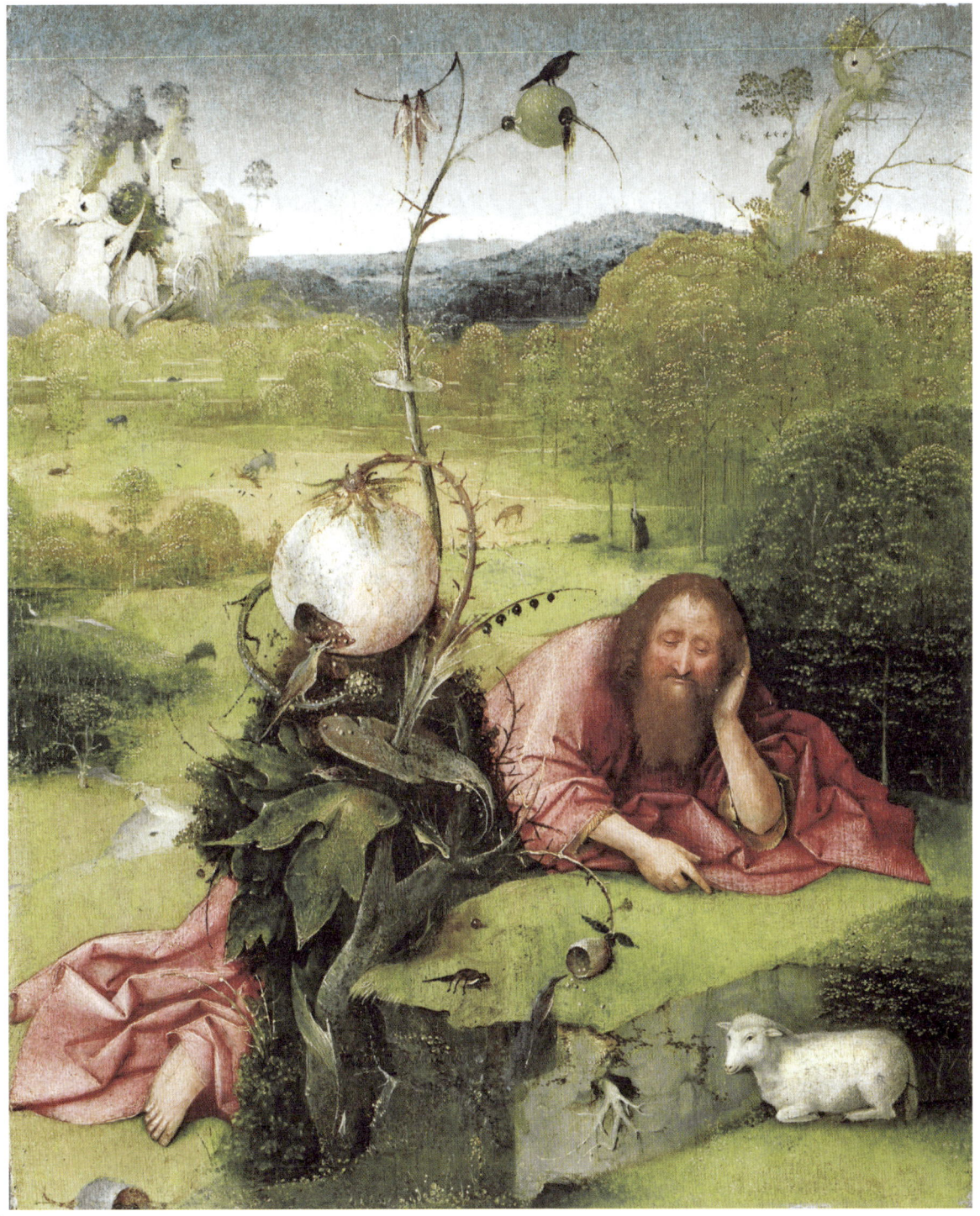

St John the Baptist in the Wilderness, *c.* 1490–95
Oil on panel, 49 x 41 cm (19⅓ x 16 in)
• Museum of Lazaro Galdiano, Madrid

St John the Baptist preached in the desert wilderness of Judea (Matthew 3:1–6). Here he is depicted at rest, similar in style to the Geerten Tot Sint Jans version of *St John the Baptist in the Wilderness*, *c.* 1485 (Staatliche Museen, Berlin, Germany).

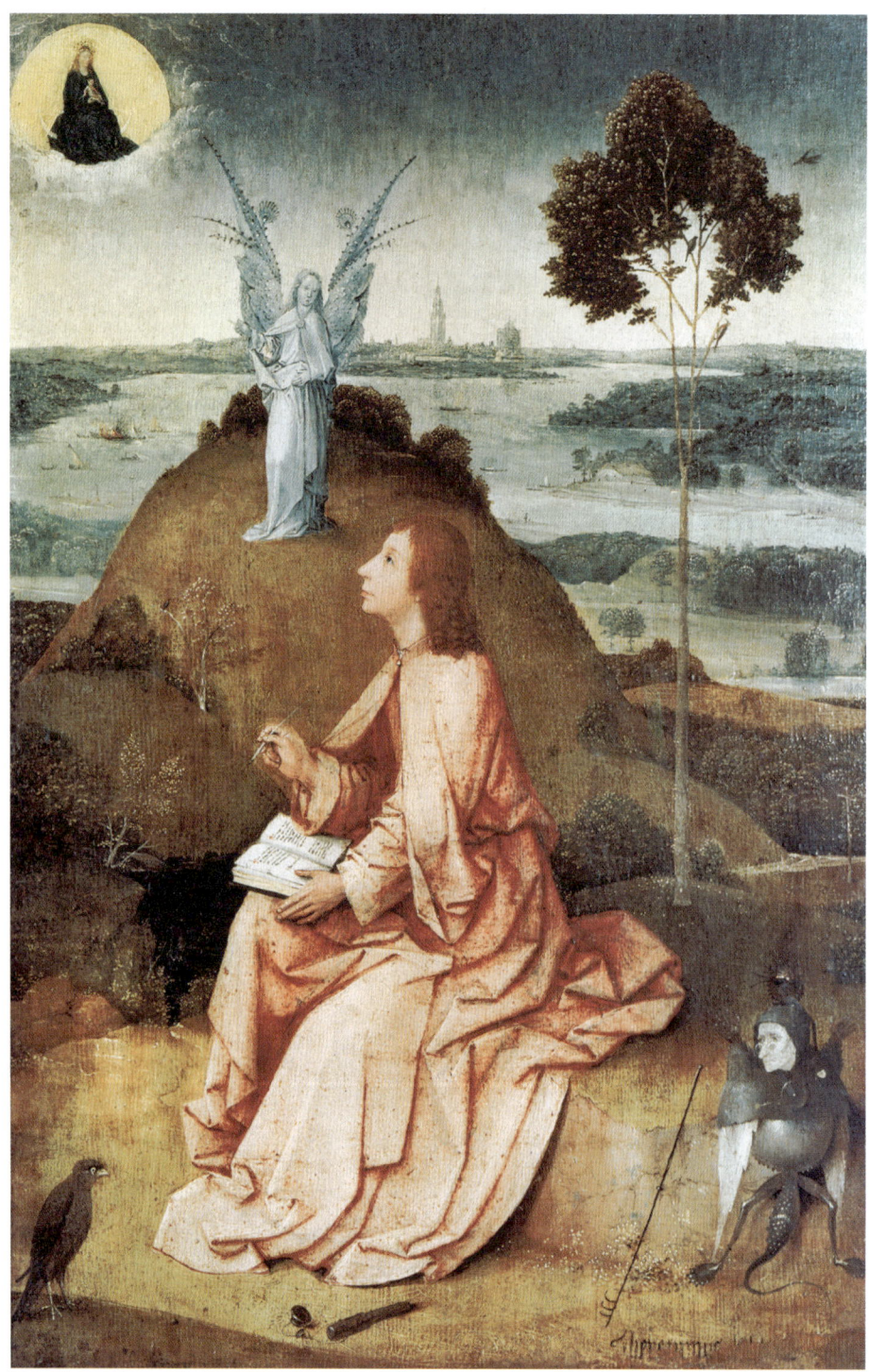

St John the Evangelist on Patmos, *c.* **1490–95**
Oil on oak panel, 63 x 43.3 cm (24¾ x 17 in)
• Bode Museum, Berlin

St John the Evangelist on Patmos may be paired with that of another hermit-saint *St John the Baptist* (Madrid), for an altarpiece in the church of Sint Jan, 's-Hertogenbosch. The reverse panel is a roundel of *The Passion of Christ.*

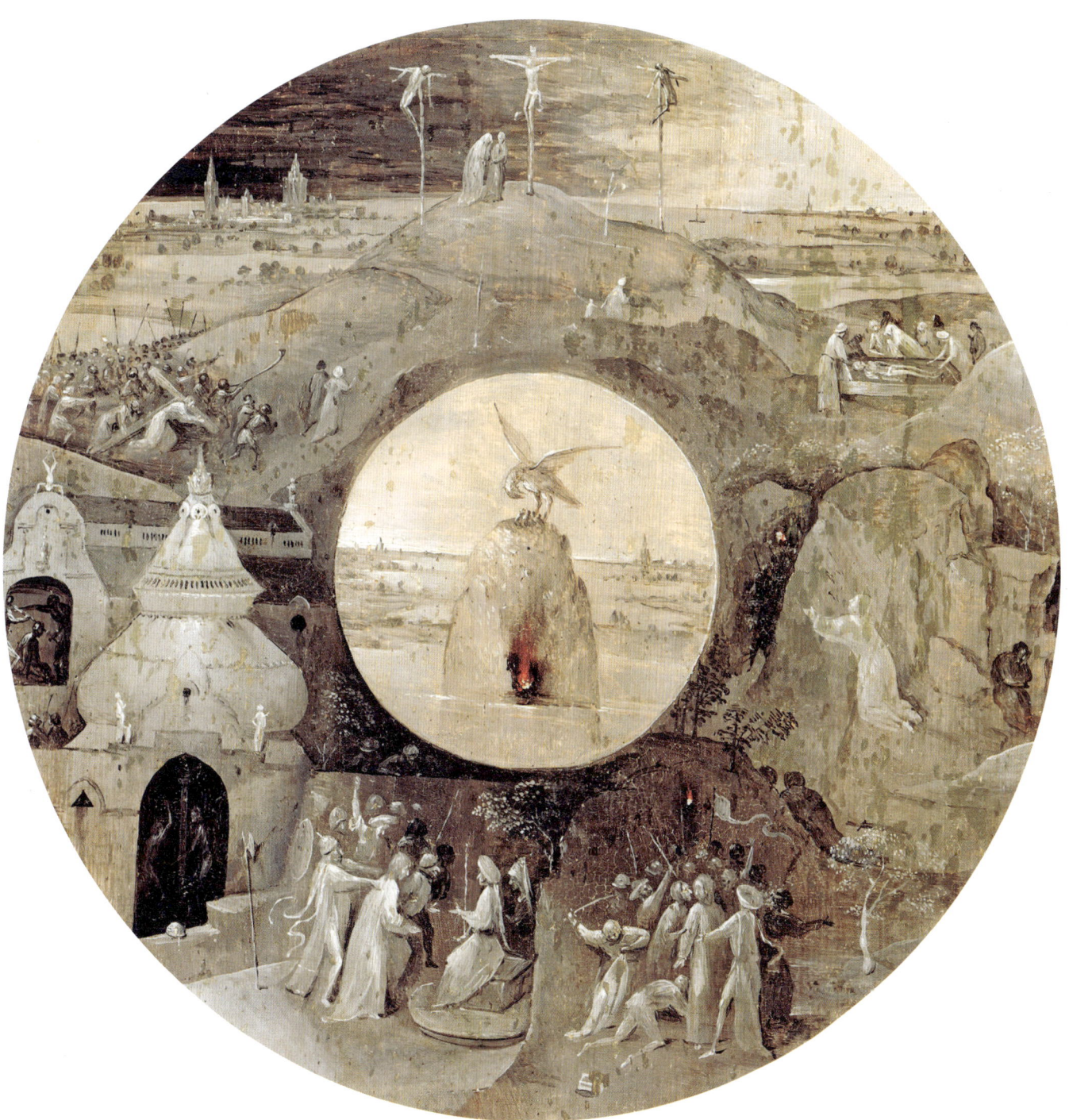

**Scenes from the Passion of Christ, *c.* 1490–95
(reverse of St John the Evangelist on Patmos)**
Oil on panel, 63 x 43.3 cm (24¾ x 17 in)
• Gemäldegalerie Museum, Berlin

Scenes from the Passion of Christ are visually narrated around a portrayal at the centre
of a pelican feeding her young with blood from her own breast so that they may live,
symbolic of Christ crucified for the salvation of mankind.

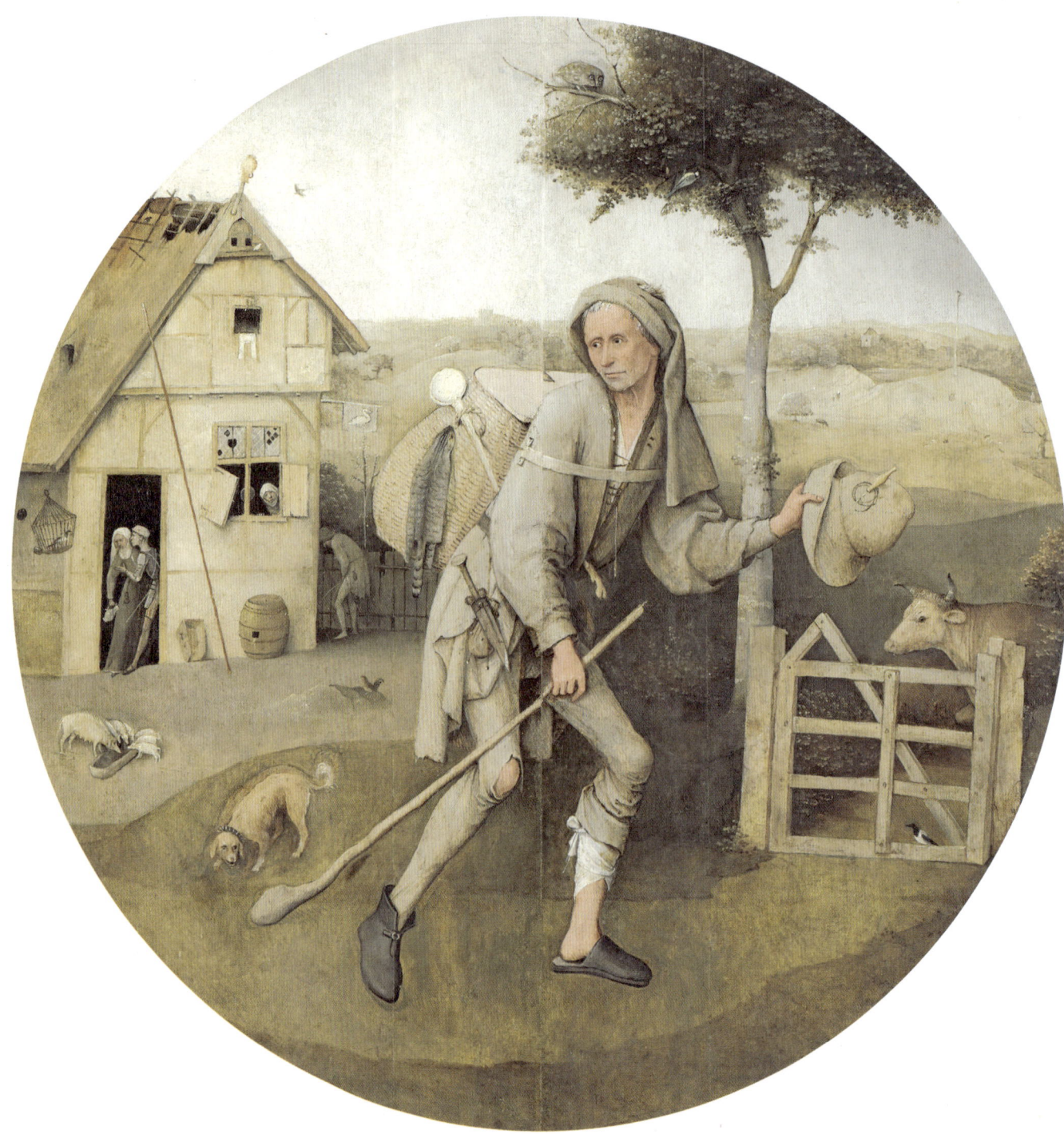

The Pedlar (The Prodigal Son/Wayfarer), *c.* **1494–1516**
Oil on panel, 71 x 70.6 cm (28 x 27¾ in)
• Museum Boijmans van Beuningen, Rotterdam

A pedlar walks past a run-down house of ill repute, a brothel with women at its windows and door. Has he indulged in their earthly pleasures or stuck to the narrow path of the higher moral ground?

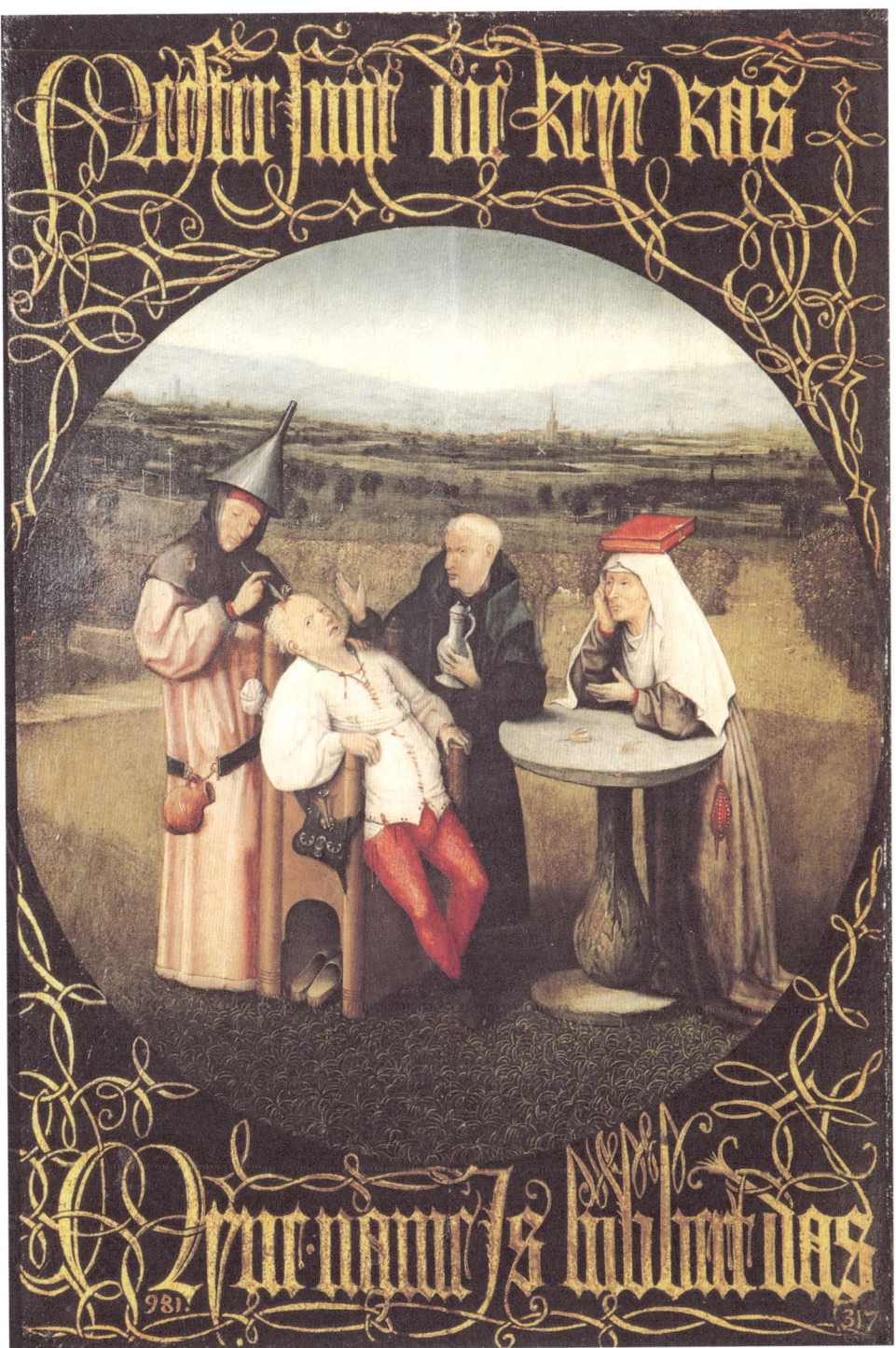

The Cure of Folly (Cutting the Stone),
c. **1494–1516, after Bosch**
Oil on panel, 47.5 x 34.5 cm (18¾ x 13⅔ in)
• Museo Nacional del Prado, Madrid

In a superb copy of a Bosch original, a medieval comic tale is richly illustrated. A quack surgeon cuts open an old man's skull to remove the stone of folly, considered the cause of his stupidity. A woman and monk mindlessly watch.

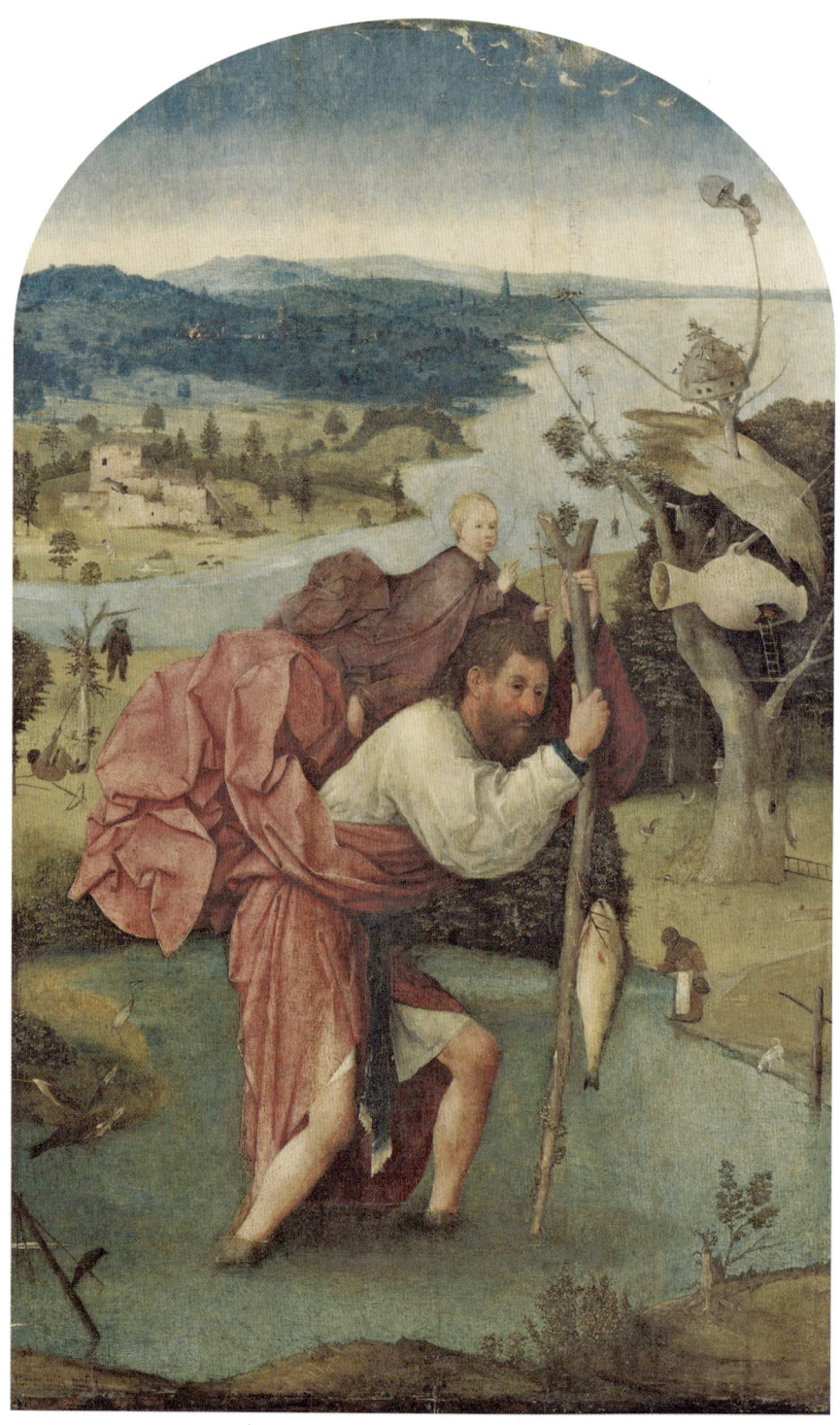

St Christopher Carrying the Christ Child, *c.* 1496–1505
Oil on panel, 113 x 71.5 cm (44½ x 28 in)
• Museum Boijmans van Beuningen, Rotterdam

St Christopher carries the Christ Child across a body of water. On the journey the child becomes heavier, symbolizing the weight of the sins of mankind carried by the young boy. St Christopher leans heavily on his staff for support.

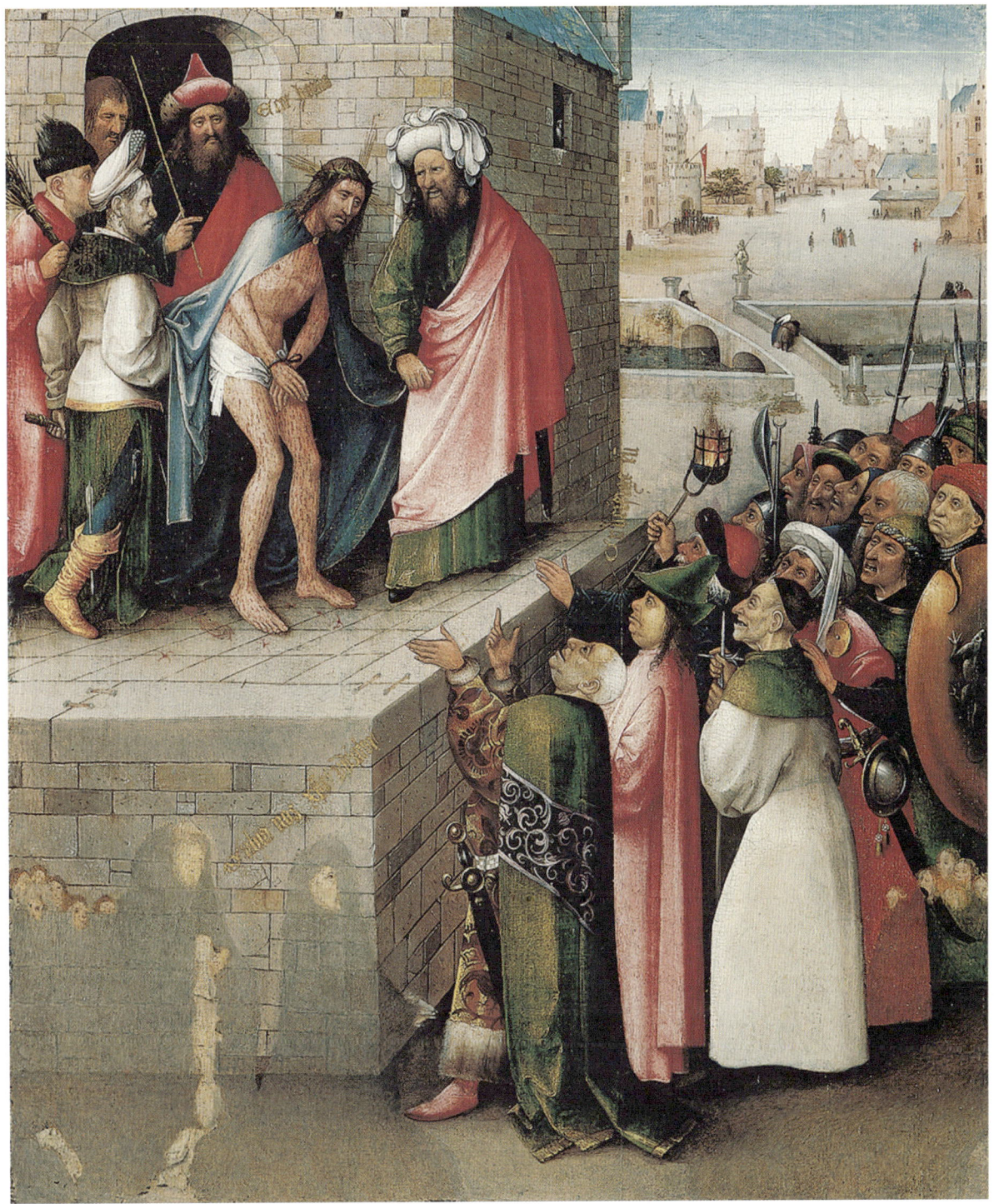

Ecce Homo, c. 1500
Oil on oak panel, 71.1 x 60.5 cm (28 x 24 in)
• Städel Museum, Frankfurt am Main

'Behold the Man' (*Ecce Homo*) are Latin words spoken by Pontius Pilate (Vulgate, John:19), as he presented the tortured Christ to jeering, aggressive crowds. Bosch divides attention between the lonely figure of Christ and the baying, bloodthirsty mob. The figures on the left, later painted out, represented donors witnessing the scene.

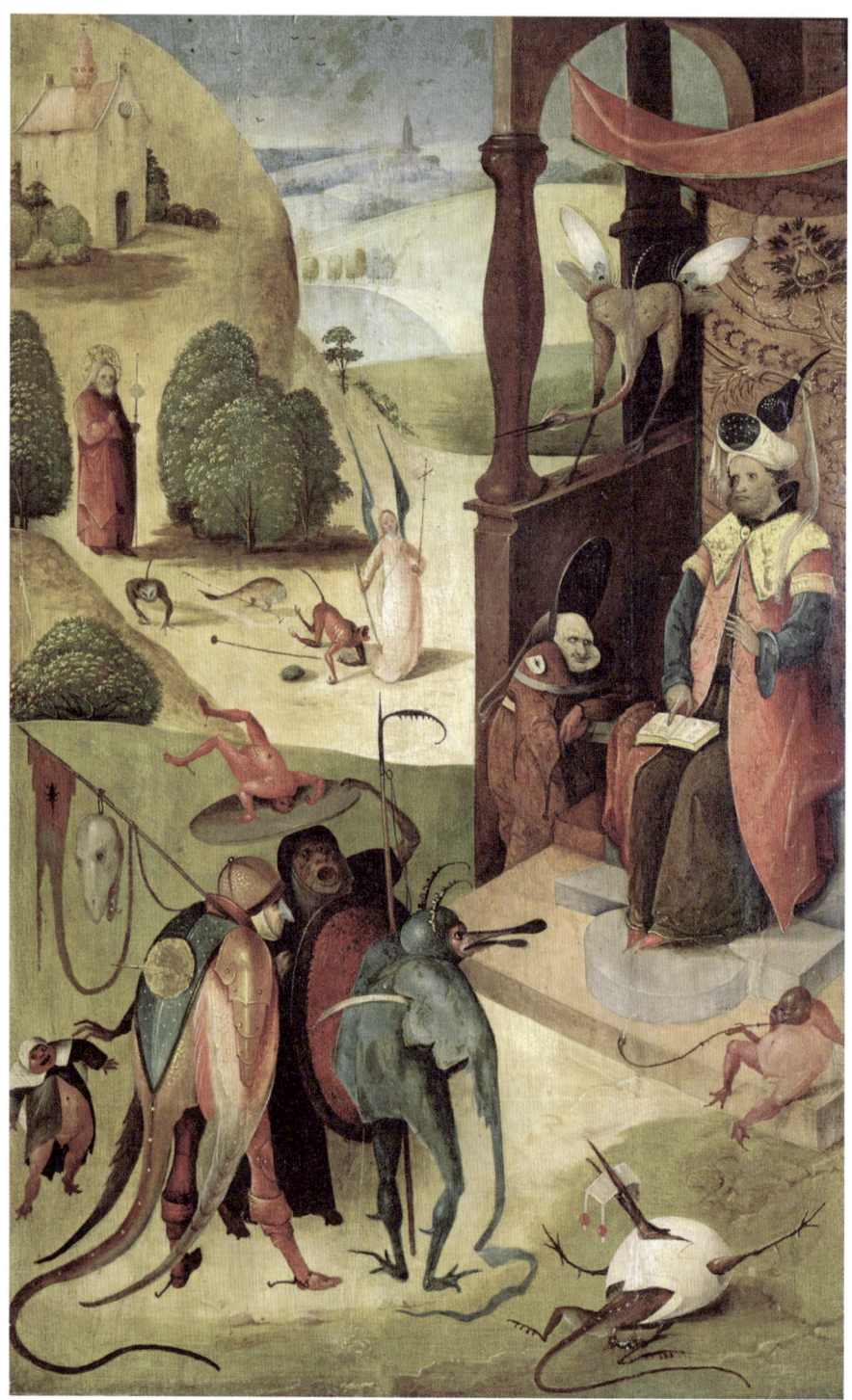

St James and the Magician, *c.* 1500, after Bosch
Oil on panel, 60 x 40 cm (23⅔ x 15¾ in)
• Musée des Beaux-Arts, Valenciennes

This panel – its reverse side is opposite – is thought to be a copy of a Bosch work. It illustrates episodes from the thirteenth-century *Golden Legend* (*see* page 19). Here, the magician Hermogenes contracts with the devils he will send to overpower St James.

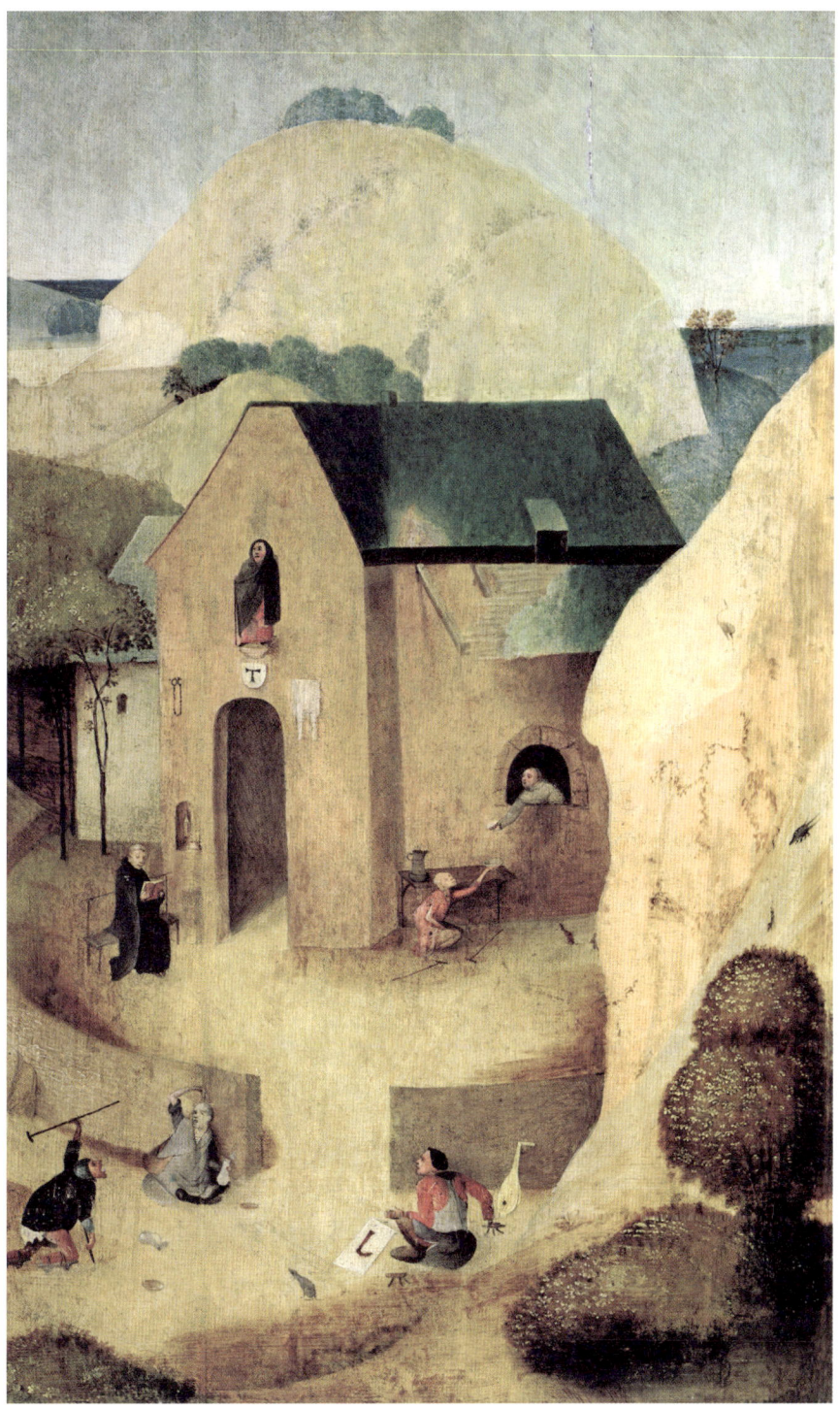

An Antonian Priory, *c.* **1500, after Bosch
(reverse of St James and the Magician)**
Oil on panel, 60 x 40 cm (23⅗ x 15¾ in)
• Musée des Beaux-Arts, Valenciennes

This is the reverse side of *St James and the Magician* (opposite), thought to be a copy of a Bosch work. It shows the healer saint, St Anthony, reading in front of a house, while at the entrance to the garden, a busker and two invalid beggars quarrel.

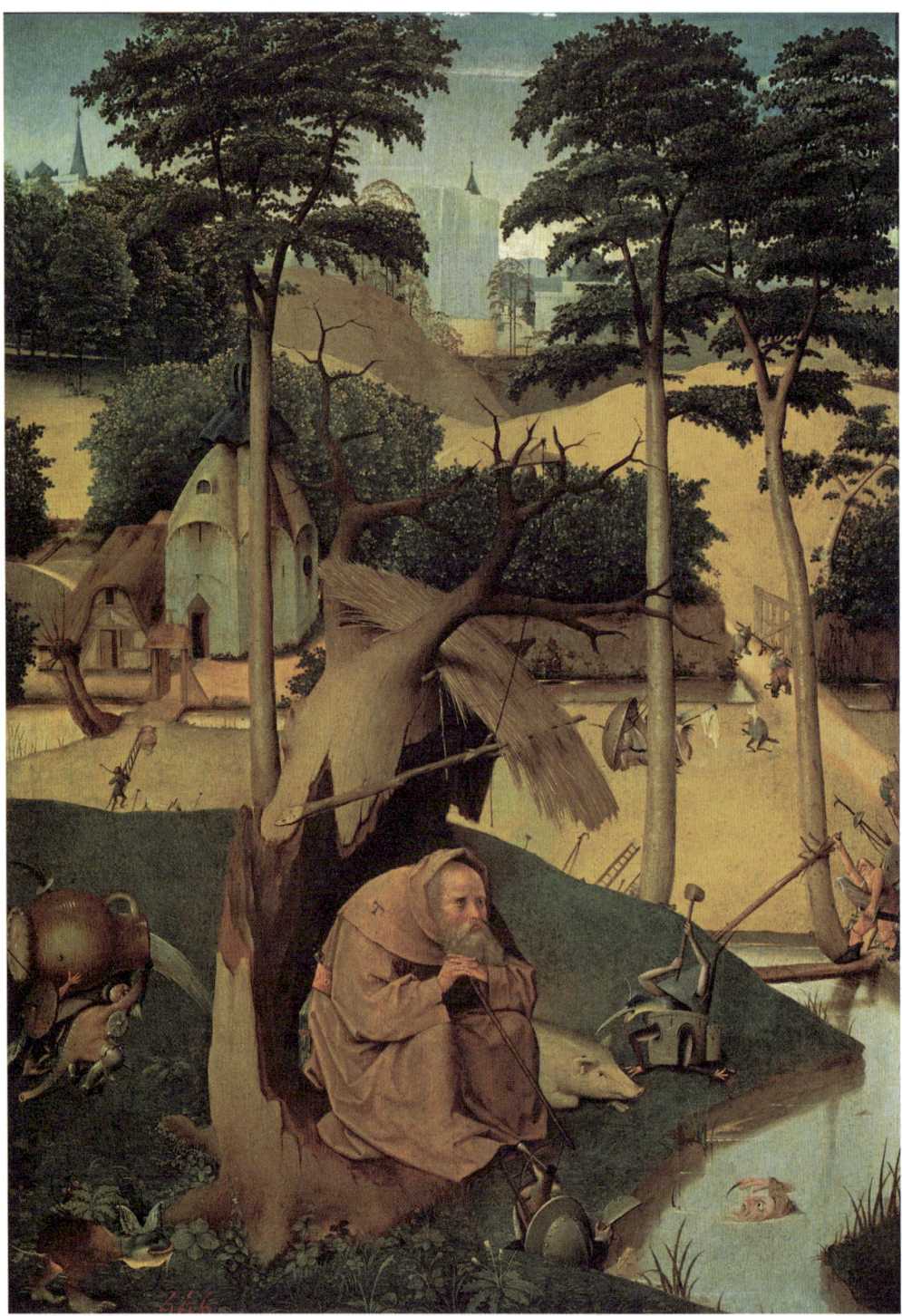

The Temptation of St Anthony, *c.* **1500 or 1530-40, follower**
Oil on panel, 73 x 52.5 cm (29 x 20¾ in)
• Museo Nacional del Prado, Madrid

An elderly monk, St Anthony, helper of the poor, sits in contemplation in a hollowed-out tree. His pig lies next to his feet. Strange occurrences are taking place in the picturesque landscape, but he ignores the material world around him.

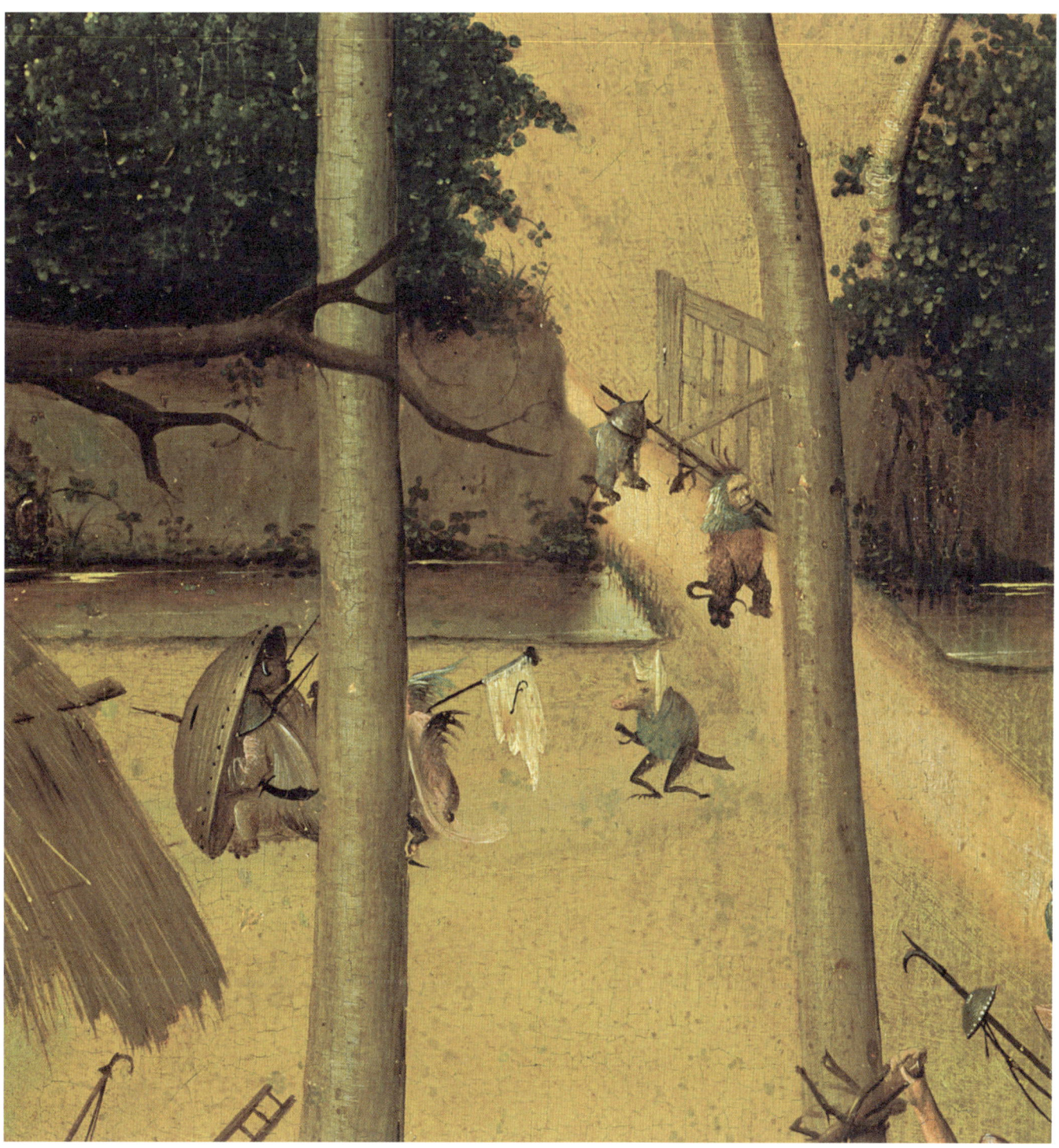

The Temptation of St Anthony, *c.* 1500 or 1530-40, follower
Oil on panel, 73 x 52.5 cm (29 x 20¾ in)
• Museo Nacional del Prado, Madrid

The artist has populated this painting with many demons intent on tempting St Anthony – or seemingly getting on with their monstrous business – copying Bosch's unlimited surreal imagination.

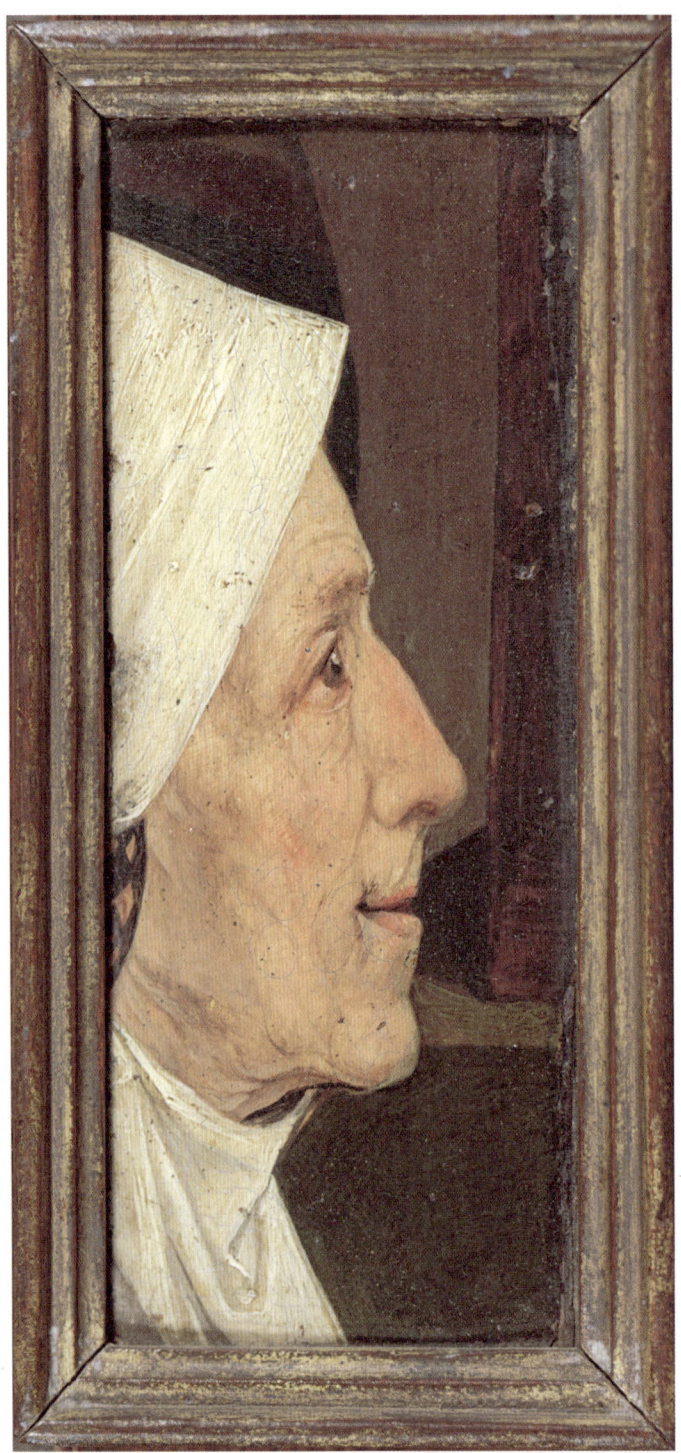

Head of an Old Woman, *c.* 1500
Oil on panel, 13 x 5 cm (5 x 2 in)
• Museum Boijmans van Beuningen, Rotterdam

A superb study of the face of an elderly woman in profile. Her skin is etched with lines, her eyes bright. The painting is a small fragment of a lost work attributed to Hieronymus Bosch.

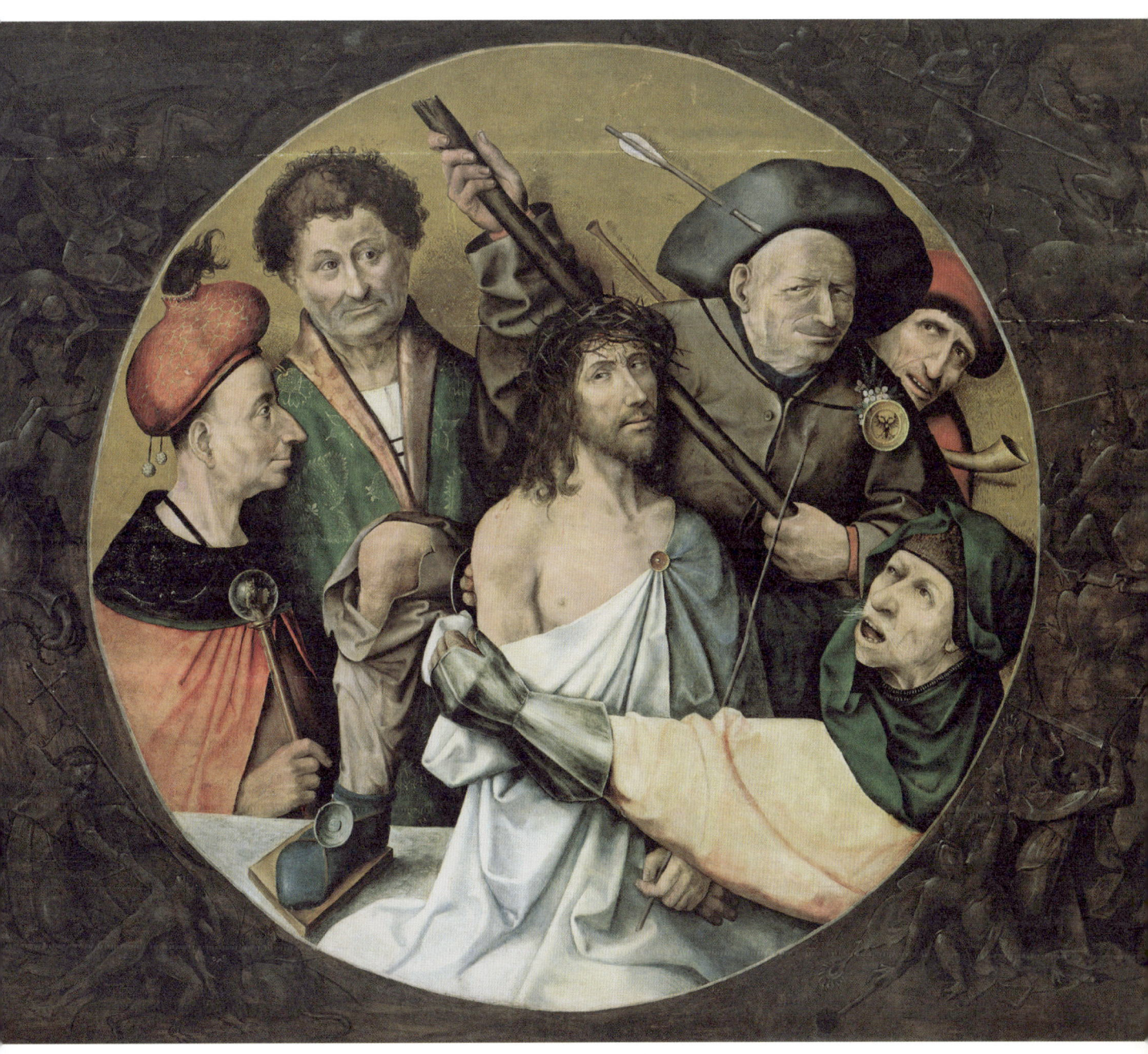

Christ Crowned with Thorns, *c.* 1500, after Bosch
Oil on wood, 165 x 195 cm (65 x 77 in) • El Escorial, Madrid

This roundel, which appears to carry Bosch's signature, is part of a triptych and in fact is a copy after Bosch. It is similar in content, not style, to *Christ Mocked (The Crowning with Thorns) (see* page 37), where a mob surrounds Christ at the centre.

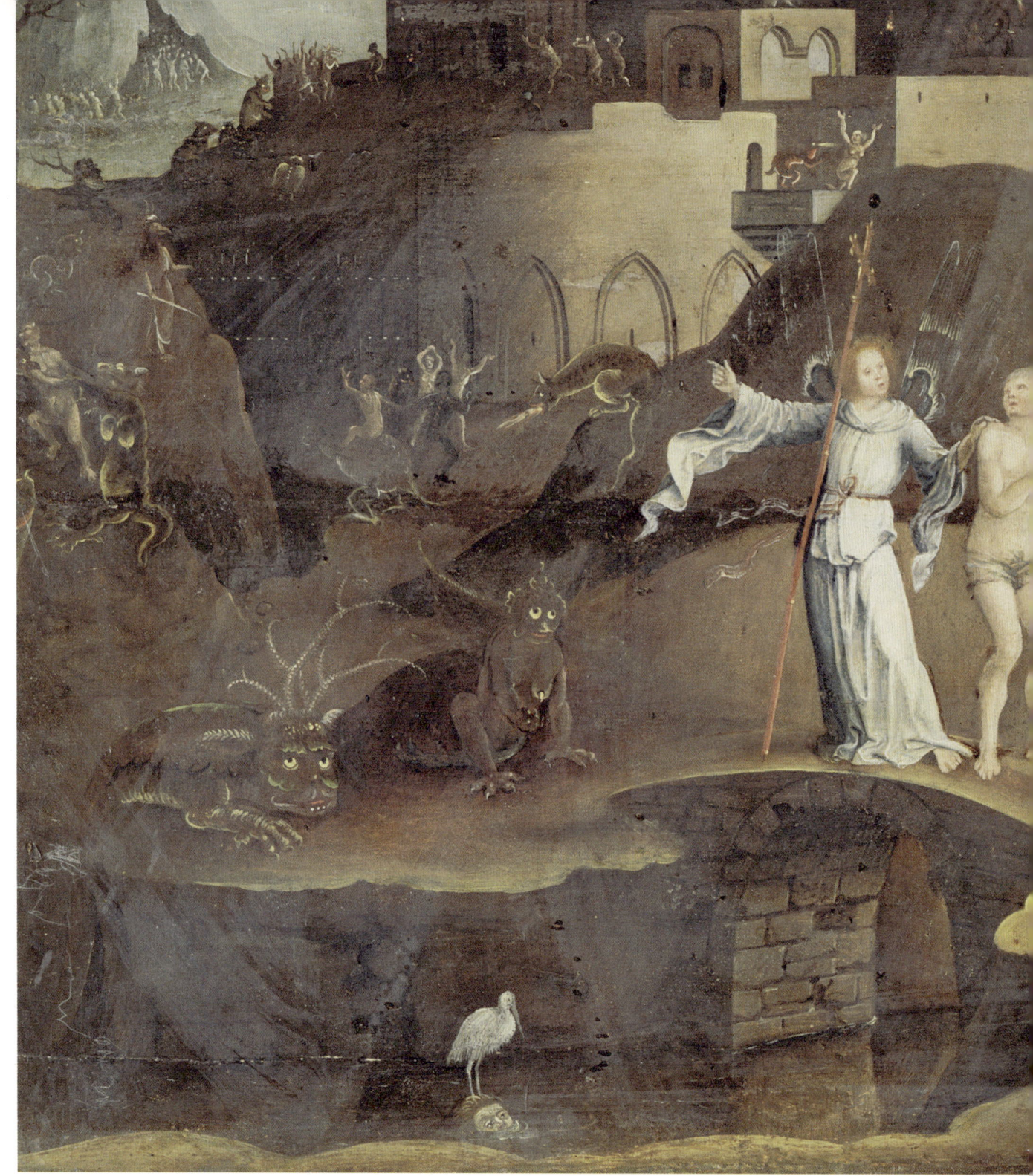

An Angel with a Soul at the Edge of Hell, *c.* **1500, after Bosch**
Oil on panel, 102 x 76 cm (40¼ x 30 in)
• London, England/Private Collection

Devils tumble from the skies in a mystical Boschian landscape, where a guardian angel guides a frightened soul to the edge of Hell. It is guarded and inhabited by otherworldly and menacing creatures.

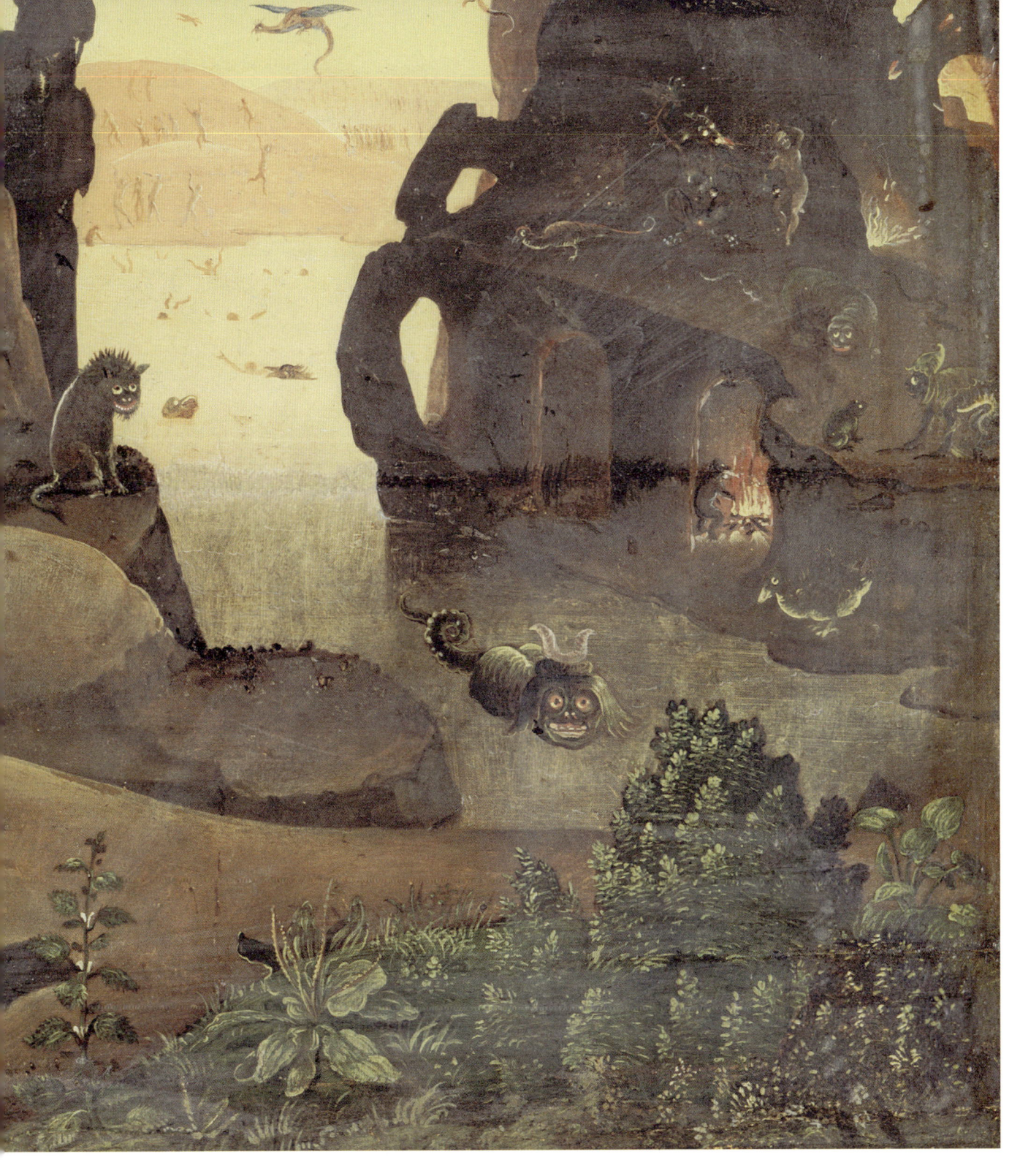

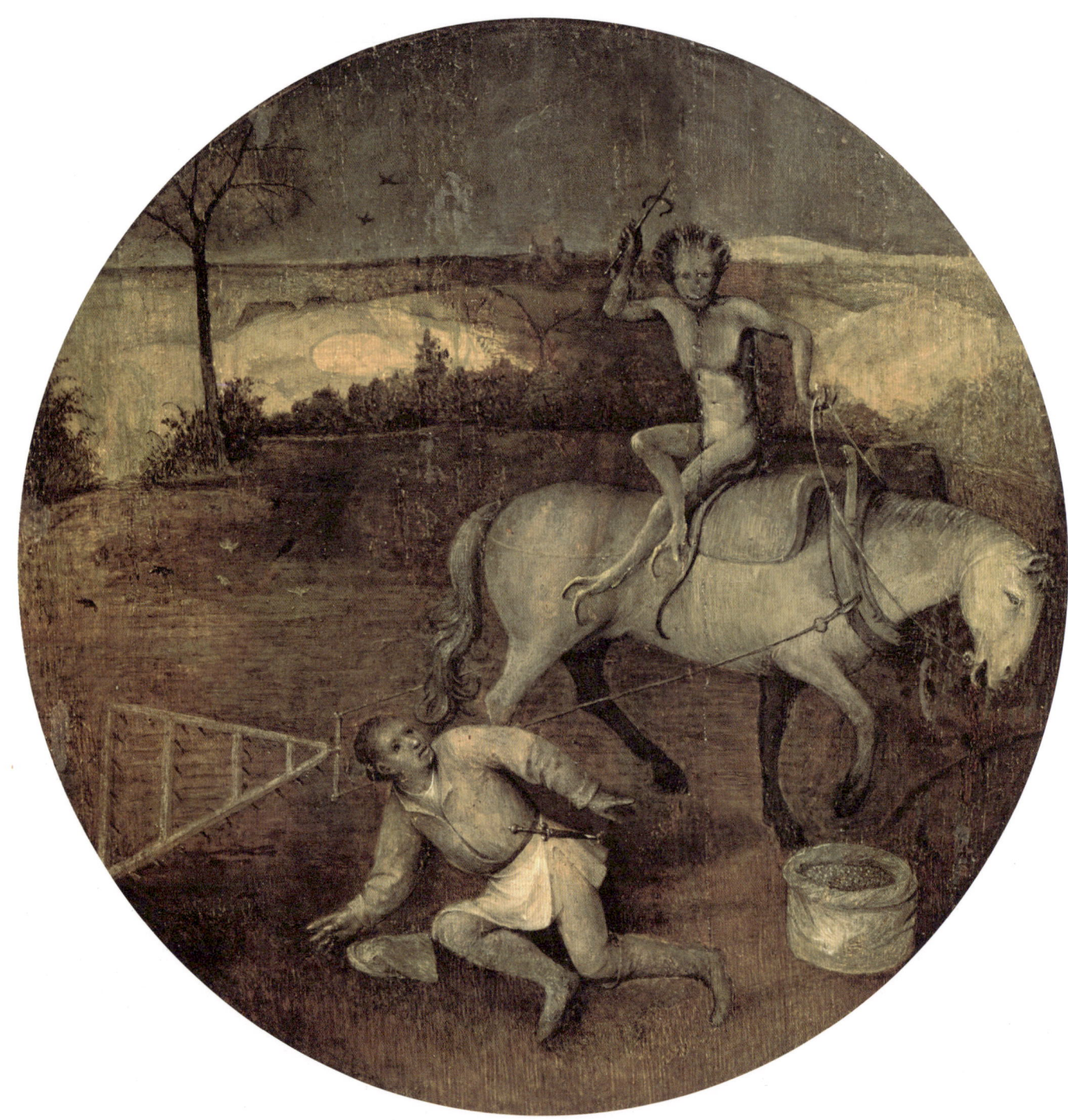

Ploughman Unhorsed by a Demon, *c.* **1500**
Oil on panel • Museum Boijmans van Beuningen, Rotterdam

A ploughman is pushed to the ground by a devil with clawed feet, who steals his horse and plough. The moral symbolism of the act may be directed at the ploughman, who should have remained vigilant against evil.

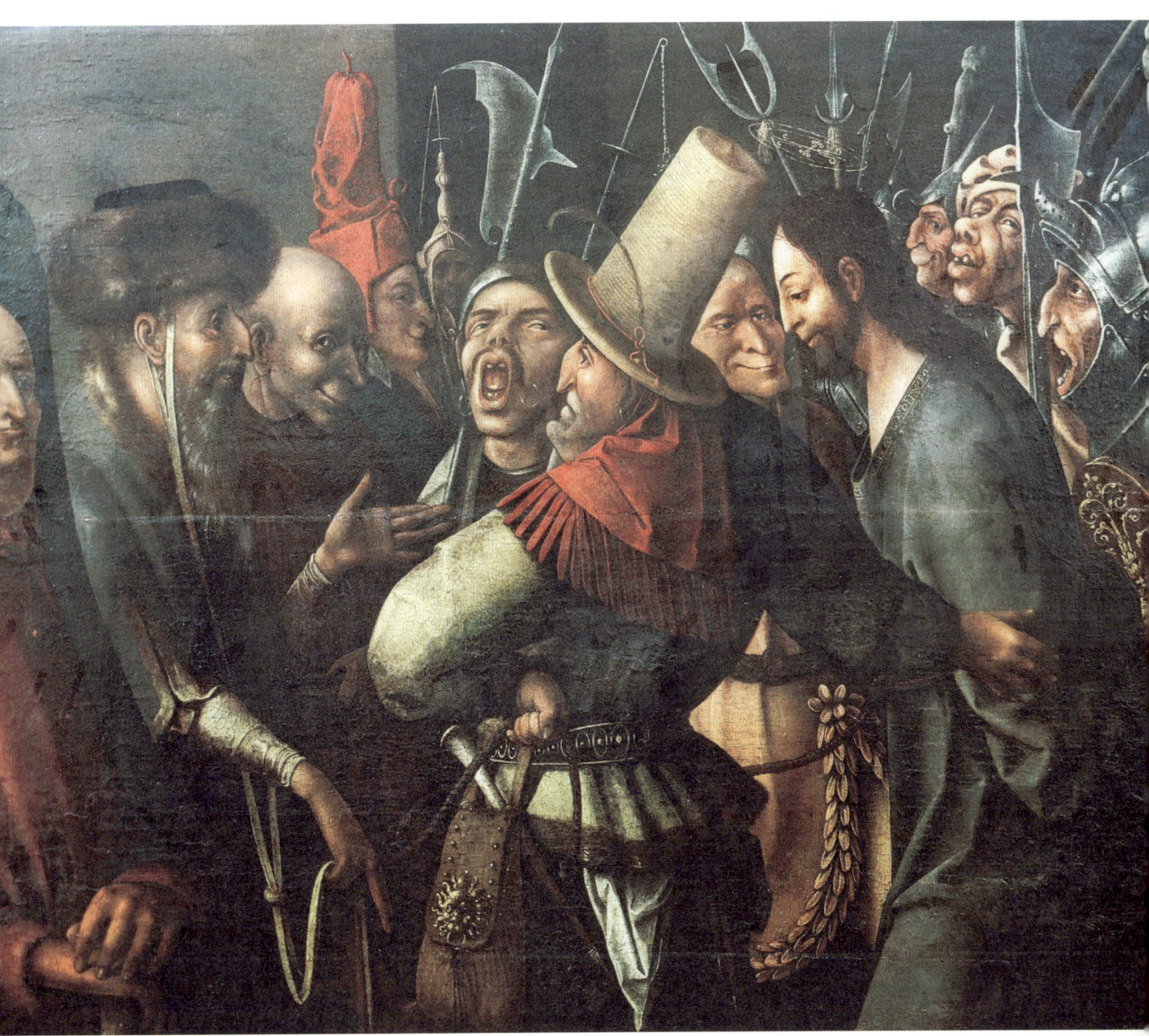

Christ Brought Before Pilate, after Bosch, *c.* 1500
Oil on panel, 61 x 77 cm (24 x 30⅓ in) • Museo de Arte, Sao Paulo

The style and content of this painting suggest a copy from a Bosch original work. Centred on the narrative of the Passion, a group of men deliver Christ to the Roman prefect Pontius Pilate, to answer charges brought against him.

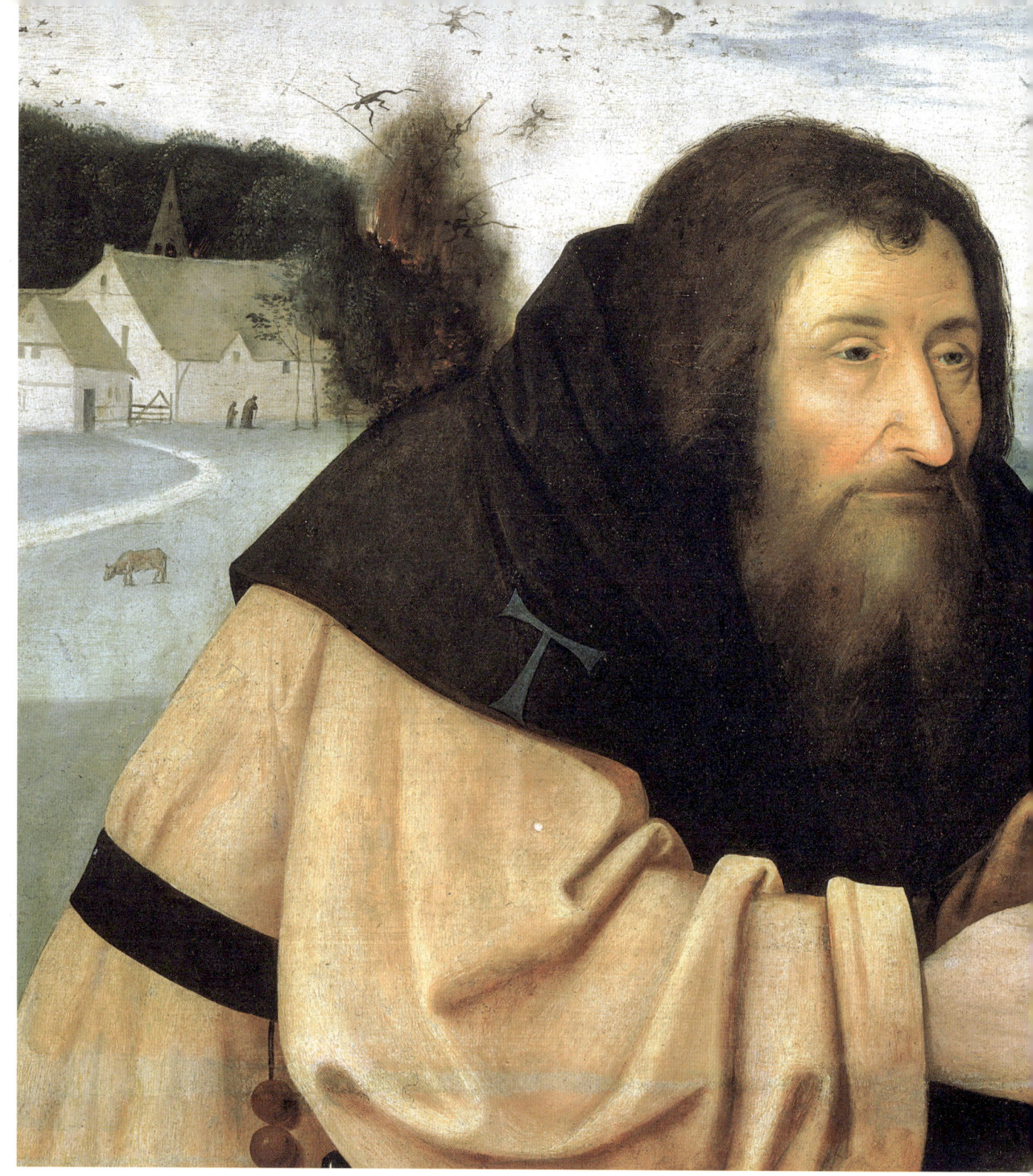

**The Temptation of St Anthony, c. 1500,
copy of Bosch's original work**

Oil on panel, 70 x 115 cm (27½ x 45⅓ in)

• Museo Nacional del Prado, Madrid

Considered to be a superb copy of one of Bosch's finest works, now lost, St Anthony is in the foreground, wearing his habit with the blue 'T' (Greek *tau*) emblem. The painter includes worldly temptations in the nearby house of prostitution.

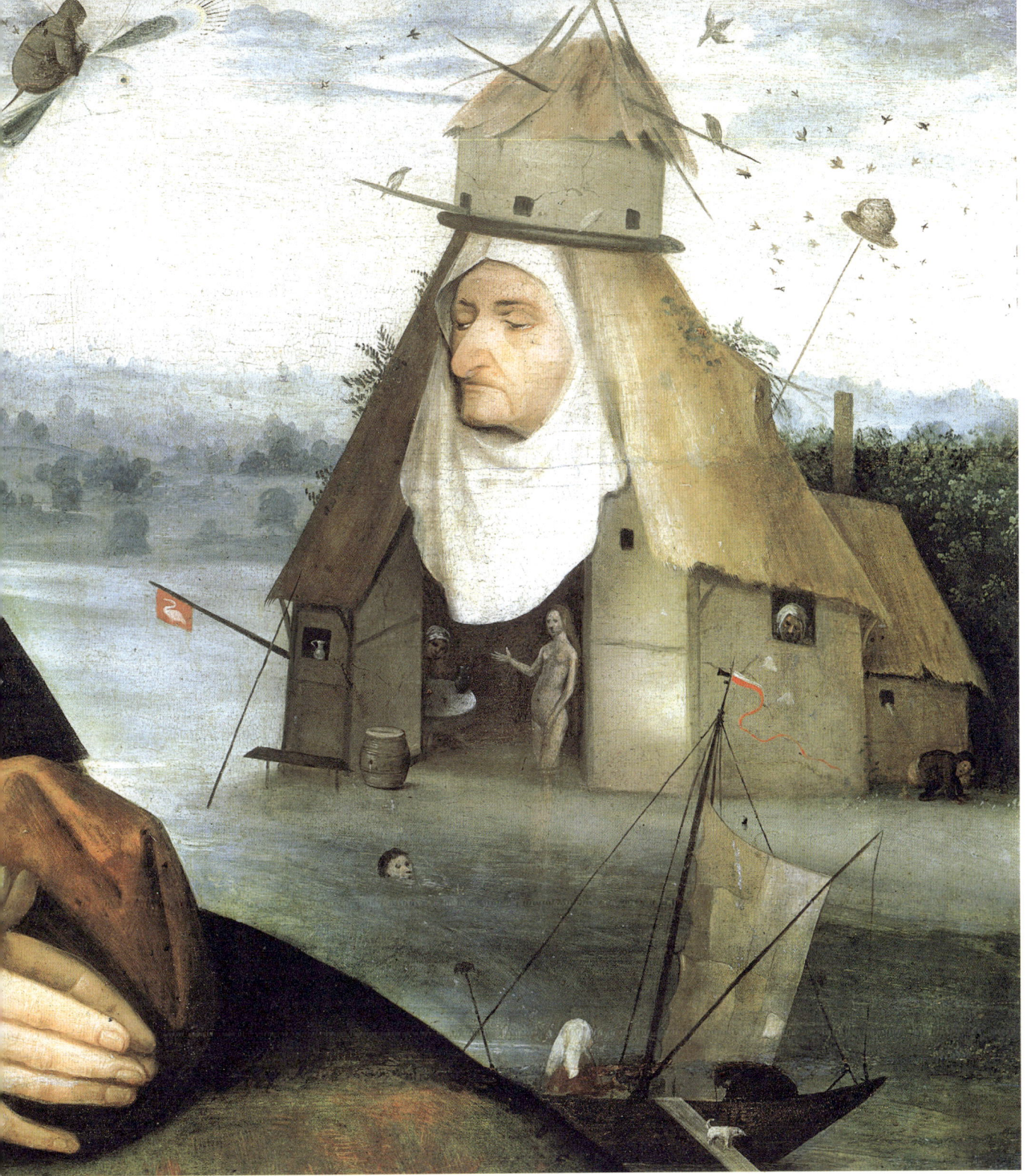

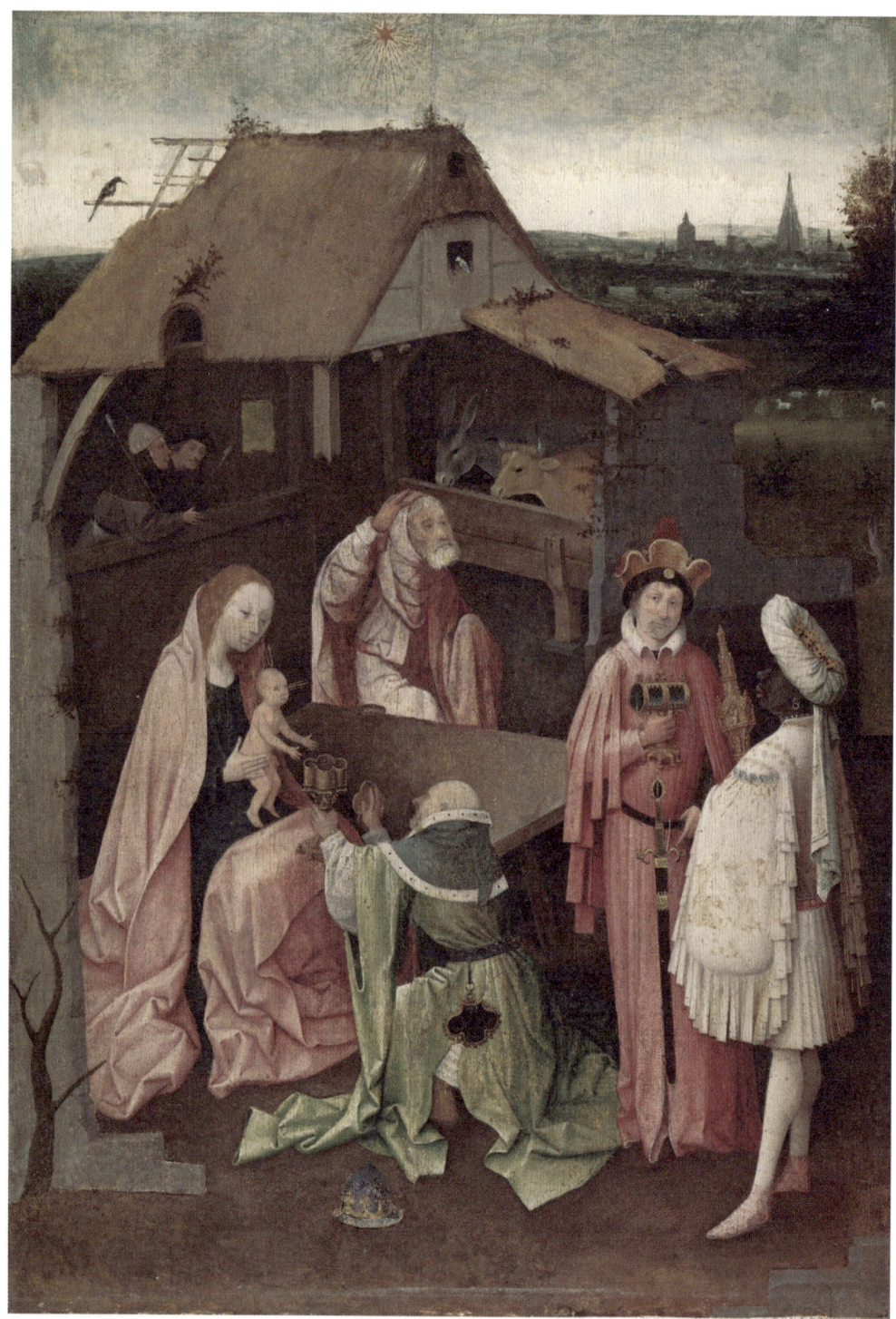

The Adoration of the Magi, c. 1500
Oil on panel, 77.5 x 55.9 cm (30½ x 22 in)
• Philadelphia Museum of Art, Philadelphia, USA

Attributed to Bosch but close in artistic style to fellow Netherlandish painters Geerten Tot Sint Jans (1455/65–85/95) and Dieric Bouts (1415–75). The richly dressed Magi meet the Holy Family within a humble stable. The infant Jesus receives their gifts.

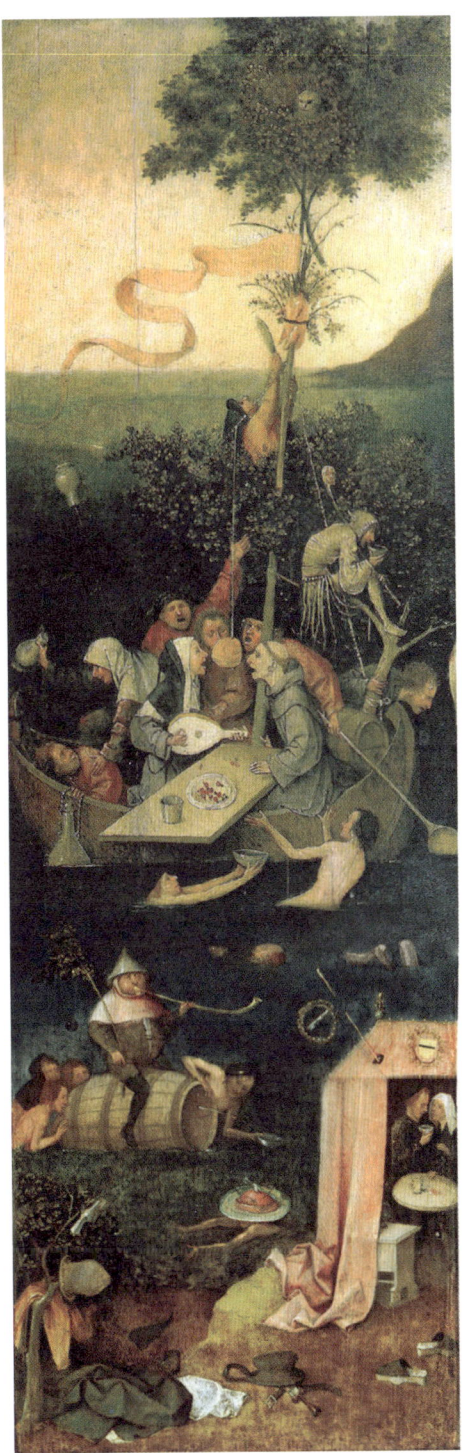
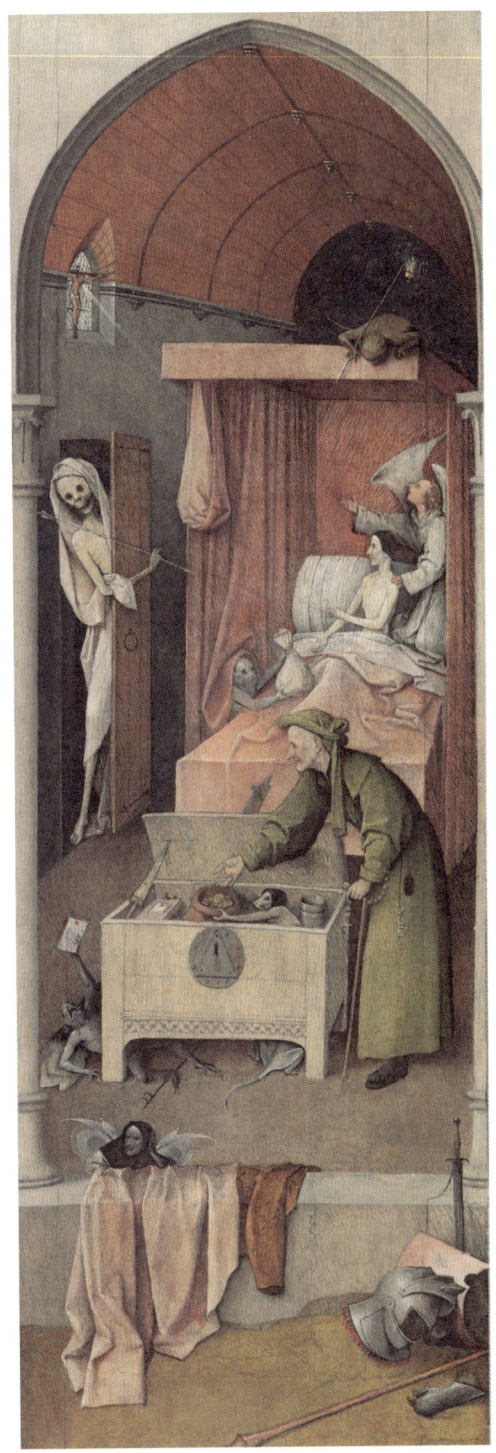

Ship of Fools/Allegory of Intemperance/Death and the Miser
Oil on panel, reconstruction of wings of possible (lost) triptych
• Louvre, Paris/Yale University Art Gallery, New Haven/
National Gallery of Art, Washington D.C.

In what was probably a triptych, the sins of Gluttony (on the left), Greed (on the right), and Lust, Sloth, Envy, Wrath and Intemperance (all probably in the missing central panel) are visually enacted. On the left, on land and in a ship sailing nowhere (a reference to the Catholic Church); on the right, a miser hoards money even as Death calls. (See overleaf.)

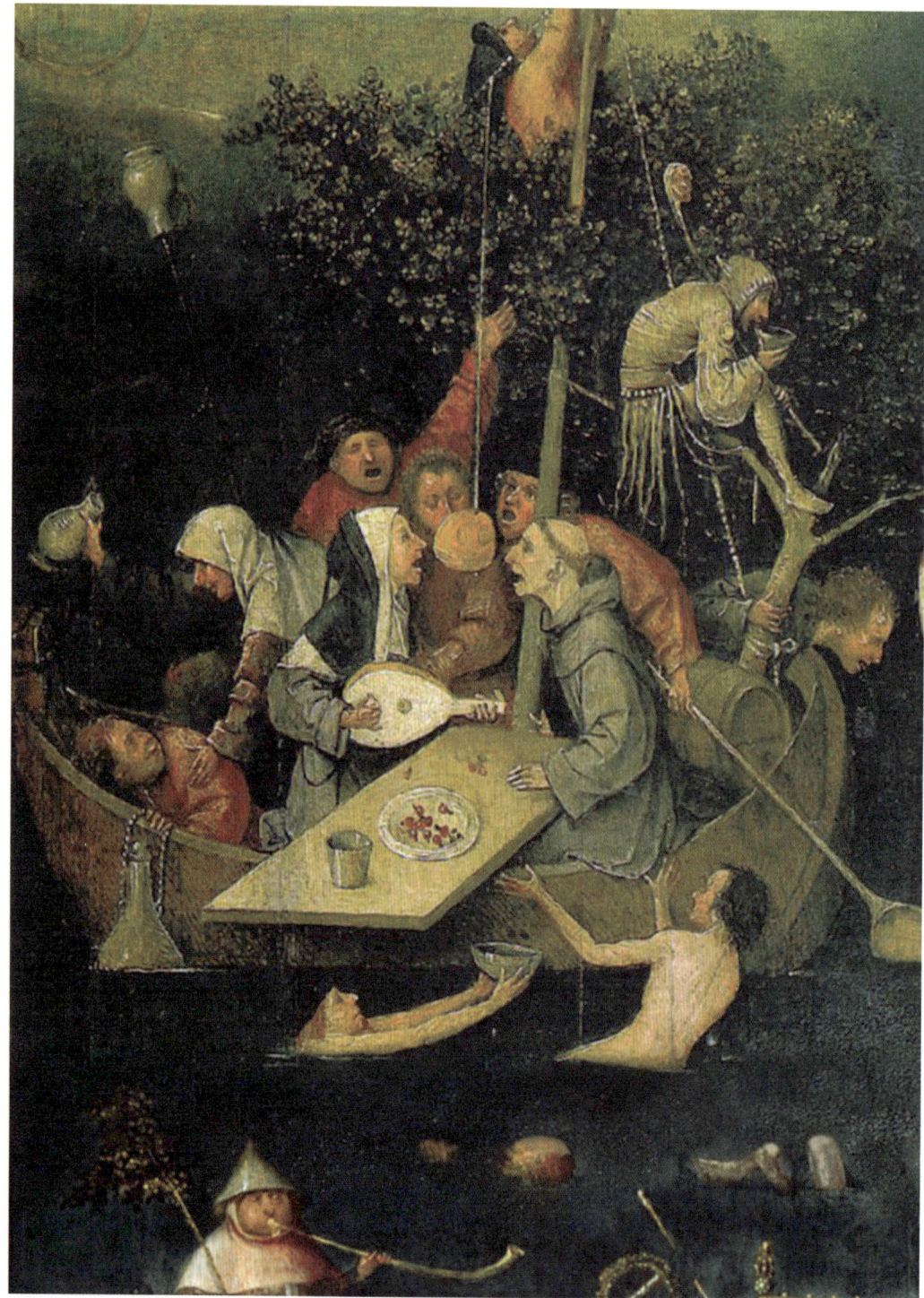

The Ship of Fools (detail), *c.* **1500–10**
Oil on panel, 58 x 32 cm (22¾ x 12⅔ in) • Louvre, Paris

The allegory of a boat or vessel without a capable helmsman to steer it was explored in a book of satirical verse, *Das Narrenschiff* ('The Ship of Fools'), by German poet Sebastian Brant, published in 1494 in many languages.

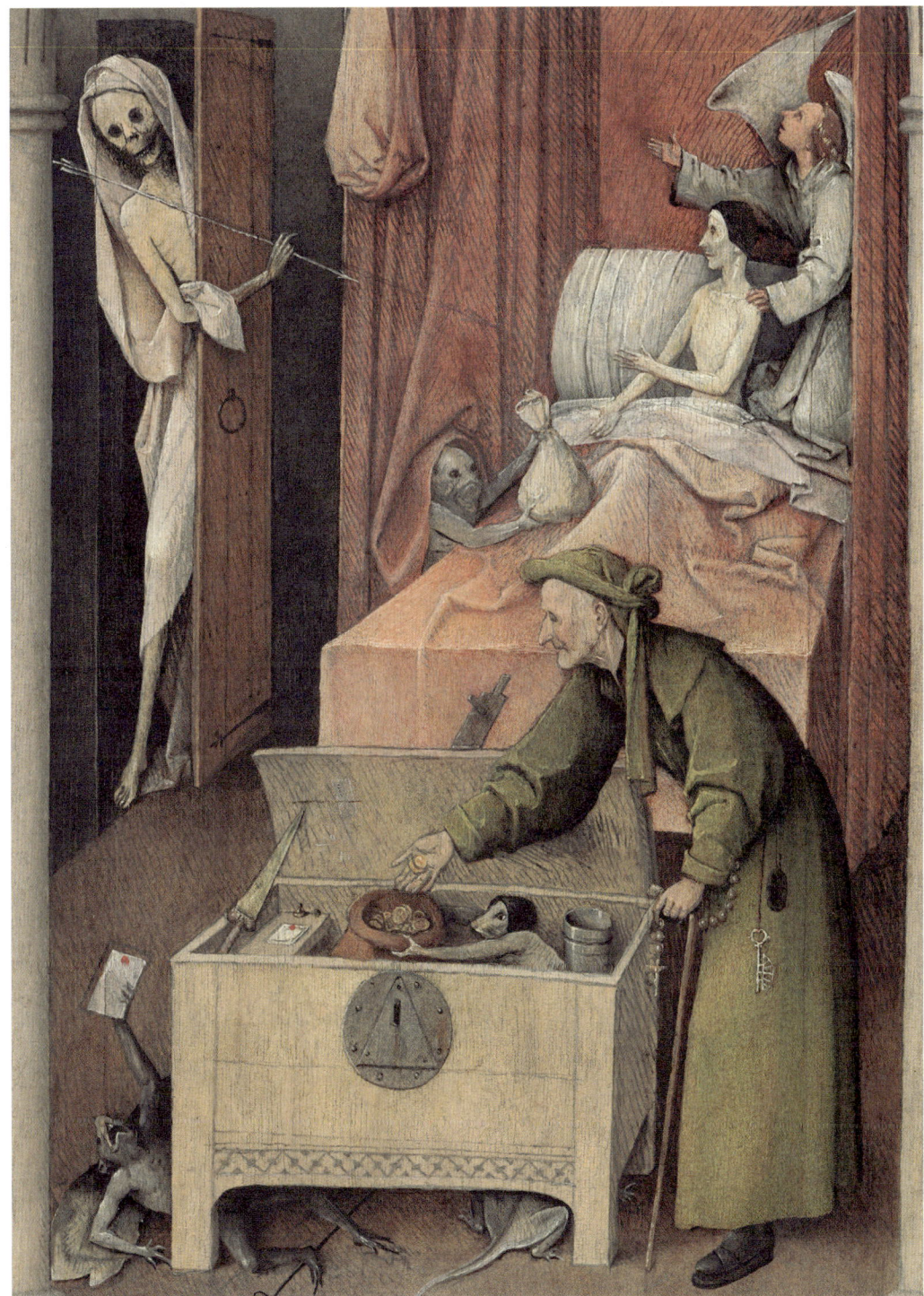

Death and the Miser (detail), *c.* **1500–10**
Oil on panel, 92.6 x 30.8 cm (36½ x 12 in)
• National Gallery of Art, Washington D.C.

In this panel, probably the right wing of the triptych, Death, the first of the Four Last Things, arrives at the house of a dying man, a miser who persists in material follies, taking a bag of money from a devil to add to his worldly treasures.

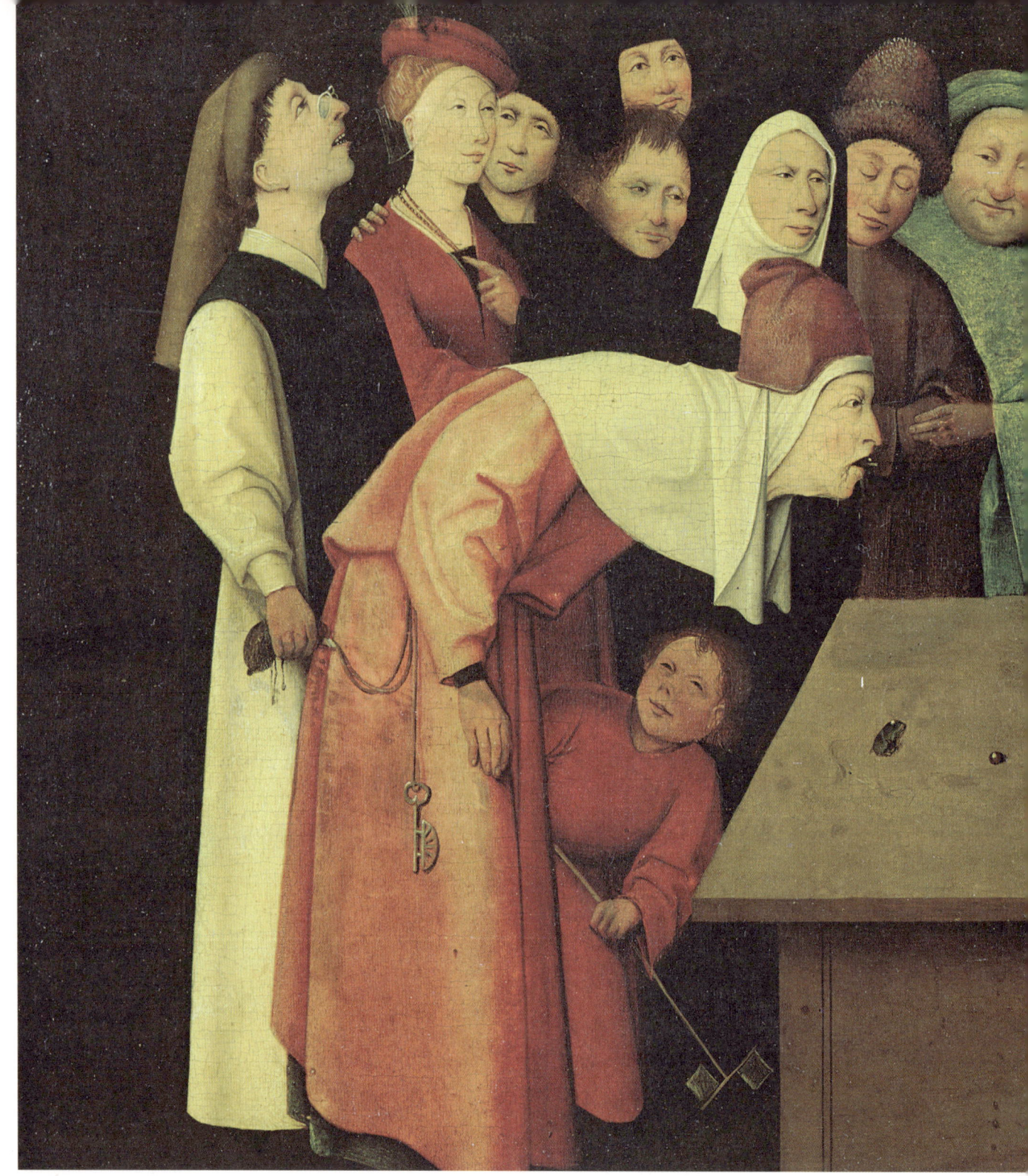

The Conjuror (The Magician), *c.* **1502–20, after Bosch**
Oil on panel, 53 x 65 cm (21 x 25⅔ in)
• Musée d'Art et d'Histoire, Saint-Germain-en-Laye

A superb copy of an original work, *The Conjuror (The Magician)* observes the duplicity of men. A conjuror brings frogs forth from the throat of a customer, while a thief cuts the gullible man's purse strings.

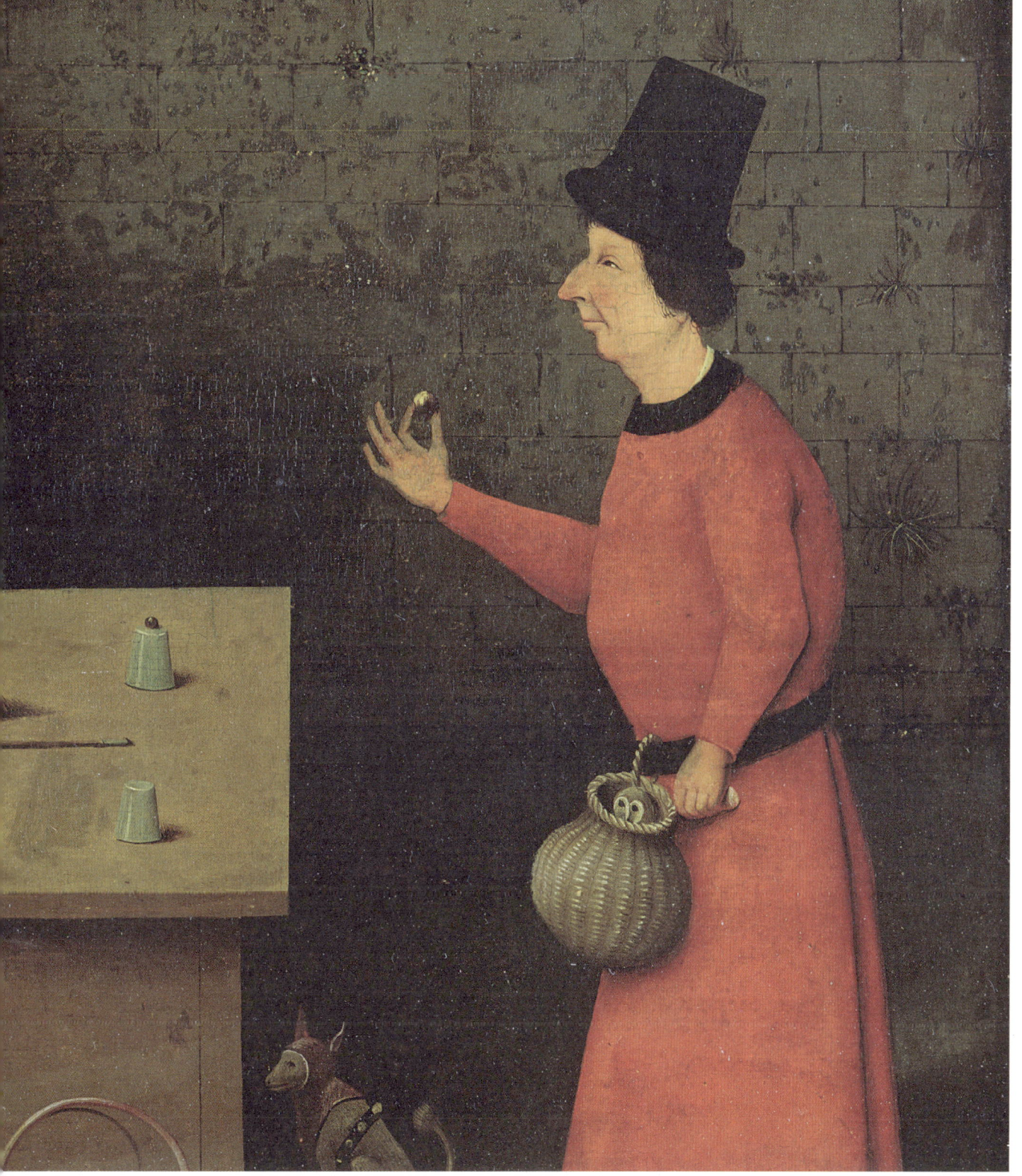

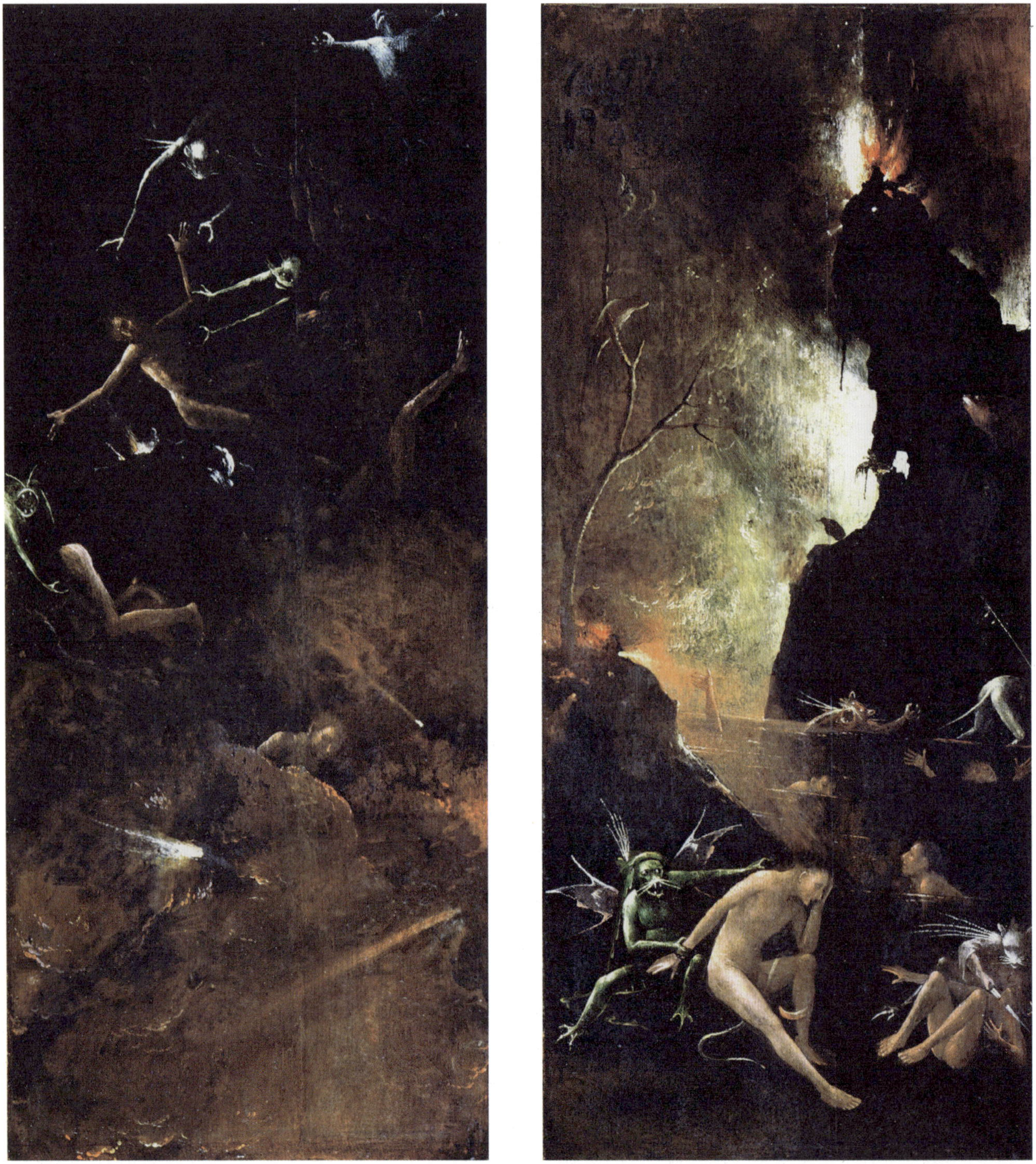

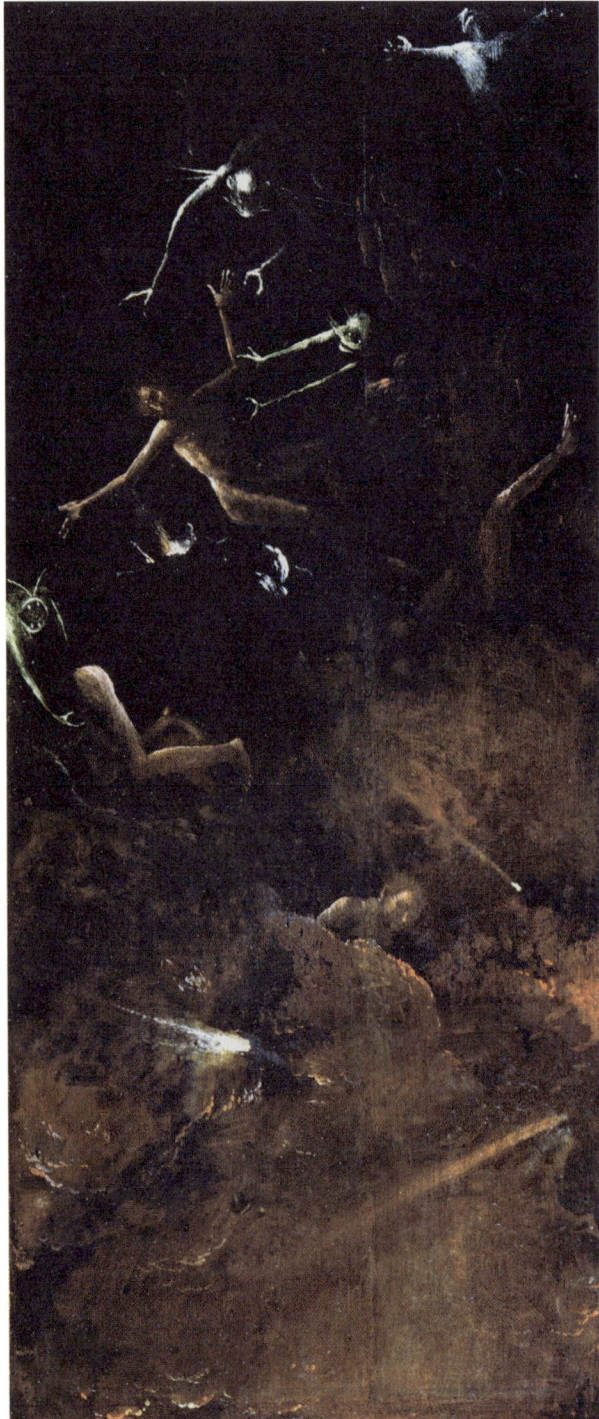

**Four Visions of the Hereafter: The Fall of the
Damned (left) and Hell (right),** *c.* **1505–15**
Oil on panel, 86.5 x 39.5 cm (34 x 15⅔ in) each
• Palazzo Ducale, Venice

Fall of the Damned and *Hell* are possibly two panels of four from a lost polyptych titled *Four Visions of the Hereafter*, attributed to Bosch through artistic style and analysis. They portray the horrendous fate of damned souls, destined for the fiery enclave of Hell, sentenced to eternal punishment.

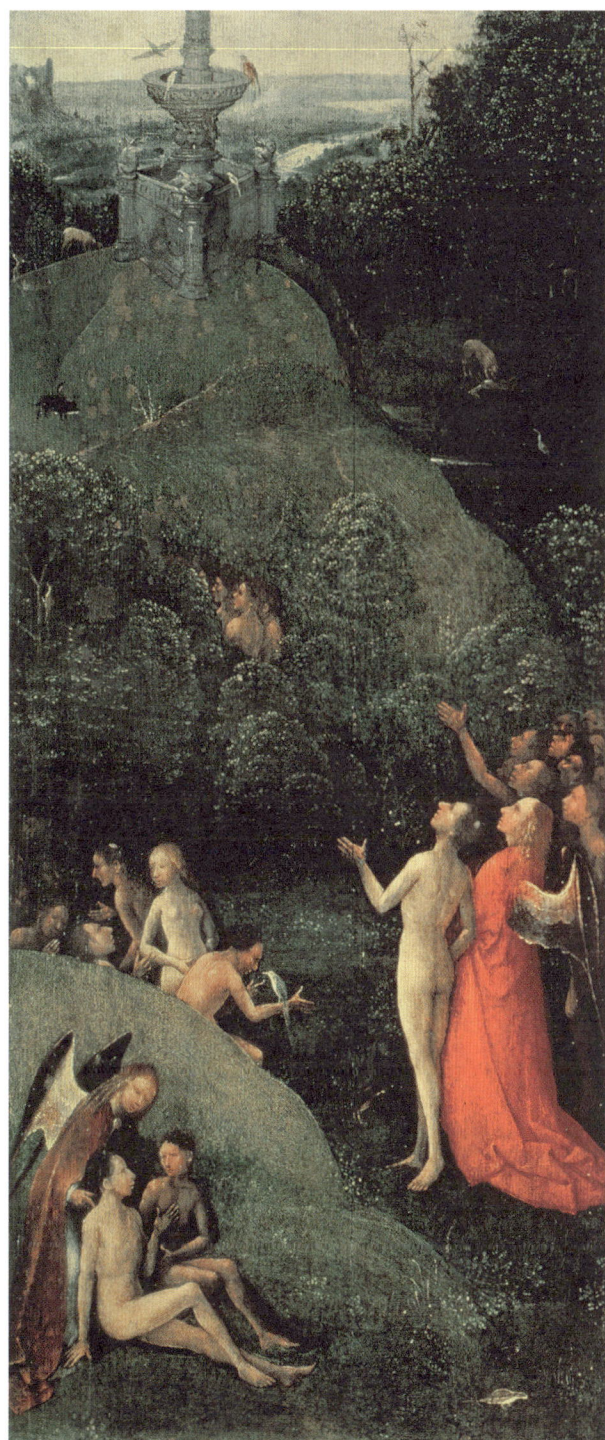 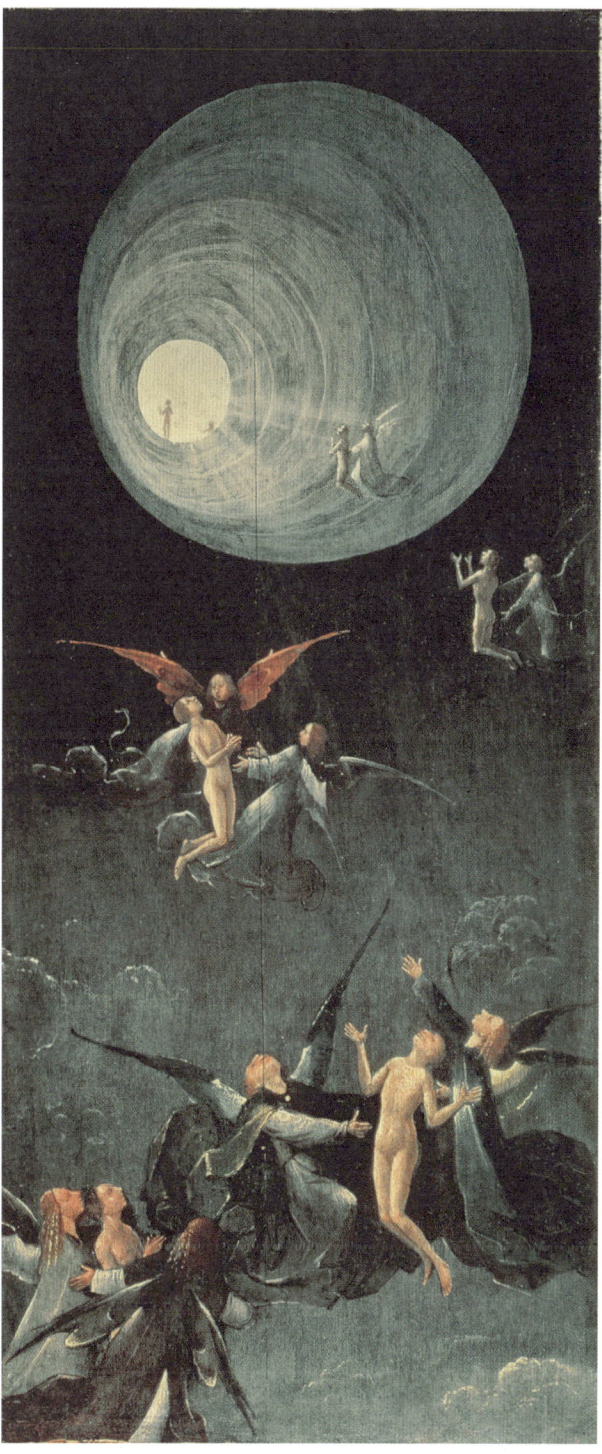

Four Visions of the Hereafter: Earthly Paradise (left) and Ascent into Heaven (right), *c.* **1505–15**
Oil on panel 86.5 x 39.5 cm (34 x 15⅔ in) each
• Palazzo Ducale, Venice

A third panel from *Four Visions of the Hereafter* depicts an earthly Paradise and shows the riches and joy of a righteous world, a considerable contrast to *The Fall of the Damned*. The final *Ascent into Heaven* may have been inspired by the mystic writings of Jan van Ruysbroeck, an Augustinian monk, describing the divine presence of God as an intensely bright light. Here, blessed souls are guided towards it by guardian angels.

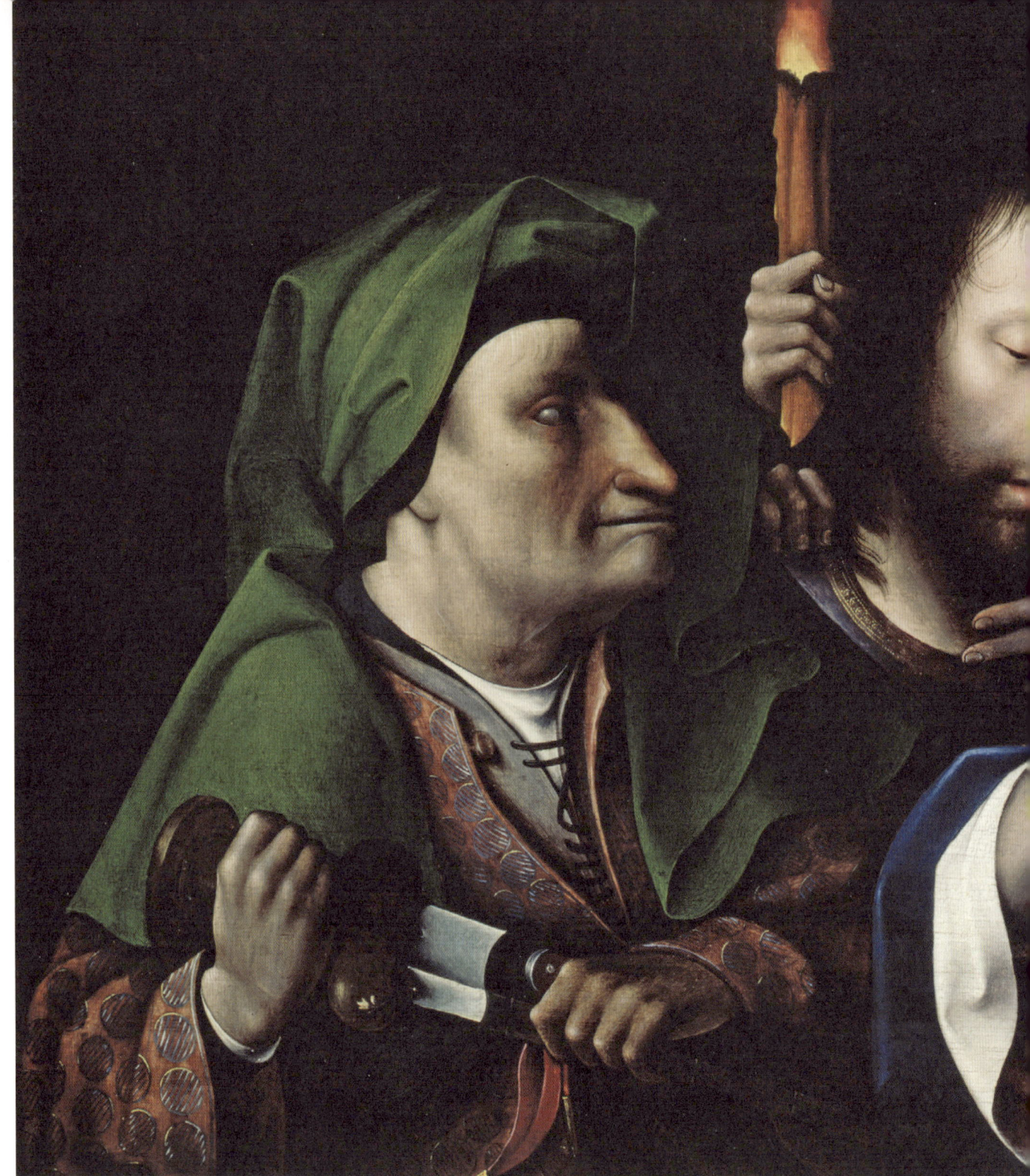

The Arrest of Christ, *c.* 1515, follower of Bosch
Oil and tempera on panel, 50.5 x 81.1 cm (20 x 32 in)
• Museum of Art, San Diego

The painting visually links to the artistic style of *Christ Carrying the Cross* (*see* page 90), and *Christ Brought Before Pilate* (*see* page 57), considered to be painted in Bosch's workshop, possibly copied from an original work.

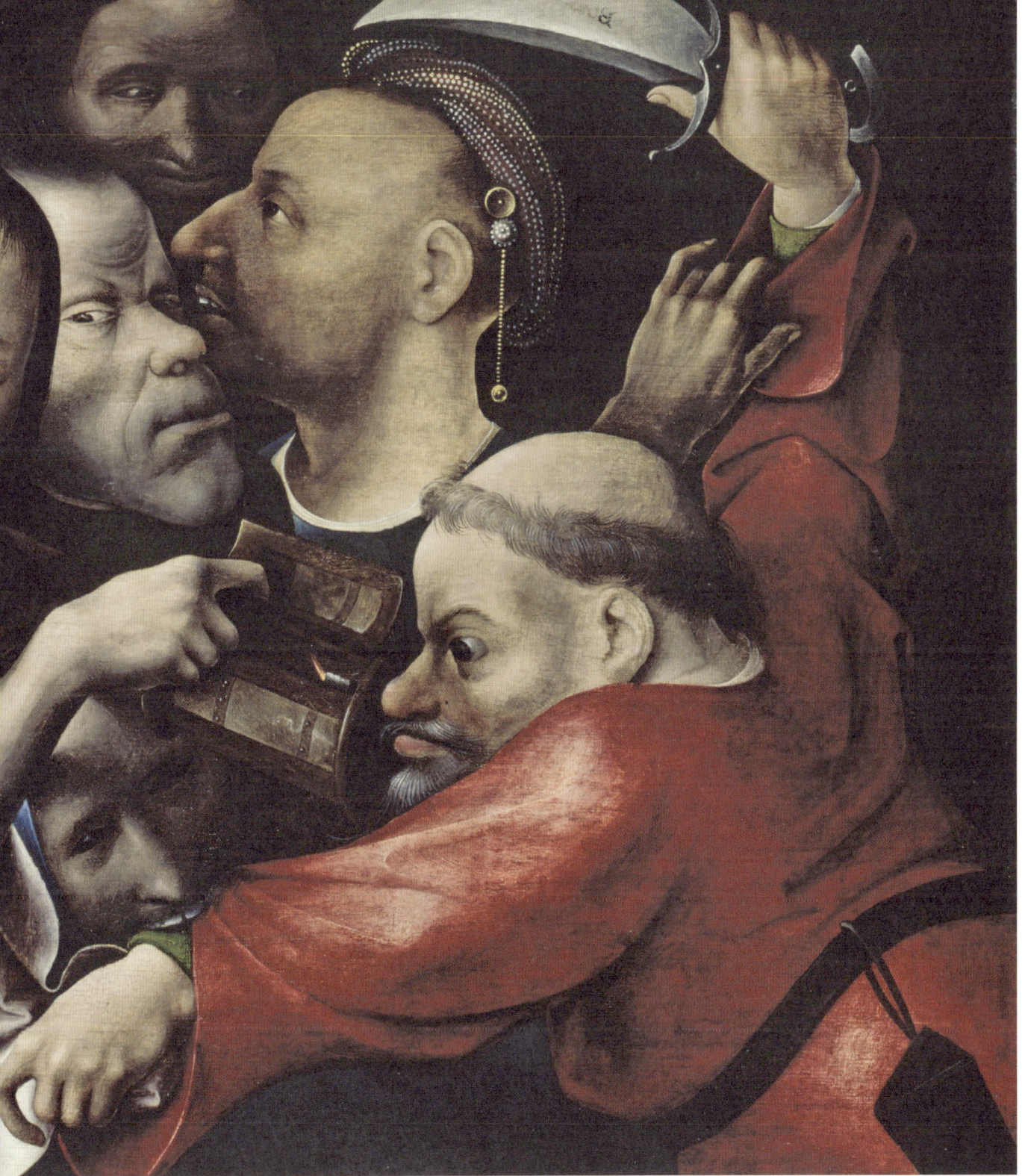

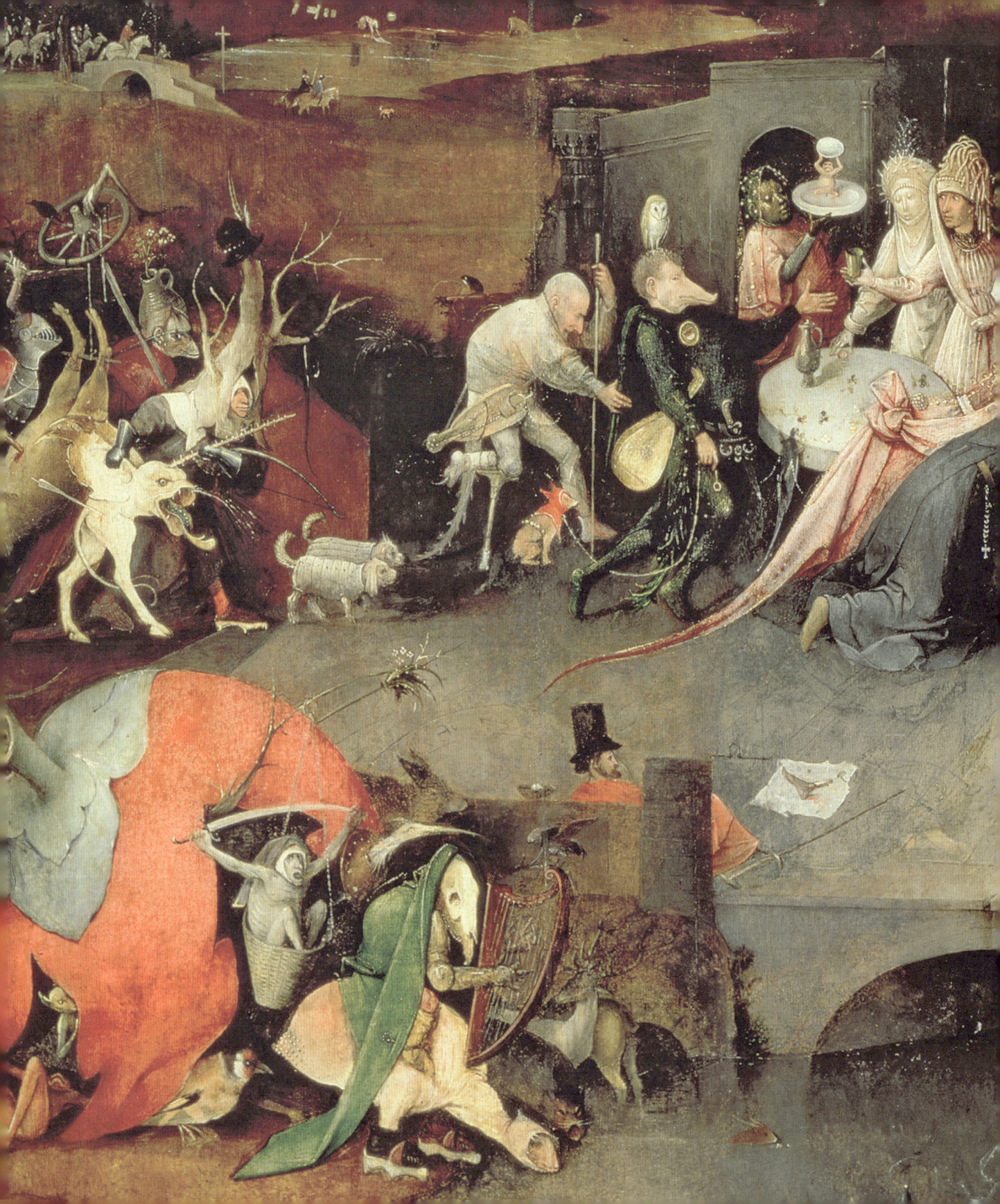

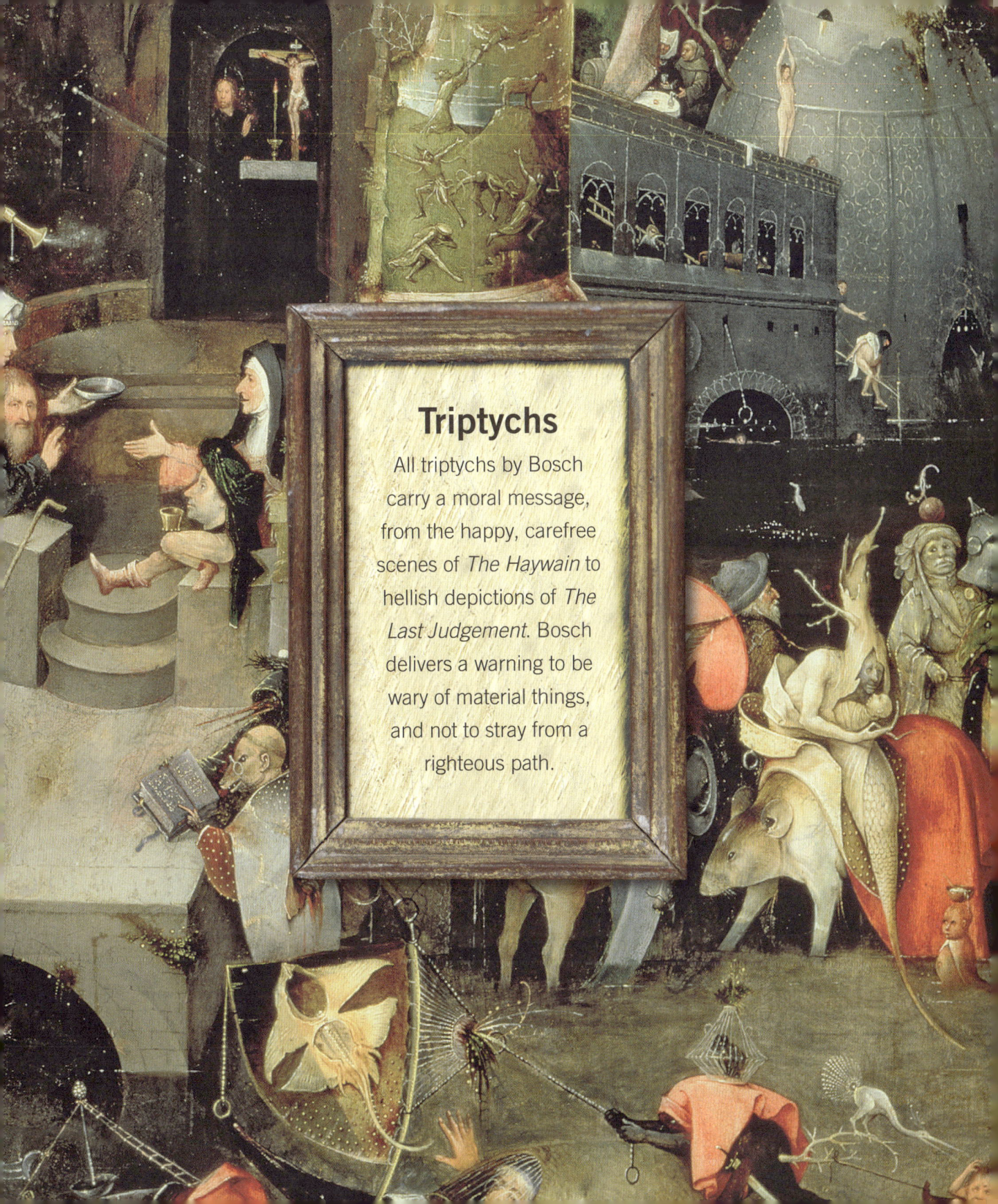

Triptychs

All triptychs by Bosch
carry a moral message,
from the happy, carefree
scenes of *The Haywain* to
hellish depictions of *The
Last Judgement*. Bosch
delivers a warning to be
wary of material things,
and not to stray from a
righteous path.

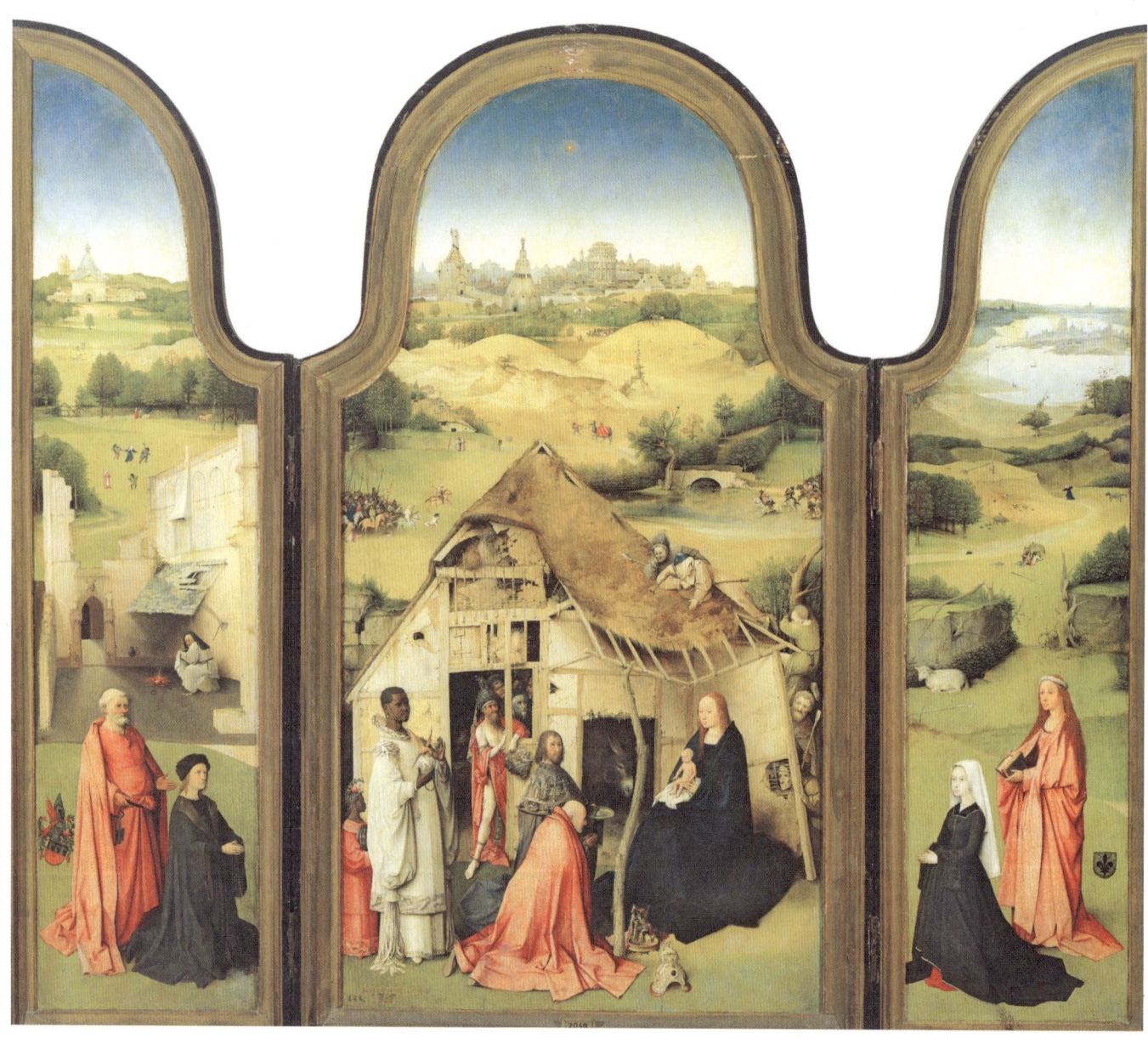

The Adoration of the Magi, *c.* 1485–1510
Oil on panel, 138 x 138 cm (54⅓ x 54⅓ in)
• Museo Nacional del Prado, Madrid

The Epiphany marks the twelfth day after Christ's birth when the infant receives a visitation from the Magi: Melchior, Caspar and Balthazar, who followed the Star guiding them to Bethlehem. This triptych is sometimes known as *The Epiphany.*

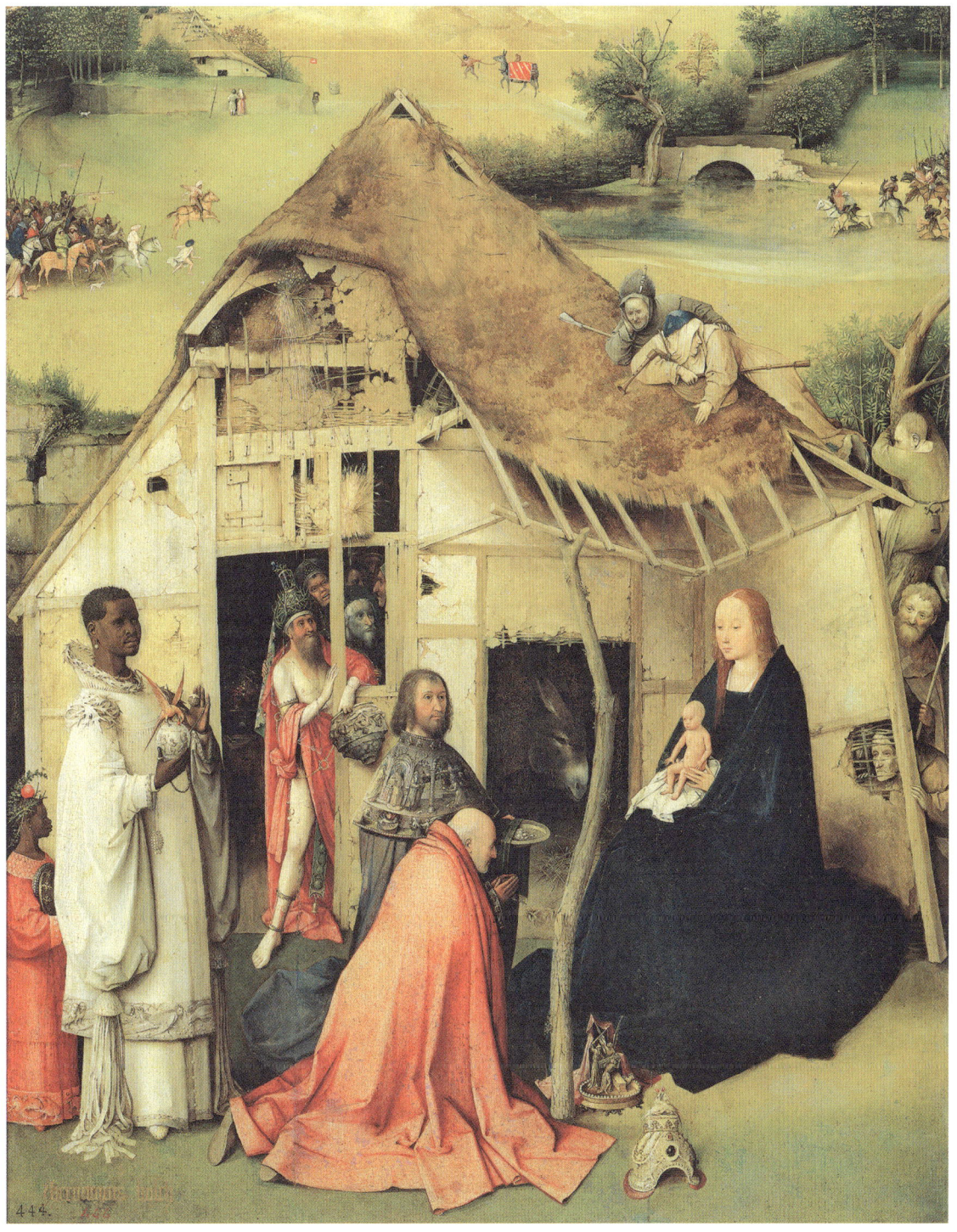

**The Adoration of the Magi
(detail of central panel),** *c.* **1485–1510**
Oil on panel • Museo Nacional del Prado, Madrid

Outside a tumbledown stable, the Magi offer their gifts of gold, frankincense and myrrh to the infant Christ, whilst a group of peasants gather round. The brightly robed but near-naked dishevelled man watching from inside the stable entrance may symbolize Herod.

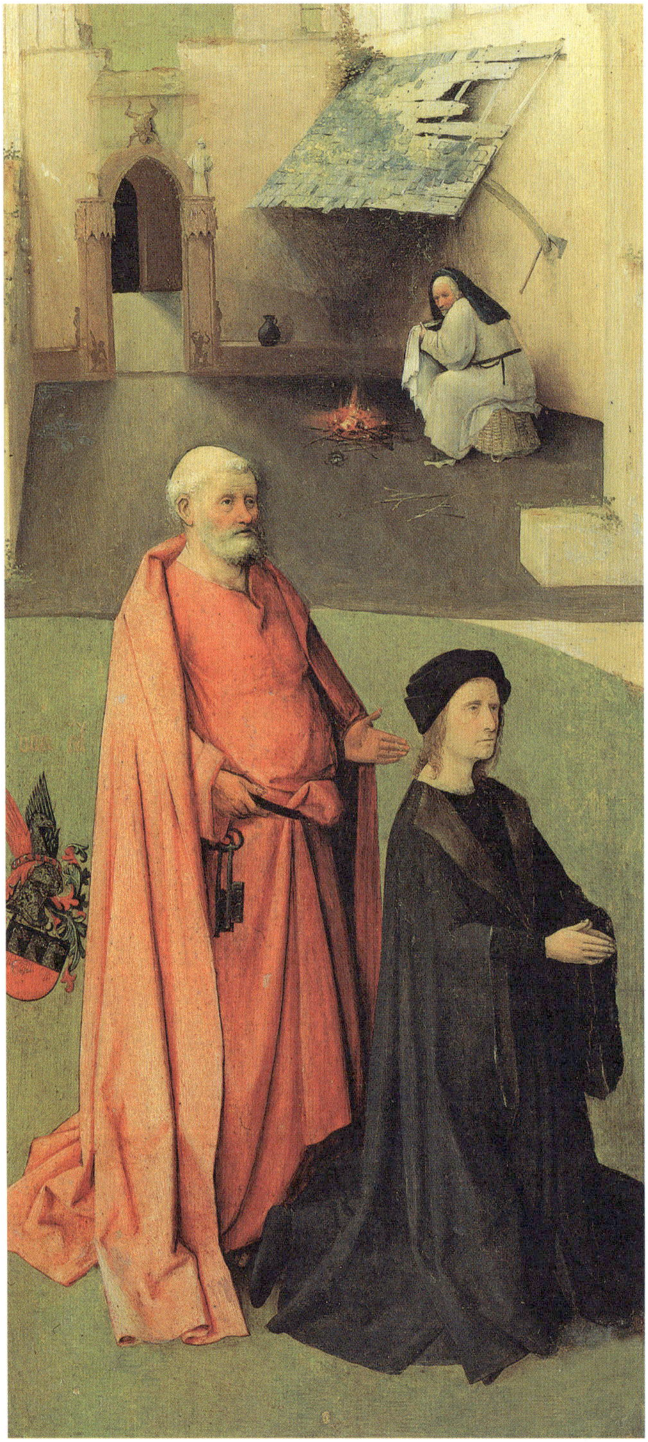

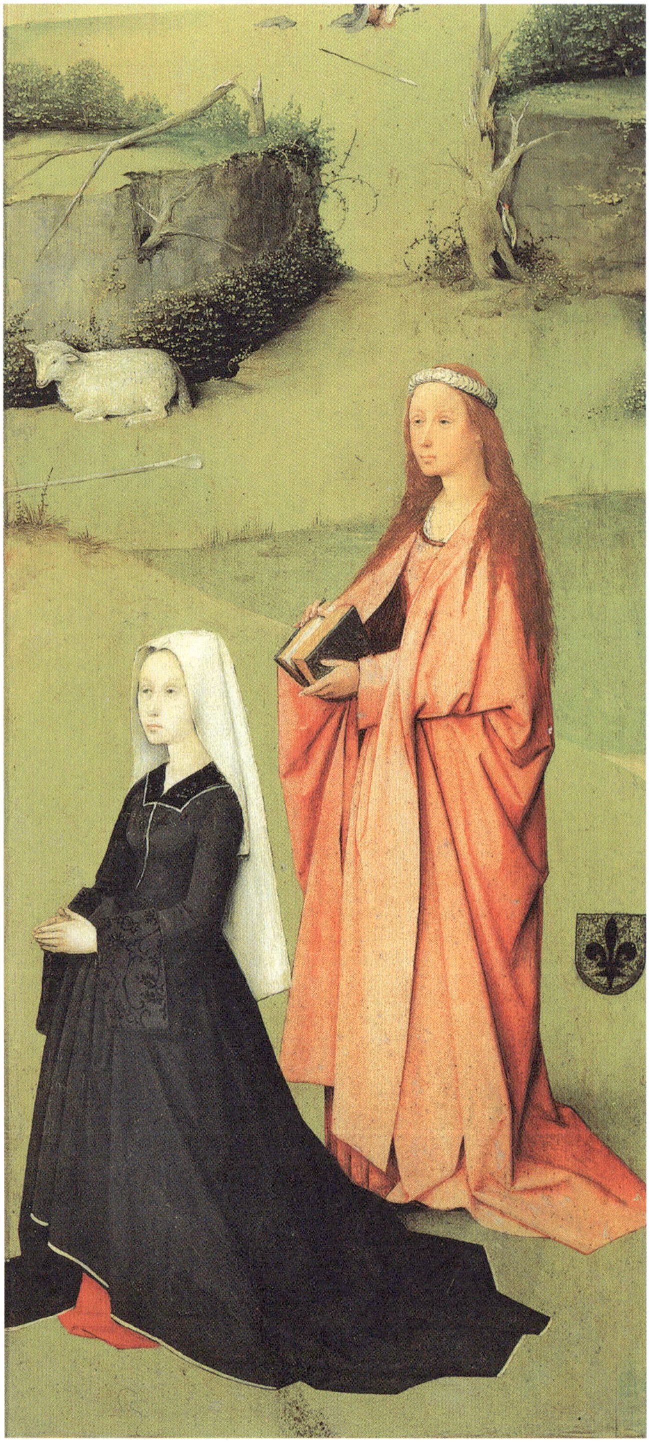

**The Adoration of the Magi
(left and right panel details),** *c.* **1485–1510**

Oil on panel • Museo Nacional del Prado, Madrid

The left panel depicts the male donor of the altarpiece kneeling towards the Adoration of the Magi supported by St Peter. In the distance a nun turns to watch the unfolding events. Complementary to the left panel, the right depicts the female donor kneeling towards the scene of the Adoration of the Magi. She is supported by St Agnes, who stands behind her.

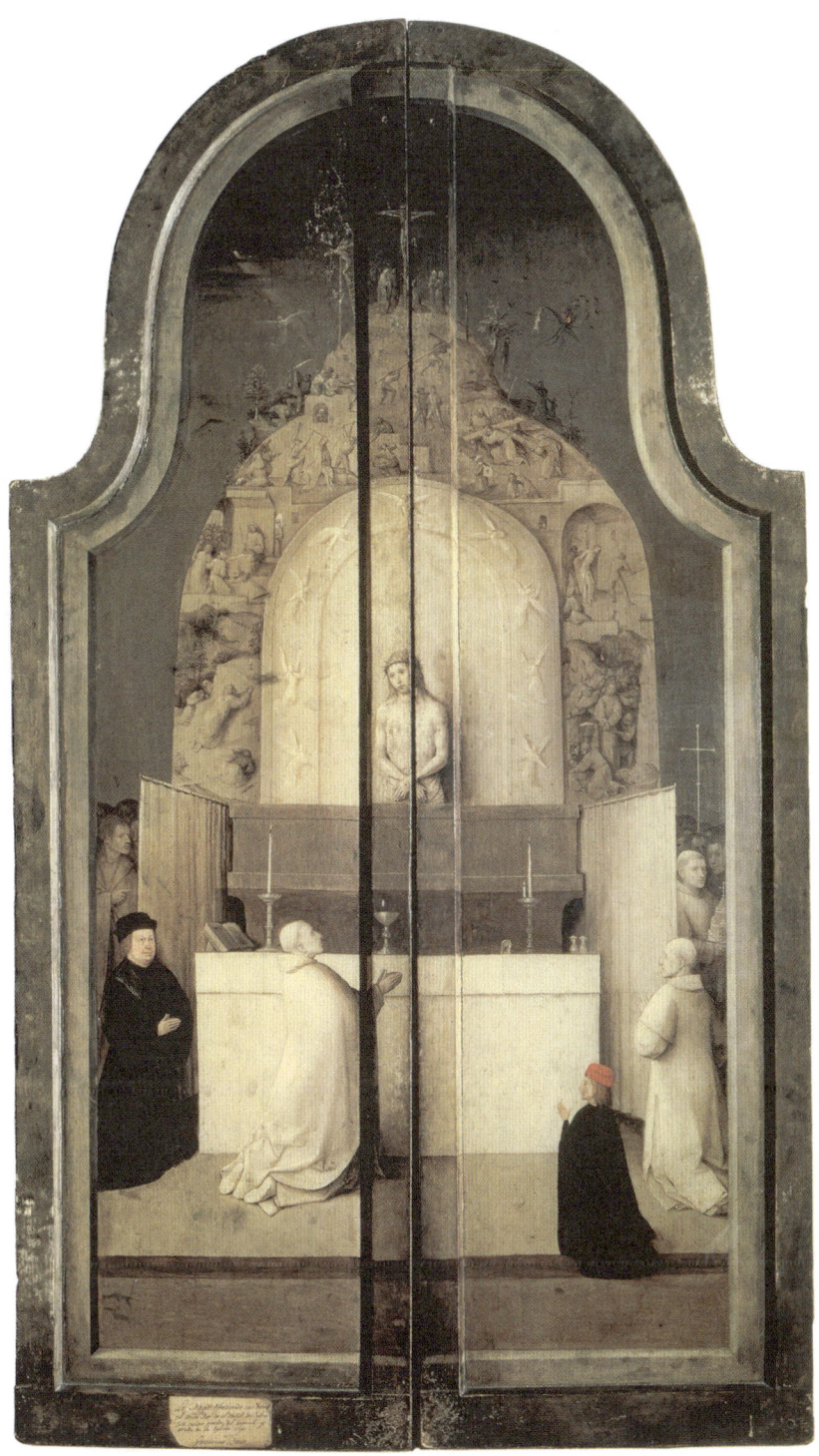

The Adoration of the Magi: The Legend of the Mass of St Gregory (closed doors), *c.* **1485–1510**
Oil on panel, 138 x 72 cm (54⅓ x 28⅓ in)
• Museo Nacional del Prado, Madrid, Spain

The Legend of the Mass of St Gregory, painted in grisaille, is depicted on the outer doors. Pope Gregory observed a Eucharist miracle, converting a disbeliever in his congregation. St Gregory, at prayer, sees Christ appear above the altar.

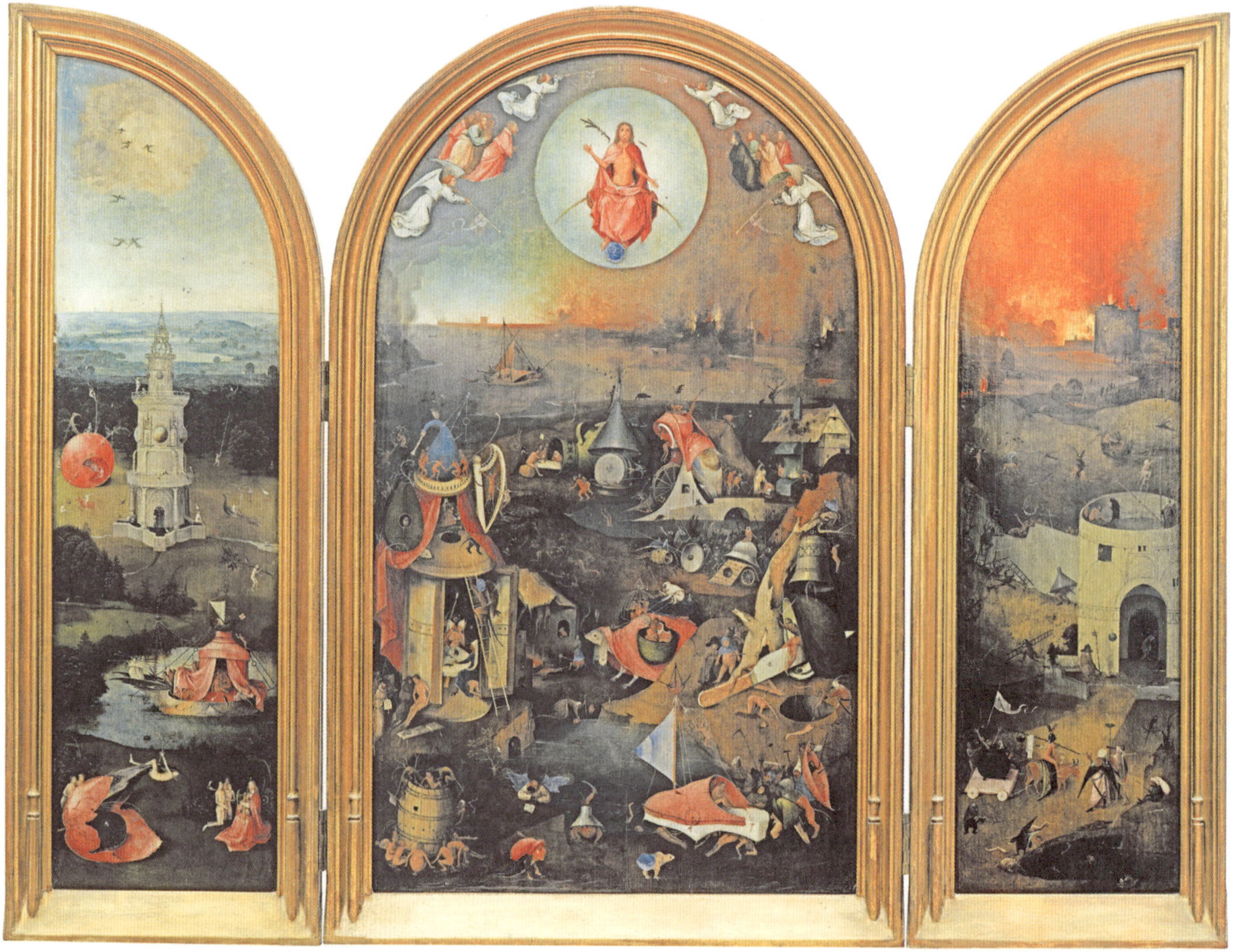

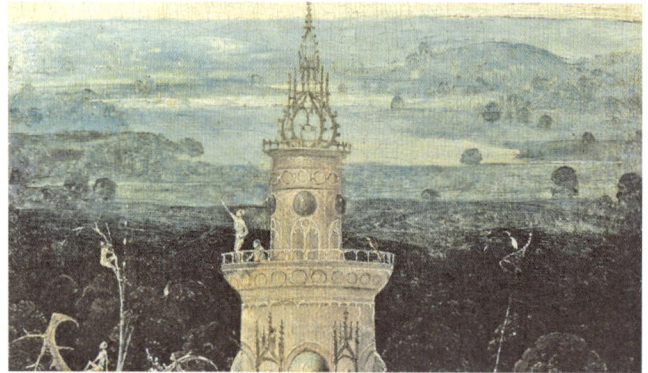

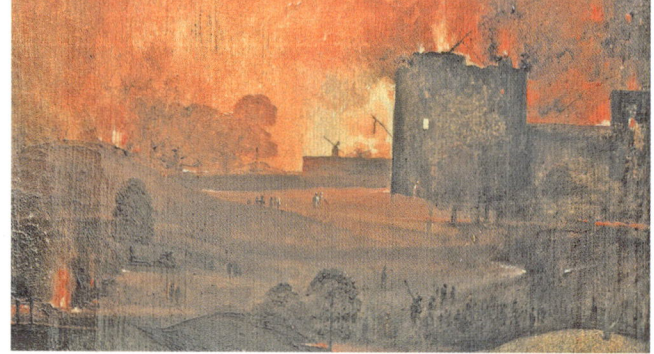

The Last Judgement (and details), *c.* **1495–1505**
Oil on panel, 99 x 117.5 cm (39 x 46⅓ in)
• Groeninge Museum, Bruges

After recent research, this triptych has been confirmed as an original work by Bosch. Across the three panels, the way towards Man's 'last judgement' unfolds. On the left, saved souls rise up; on the right, buildings are fully ablaze in the hellish land of lost souls.

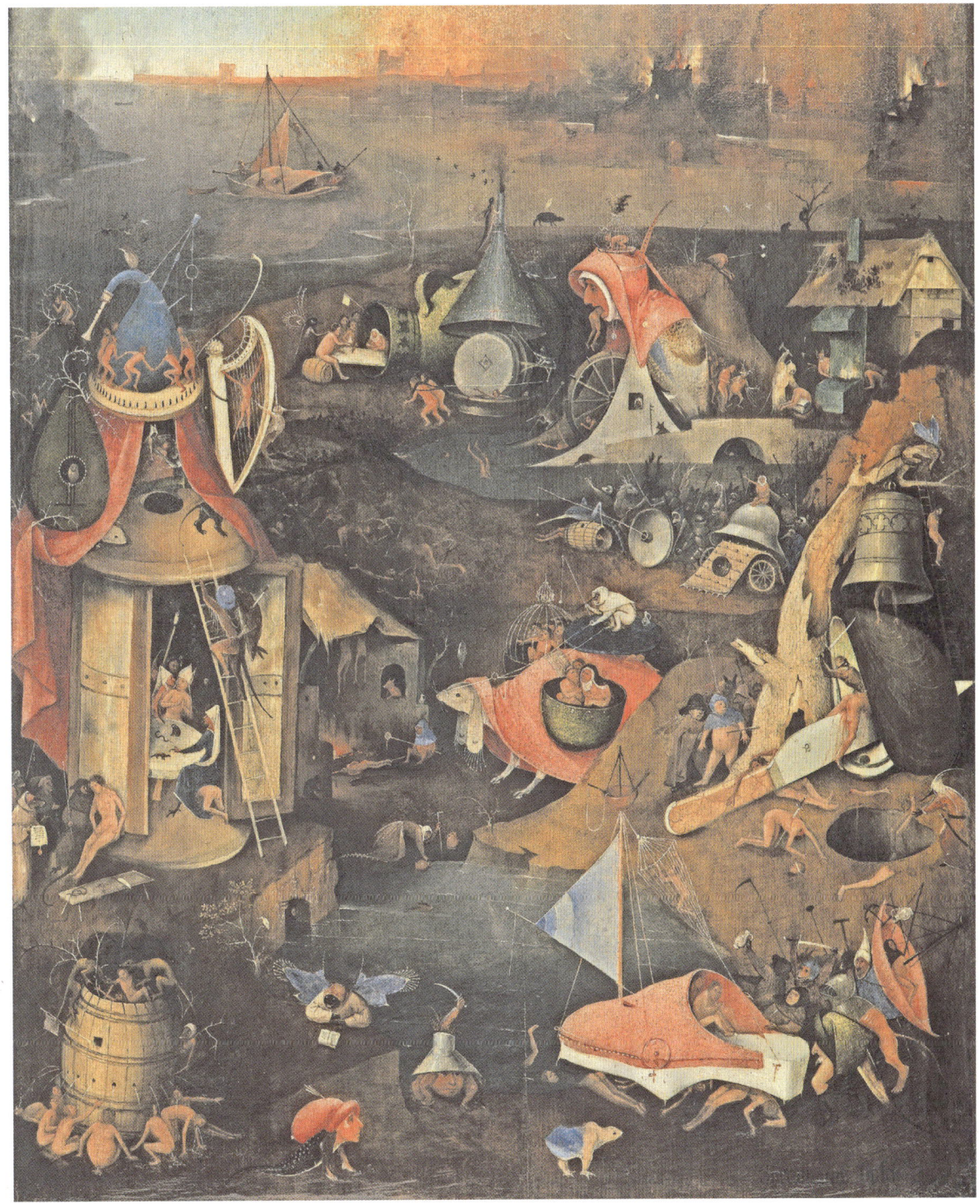

The Last Judgement (central panel), *c.* **1495–1505**
Oil on panel • Groeninge Museum, Bruges

Set in a landscape stretching from left to right panels, at the centre Christ appears in a beam of light, surrounded by a heavenly choir. Below him, scenes of torture, lust and wanton abandon take place.

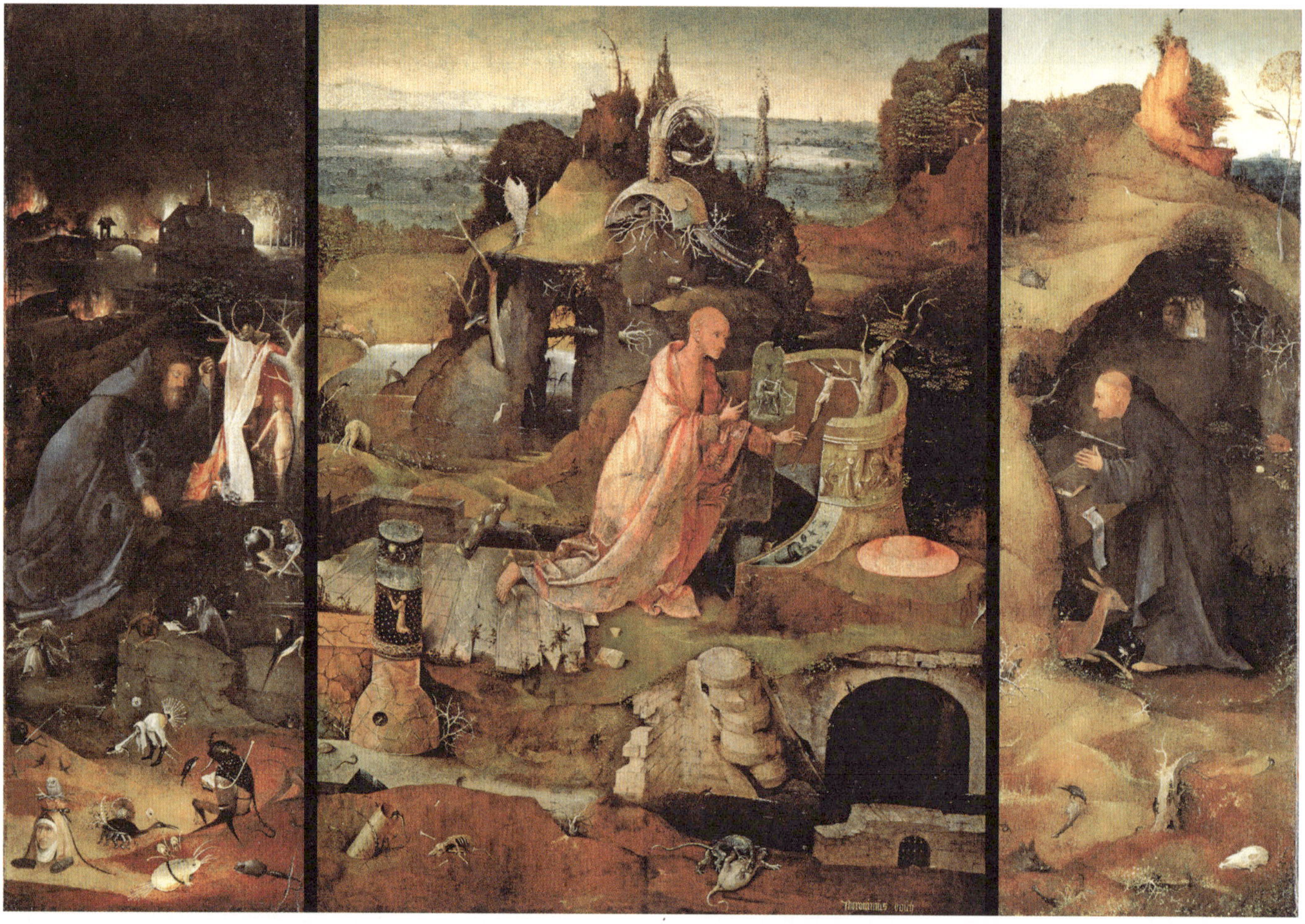

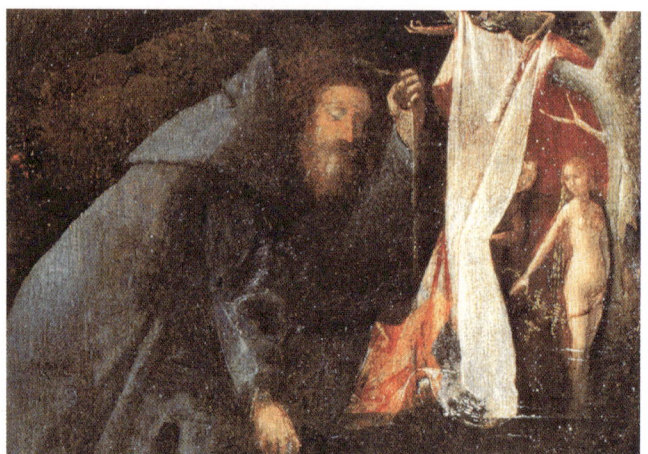

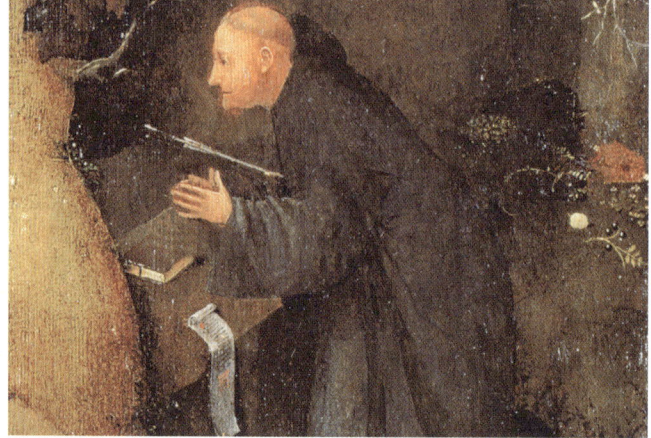

The Hermit Saints (and details), *c.* **1495–1505**
Oil on panel, 86 x 60 cm (34 x 24 in)
• Palazzo Ducale, Venice, Italy

Three revered hermit saints, St Anthony, St Jerome and St Giles, depicted with their attributes, are portrayed in unsettling, desolate landscapes, each man praying to receive the wisdom and blessing of God. On the left St Anthony is surrounded by temptations, including the carnal beauty of a She-Devil; on the right St Giles removes an arrow from his beloved animal companion.

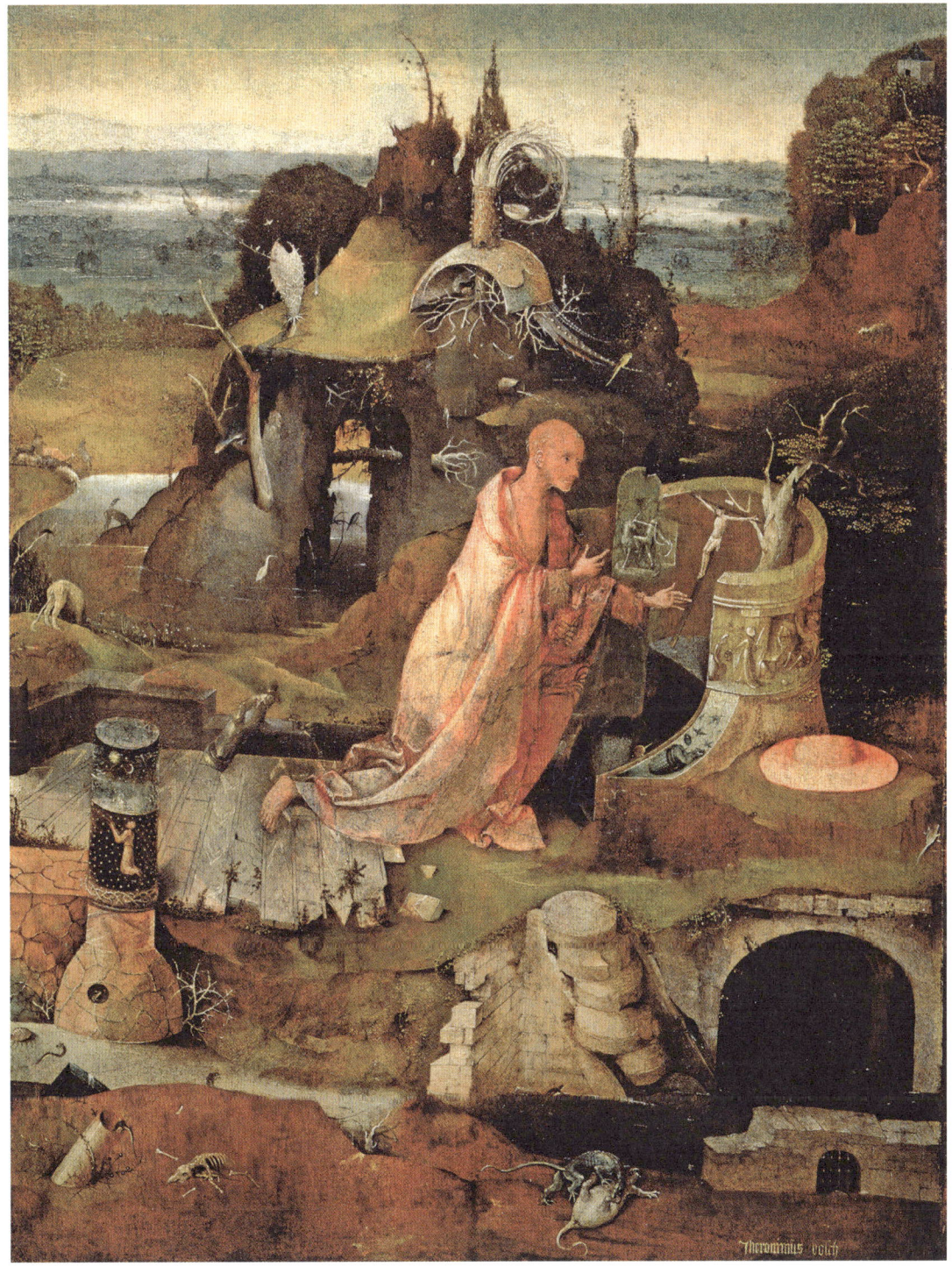

**The Hermit Saints
(central panel),** *c.* **1495–1505**

Oil on panel • Palazzo Ducale, Venice, Italy

St Jerome, praying in the ruins of a pagan building, kneels before a crucifix. His calm demeanour underlines the contemplative life of a hermit, quite oblivious to the fatal skirmish played out by small creatures in the foreground.

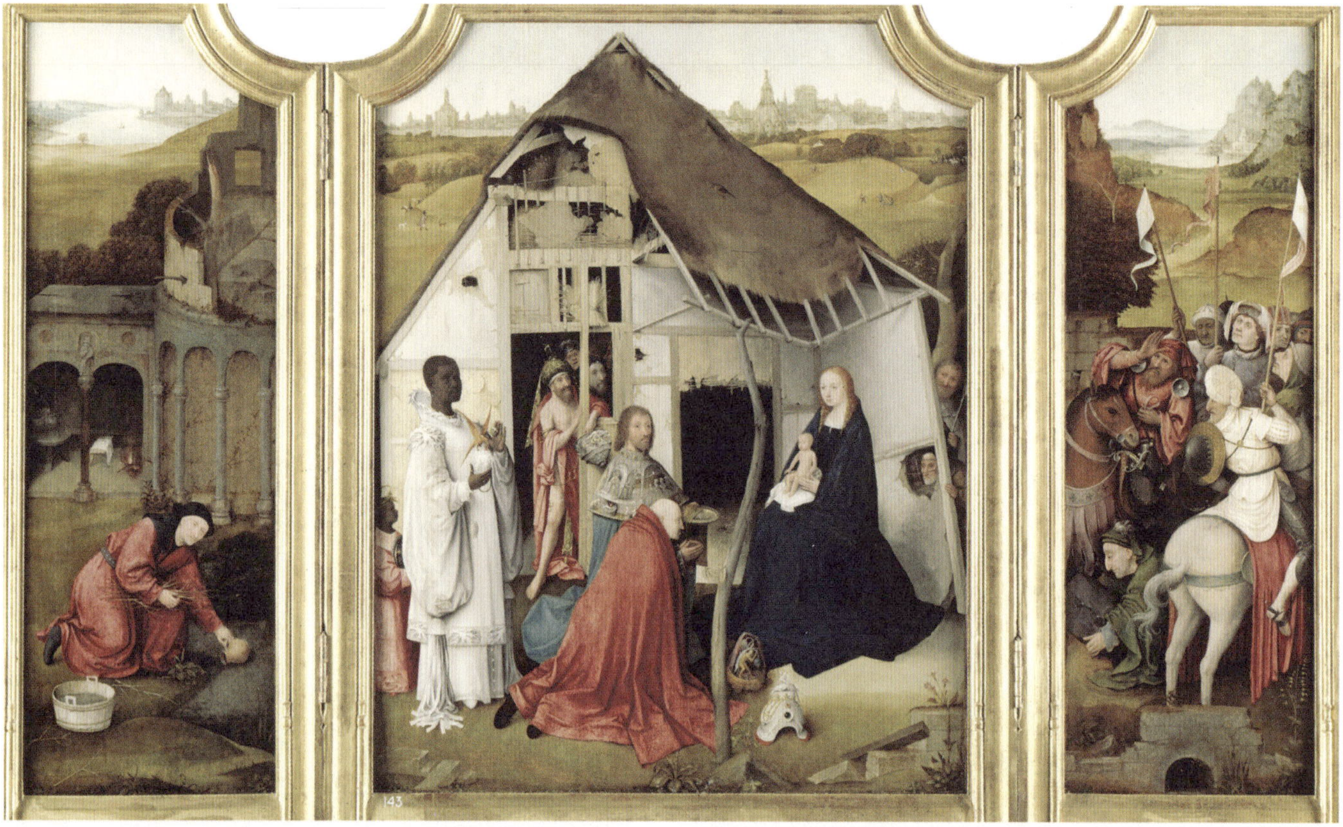

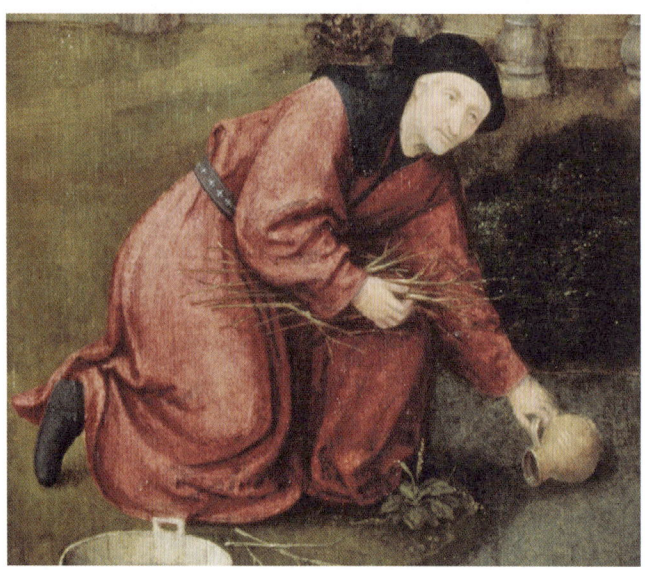

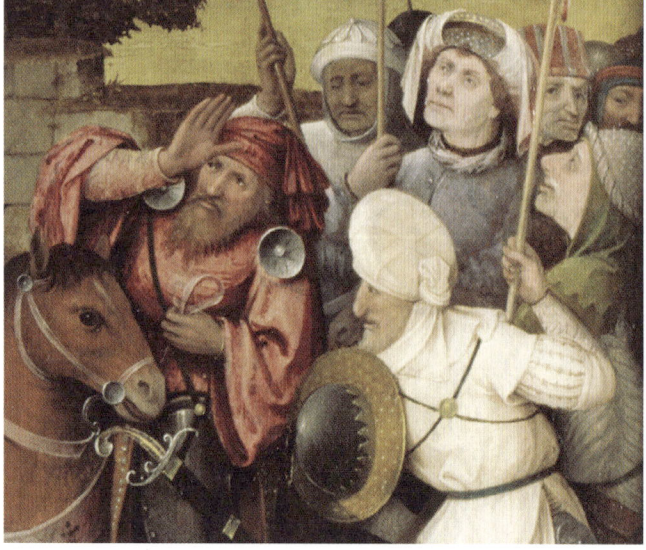

The Adoration of the Magi, *c.* 1495
Oil on panel, 91.4 x 144.8 cm (36 x 57 in)
• Upton House, Warwickshire, England

The painting is attributed to Hieronymus Bosch. The illustrative content of the central panel of the triptych is strikingly similar to the central panel of the *Adoration of the Magi*, 1510, in the Prado, Madrid (*see* pages 72-75).

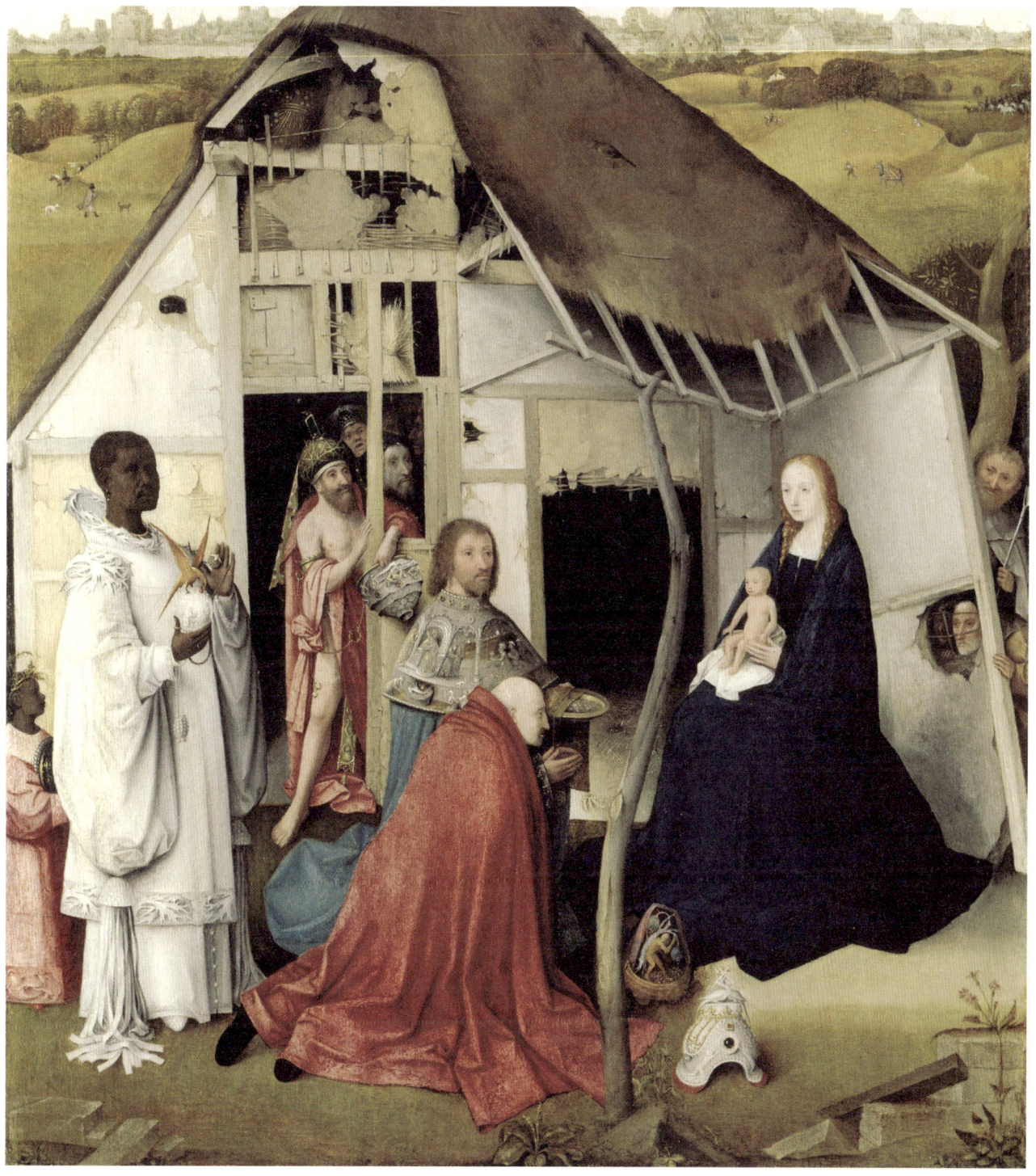

**The Adoration of the Magi
(central panel),** *c.* **1495**

Oil on panel • Upton House, Warwickshire, England

Outside the stable where Christ was born, the seated Virgin Mary holds the infant Christ,
to receive the Magi, three kings from the East. Standing at the entrance to the stable, a
semi-robed man, possibly representing Herod, watches the proceedings.

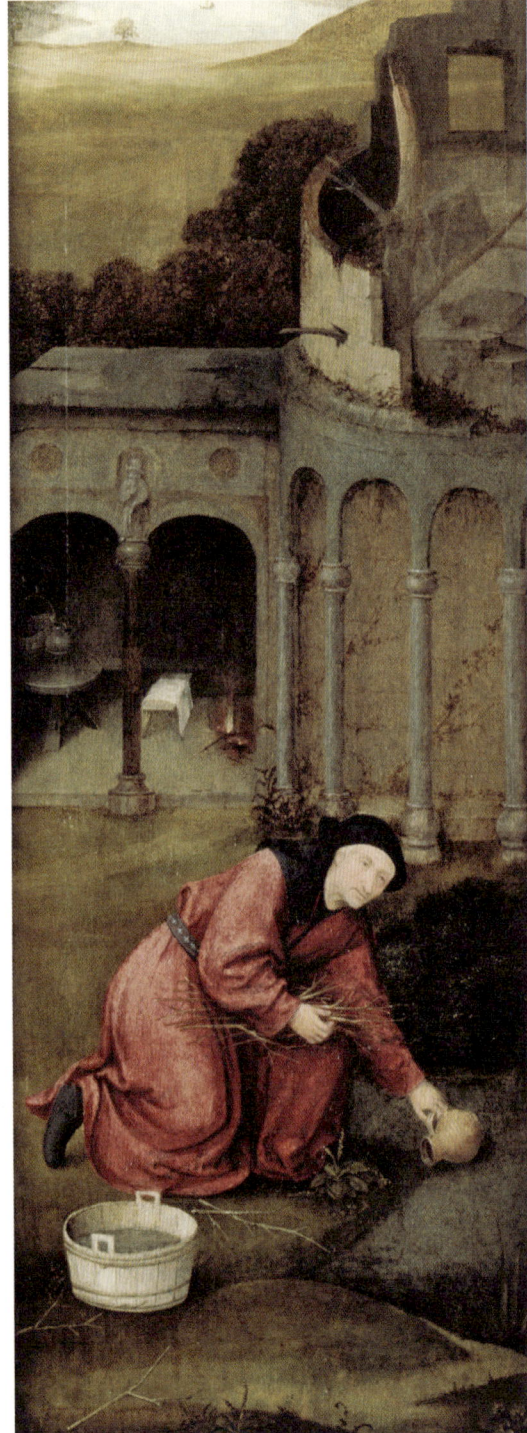
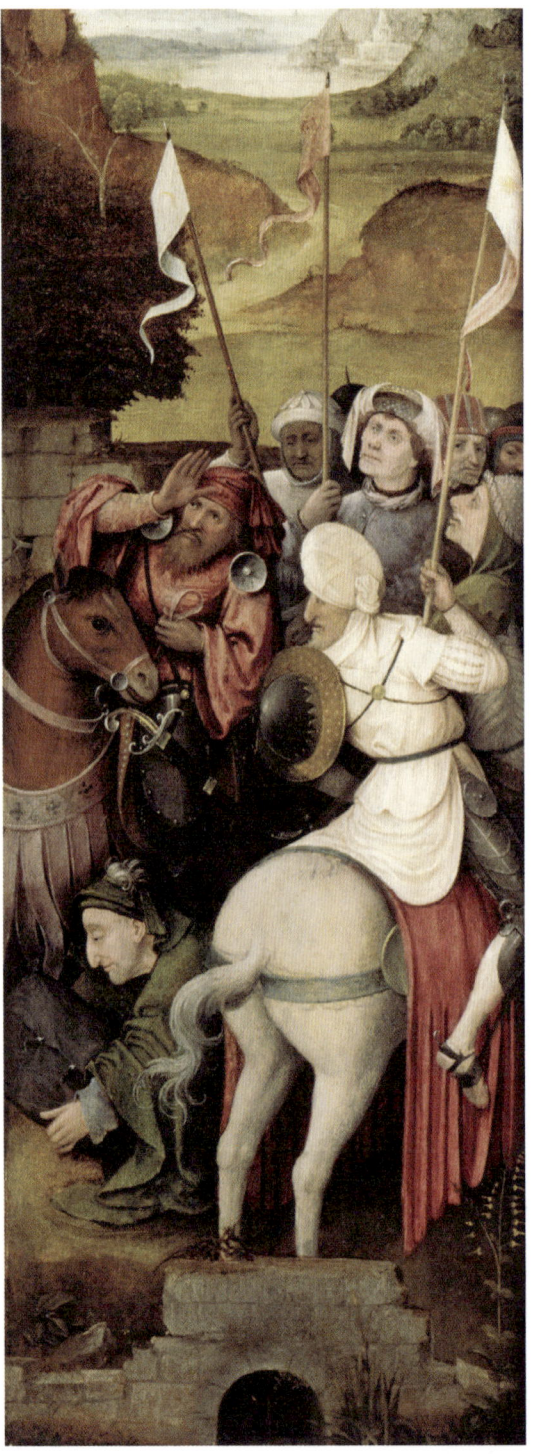

The Adoration of the Magi (left and right panels), *c.* **1495**
Oil on panel • Upton House, Warwickshire, England

In the left panel of the triptych we see Joseph collecting water for his family; while on the right is the retinue of the three kings.

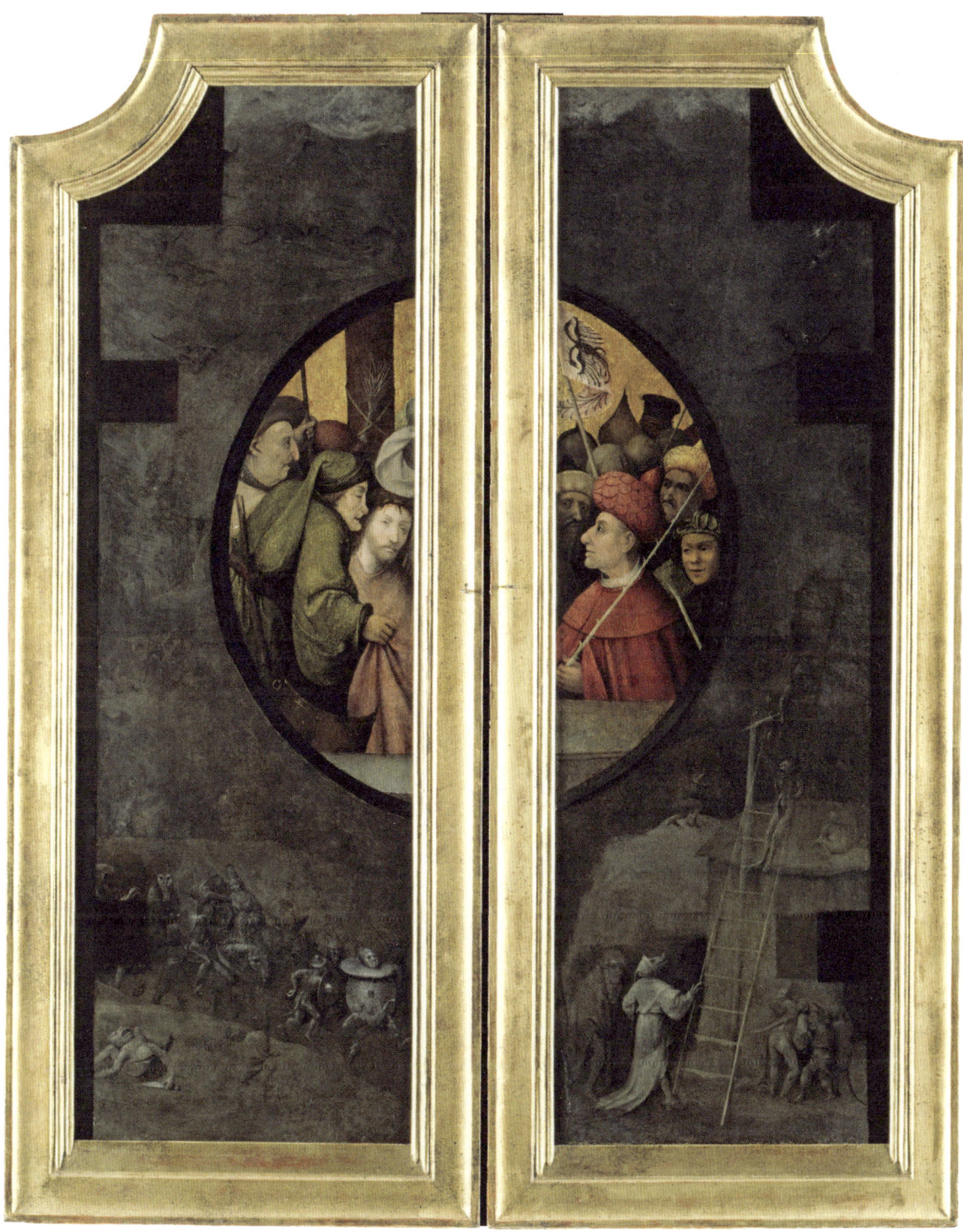

**The Adoration of the Magi: Christ Before Pilate
(closed doors),** *c.* **1495**

Oil on panel • Upton House, Warwickshire, England

The symbolic appearance of Herod, witnessing the Adoration of the Magi and his subsequent orders to murder the infant, links to the closed doors depicting Christ before Pontius Pilate, leading the narrative from Christ's birth to his death.

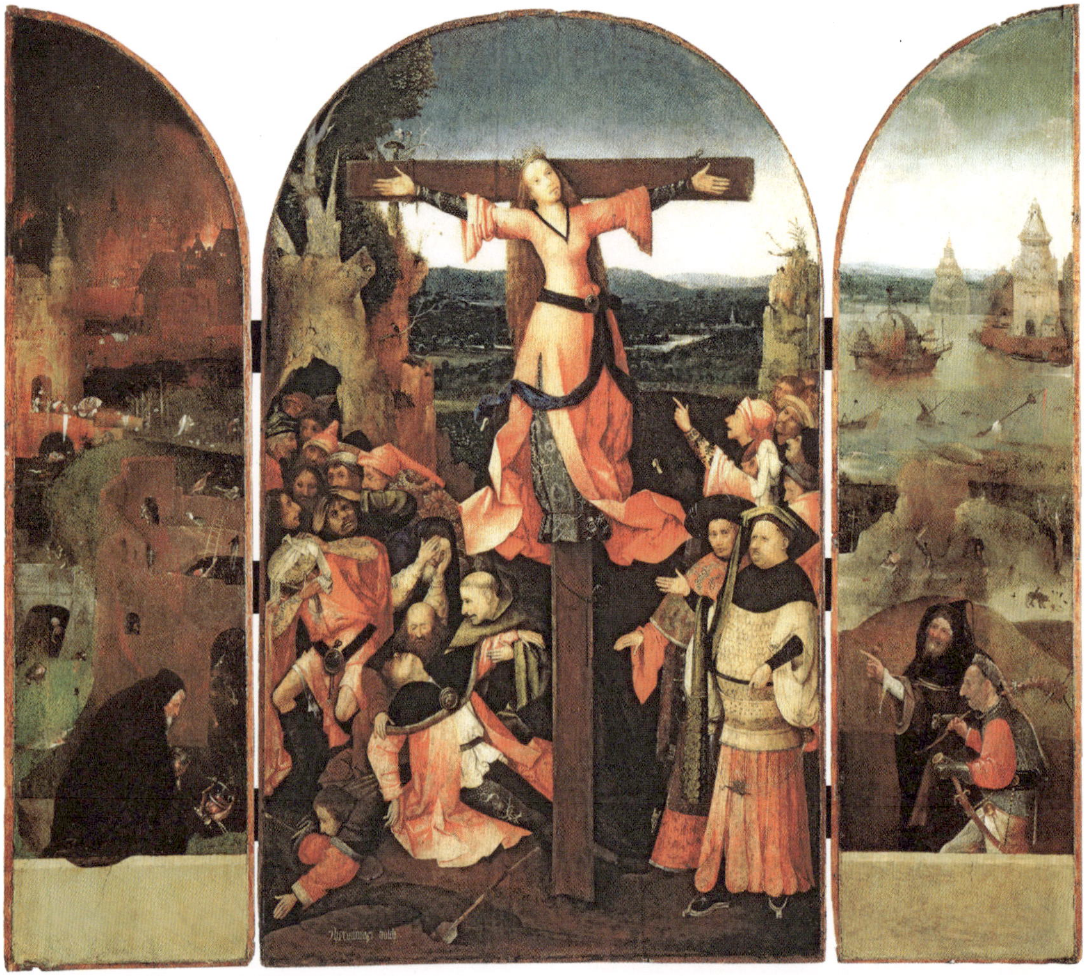

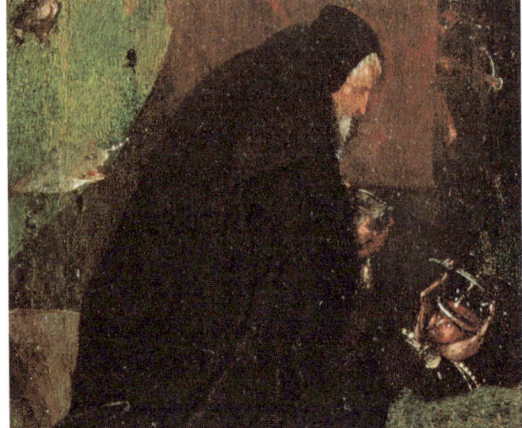

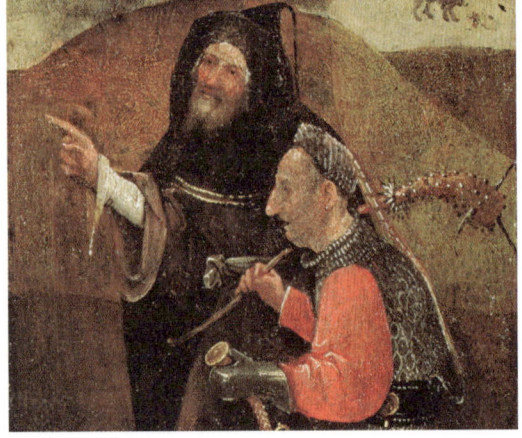

The Crucifixion of St Julia (and details), *c.* **1497**
Oil on panel, 104 x 119 cm (41 x 47 in)
• Palazzo Ducale, Venice

St Julia was the daughter of a pagan king. He ordered her death by crucifixion when she took a vow of chastity to avoid his choice of pagan suitors. On the left is St Anthony in meditation, while the right wing portrays a monk directing a soldier. Kneeling donors in each side panel were painted out, but are visible today through infrared photography.

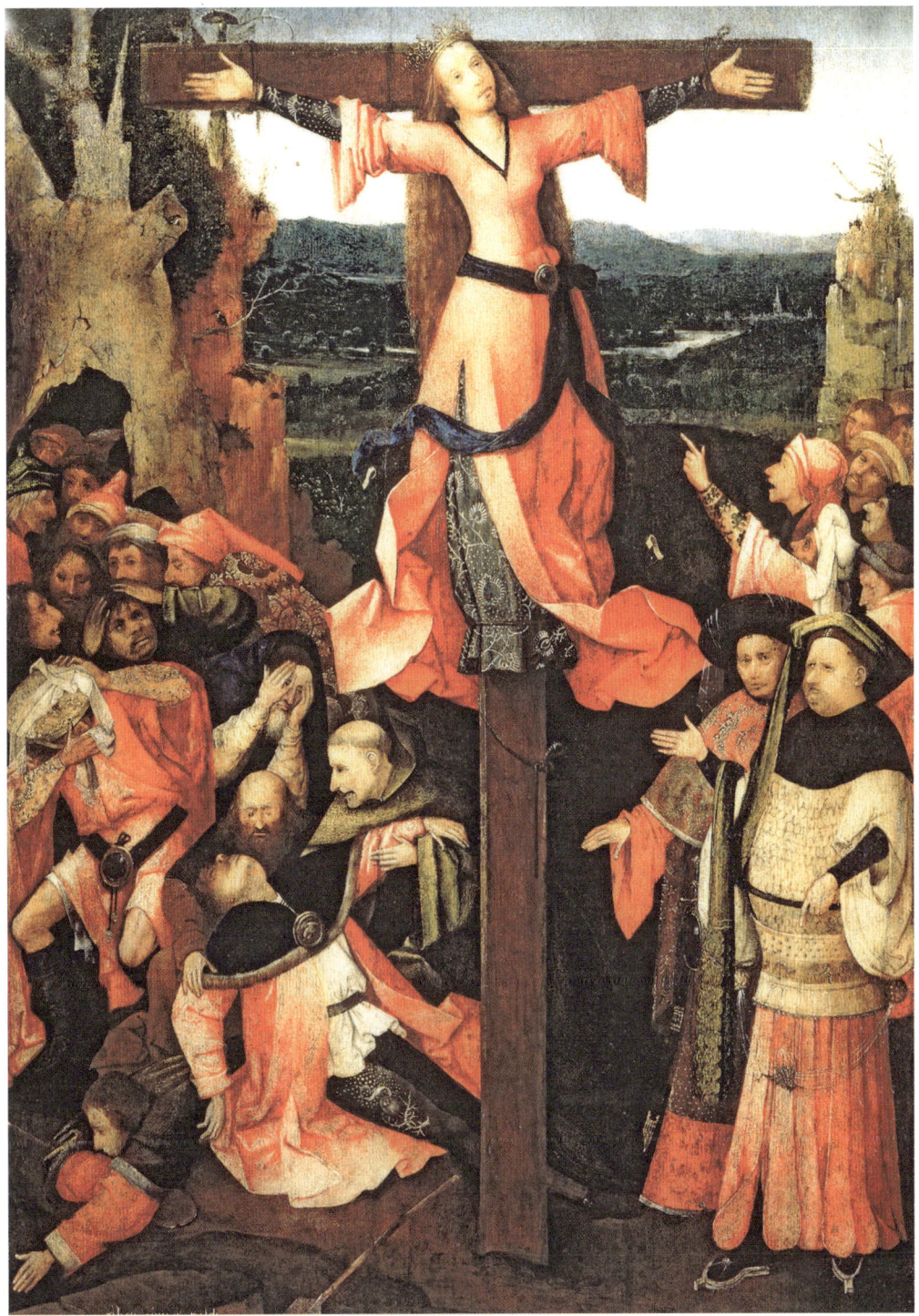

The Crucifixion of St Julia (central panel), *c.* 1497
Oil on panel • Palazzo Ducale, Venice

St Julia (also known as St Liberata, St Uncumber and St Wilgefortis), the first female Christian martyr, converted to Christianity and with spiritual help through prayer grew a beard to make herself unattractive to the pagan suitor her father wished her to marry. The painted beard is visible today under infrared light.

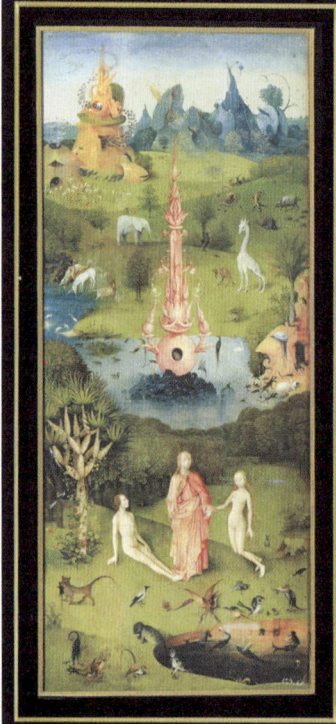
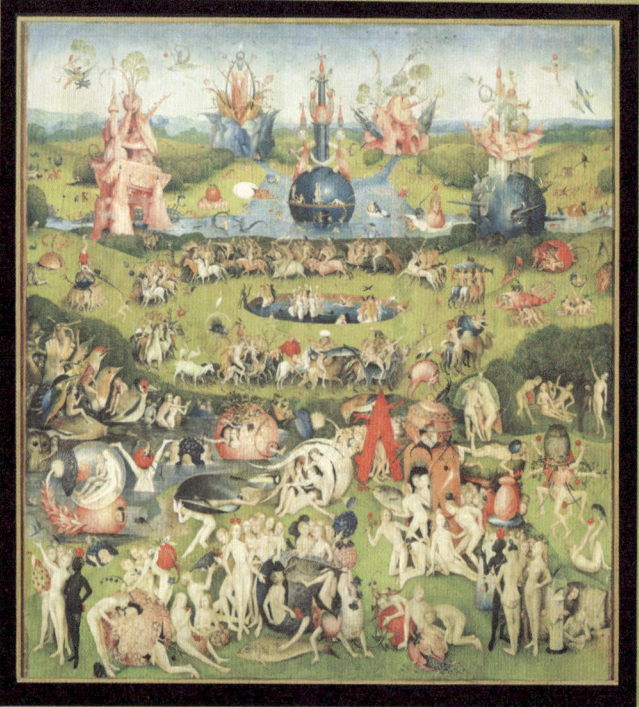
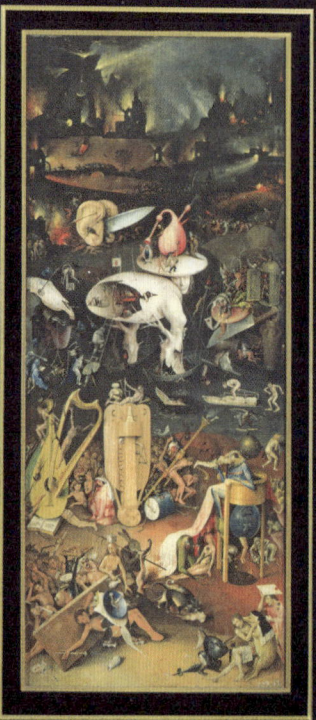

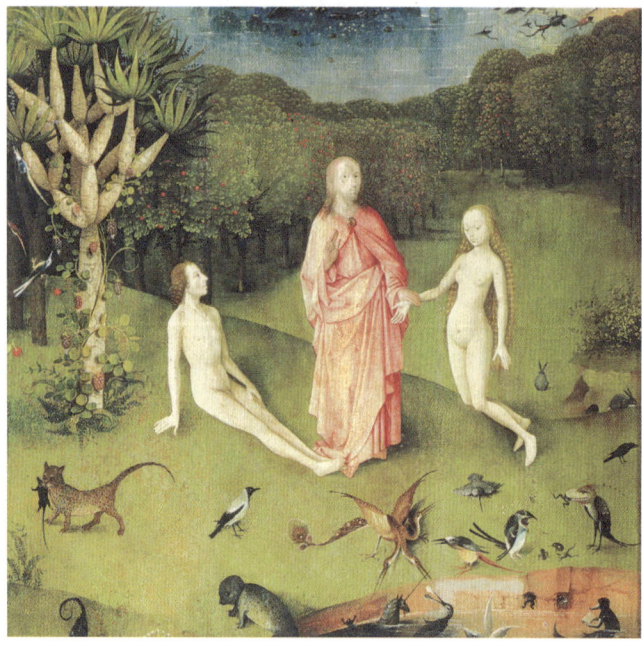
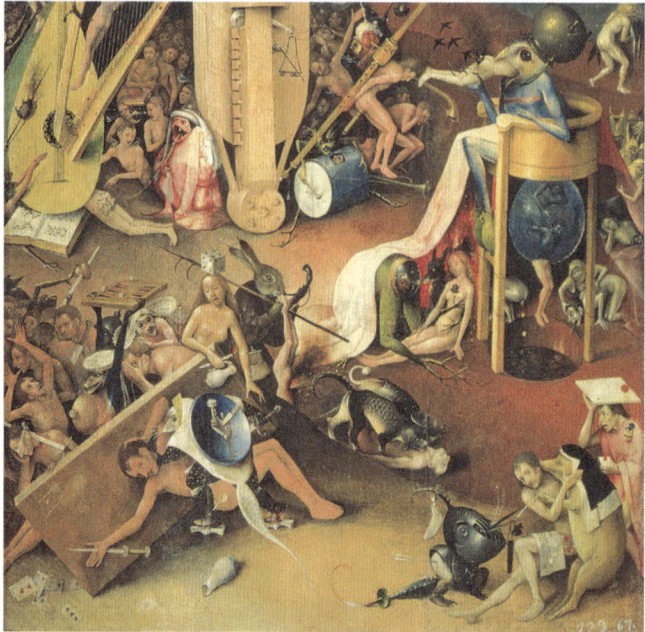

The Garden of Earthly Delights (and details), *c.* **1500**
Oil on panel, 220 x 389 cm (86⅔ x 153 in)
• Museo Nacional del Prado, Madrid

The artist paints a sumptuous vision of an earthly Paradise filled with material vanities.
It includes a vision of Hell and uses visual puns of popular metaphors of contemporary
times to make a moral point.

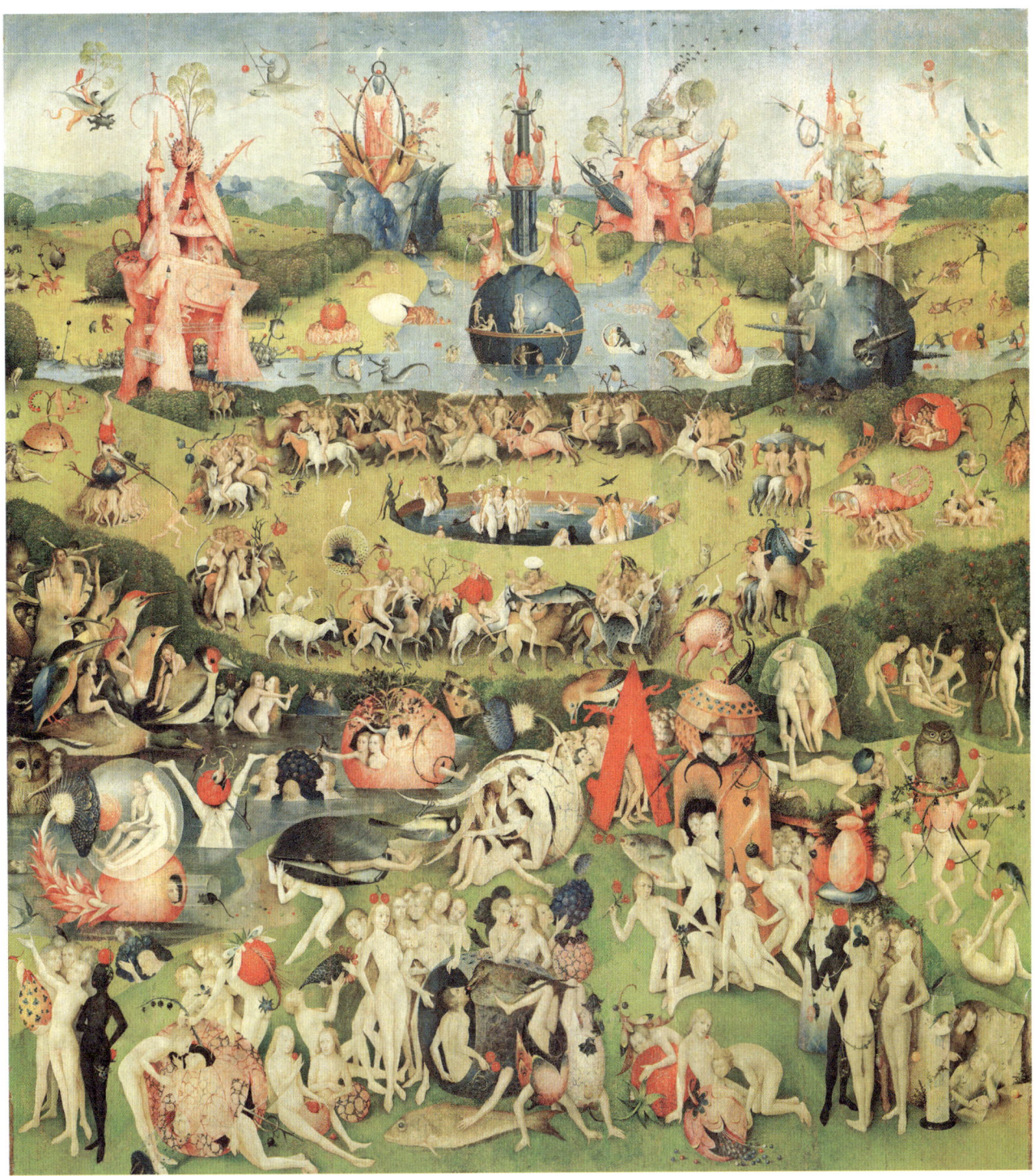

**The Garden of Earthly Delights: Allegory of Luxury
(central panel),** *c.* **1500**

Oil on panel • Museo Nacional del Prado, Madrid

The central panel focuses explicitly on lust, picturing crowds of men and women romping naked in a landscape of pleasure domes, experiencing sinful excesses, riding strange animals, swimming with bestial creatures and promiscuously mixing with strangers.

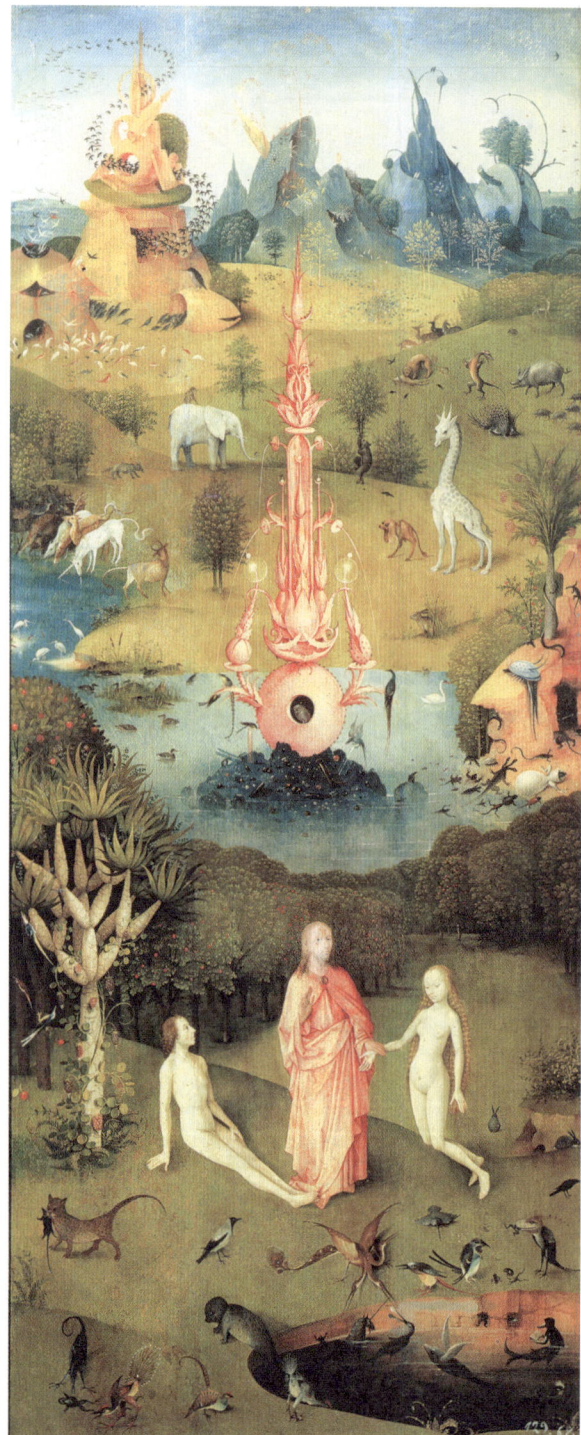
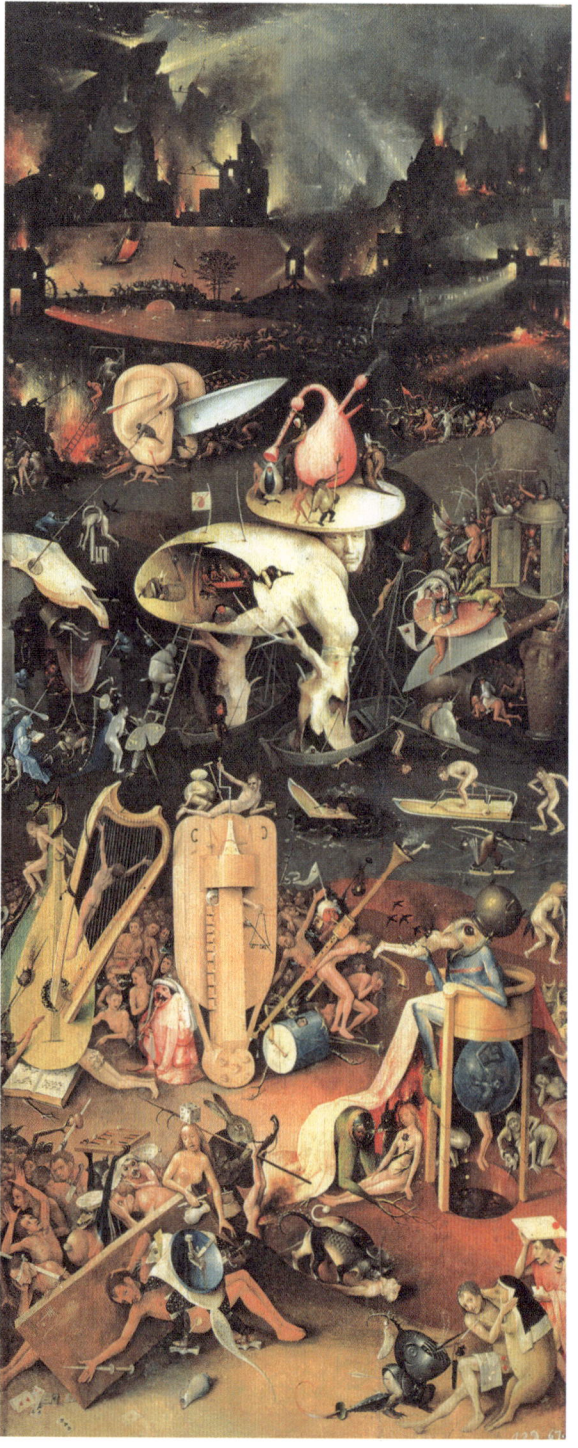

The Garden of Earthly Delights:
The Garden of Eden (left) and Hell (right), *c.* 1500
Oil on panel • Museo Nacional del Prado, Madrid

God's creation of the world is reconstructed in circular planes of landscape where many different creatures cohabit. Adam looks on as Christ, representing God, creates Eve. The cacophony of Hell is played by tortured musicians in the artist's interpretation of sin's consequences. A 'tree-man' with a human face carries a 'ship of fools' in his broken body.

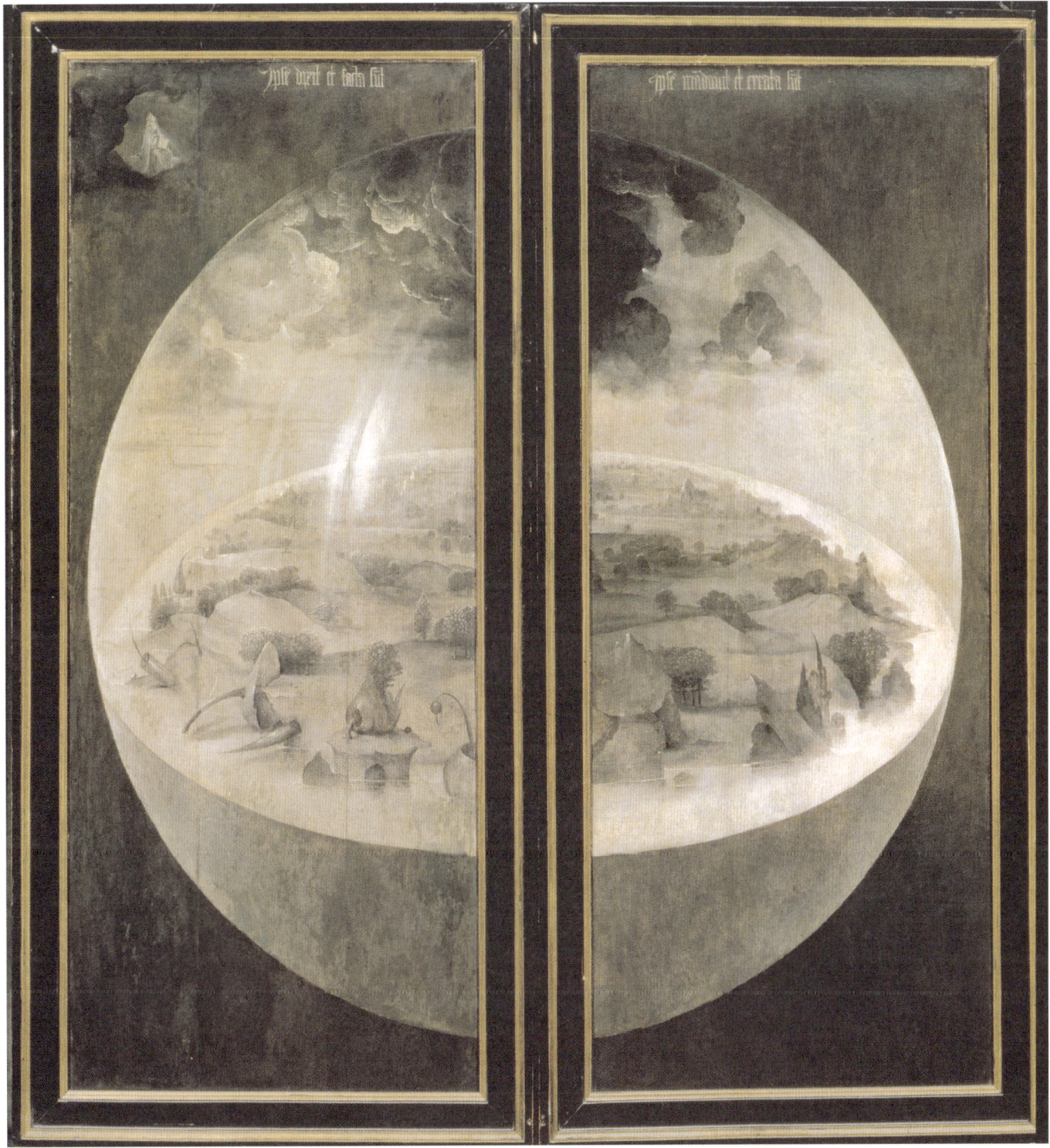

The Garden of Earthly Delights:
The Creation of the World (closed doors), *c.* **1500**
Oil on panel • Museo Nacional del Prado, Madrid

The celestial space around Earth leads the eye to a city that might be 's-Hertogenbosch. It is a tranquil introduction to the visions of the material and spiritual life on the panels within.

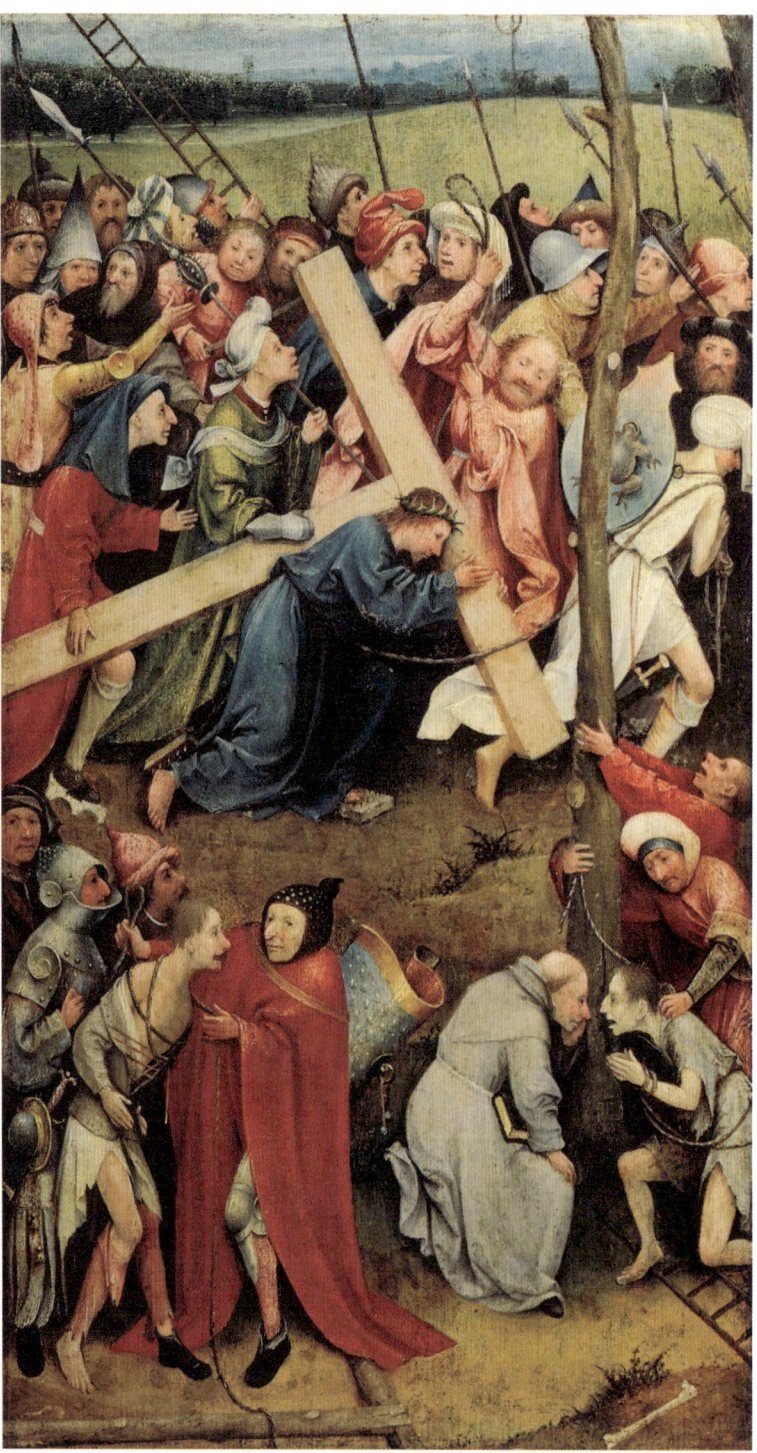

Christ Carrying the Cross (inner left panel of a triptych), *c.* **1490–1510**
Oil on panel, 57.2 x 32 cm (22½ x 12⅔ in)
• Kunsthistorisches Museum, Vienna

The reverse panel, illustrating a young child pushing a wooden frame, links Christ's birth to his death by crucifixion. On this panel Christ bears the Cross, which symbolizes the burden of the sins of mankind he carries.

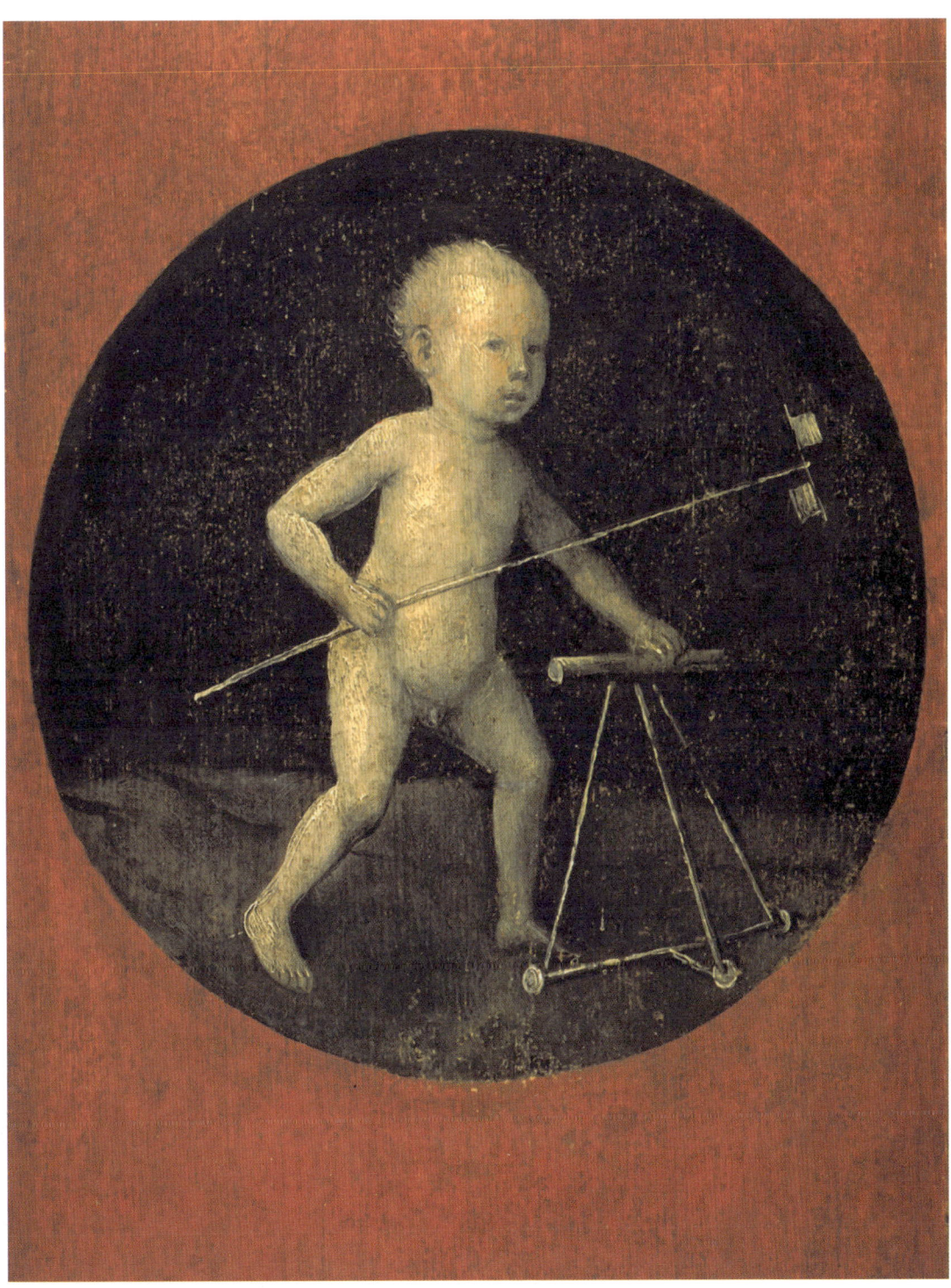

Christ Child with a Walking Frame (painted on the reverse of Christ Carrying the Cross), c. 1490–1510
Oil on panel, 57.2 x 32 cm (22½ x 12⅔ in)
• Kunsthistoriches Museum, Vienna

On a blood-red background, the artist portrays a young child pushing a wooden frame. The portrayal links the infant Christ's birth to his later death by crucifixion in *Christ Carrying the Cross* (reverse panel).

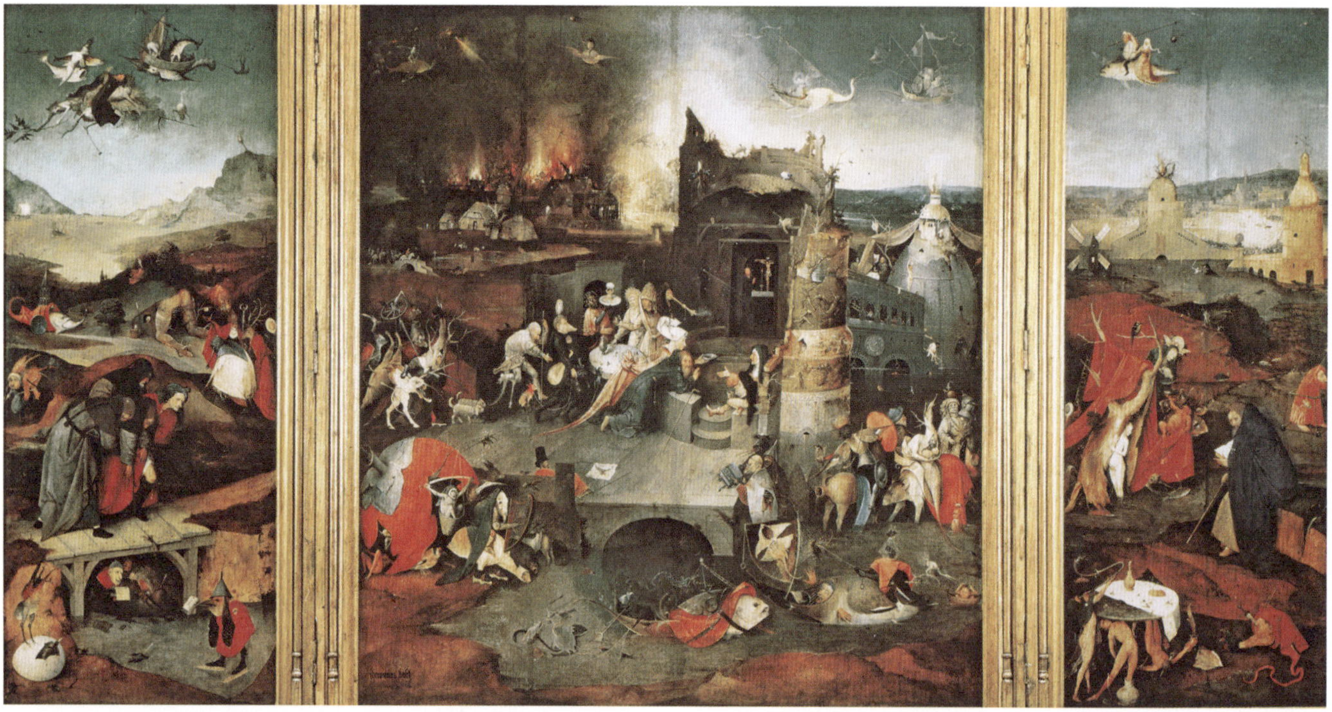

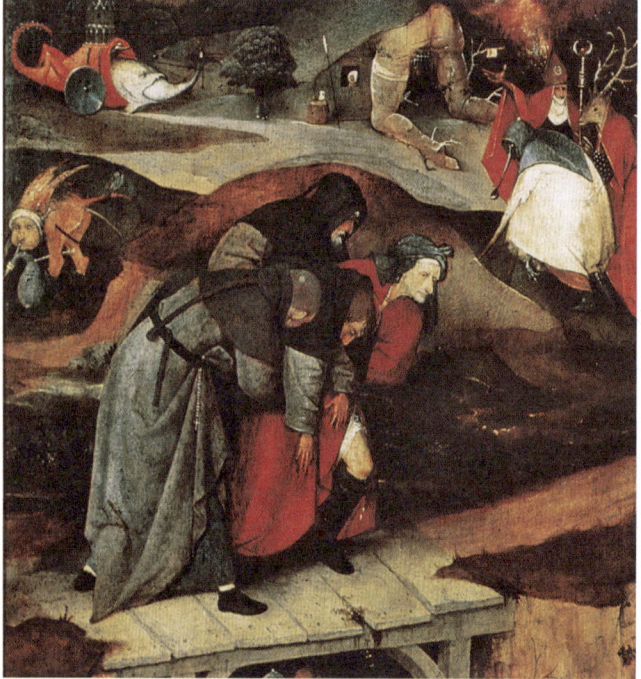

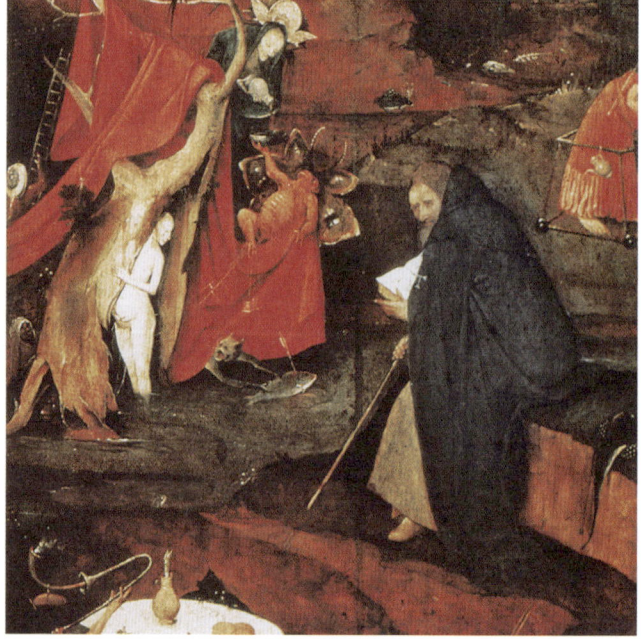

The Temptation of St Anthony (and details), *c.* 1501
Oil on panel, 131 x 228 cm (52 x 90 in)
• Museu Nacional de Arte Antiga, Lisbon

A triptych which follows the life of St Anthony, in supernatural and worldly experiences, revealing the temptations that can turn a spiritual man away from God unless he is steadfast in prayer.

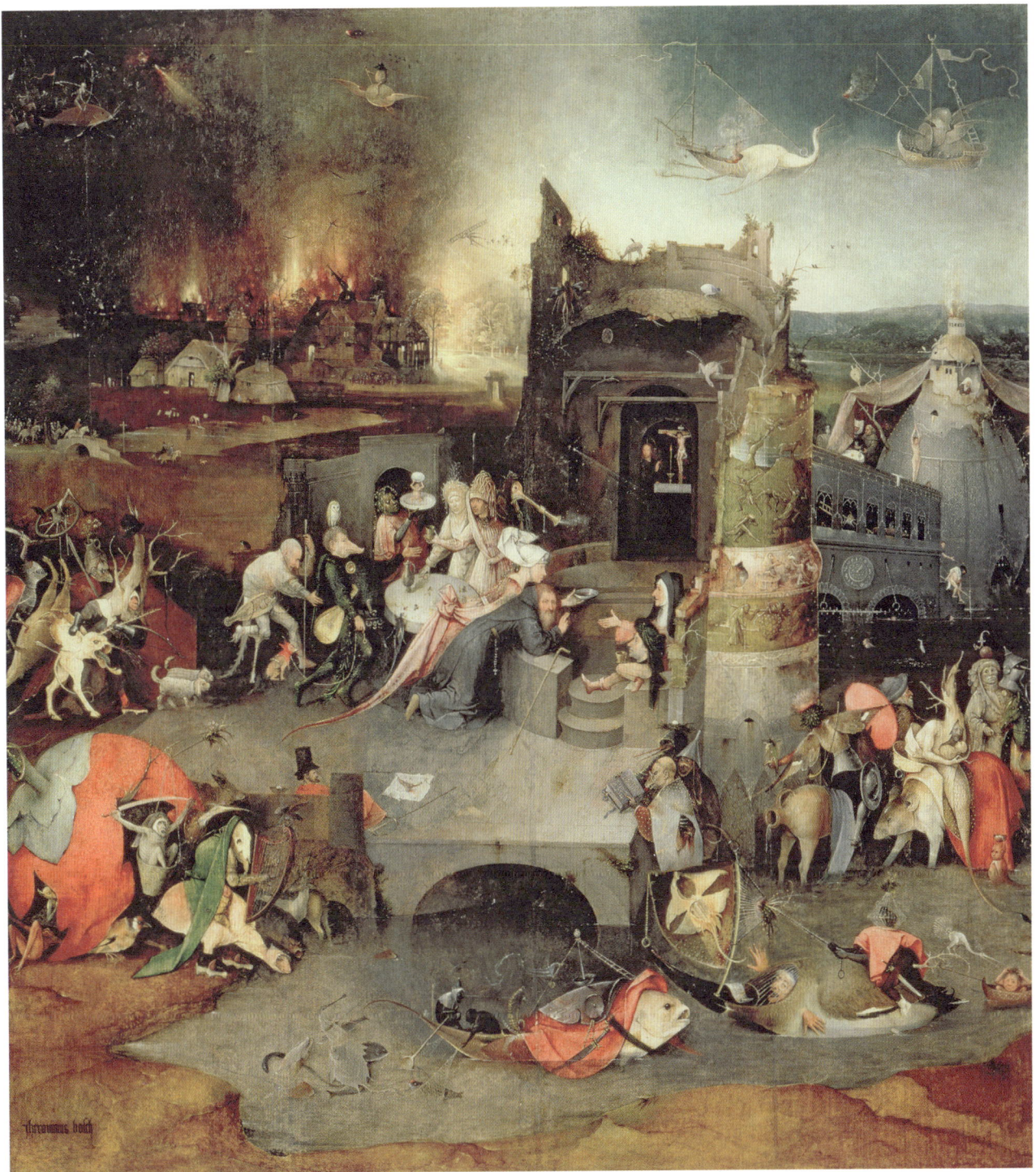

The Temptation of St Anthony (central panel), *c.* **1501**
Oil on panel • Museu Nacional de Arte Antiga, Lisbon

The central panel shows the saint at prayer in a ruined building, surrounded by the material greed of soothsayers, false preachers and tempters. Burning buildings and wreckage depict the world as a ruinous place where one must follow the righteous path.

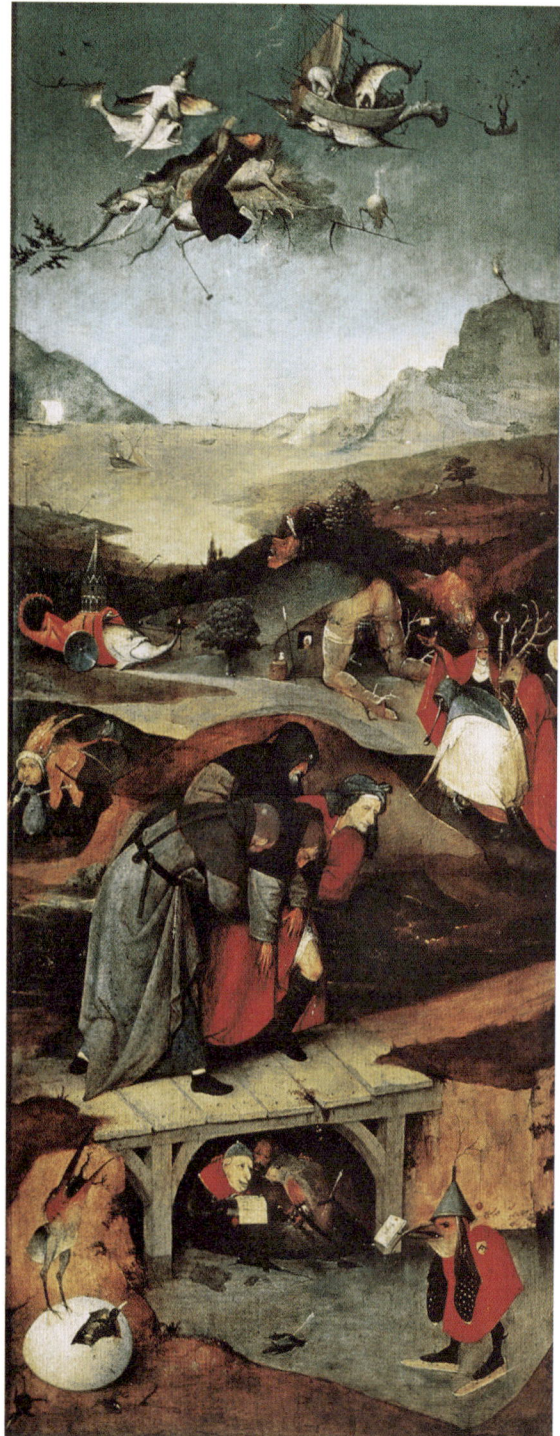

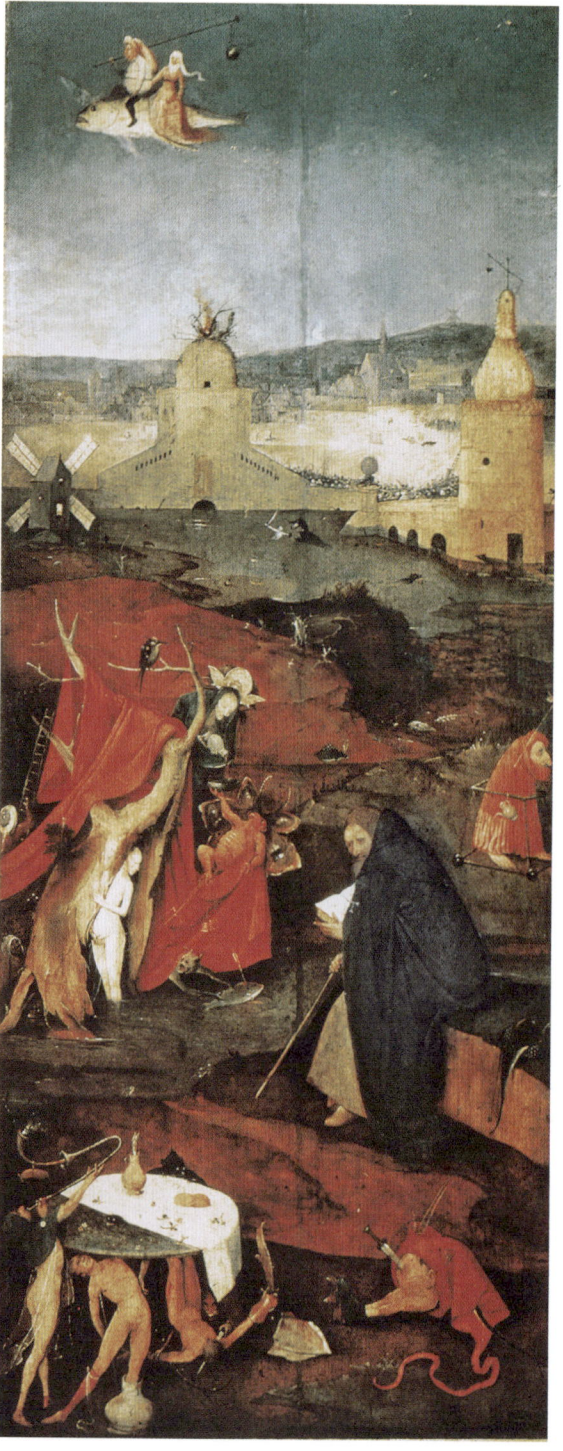

**The Temptation of St Anthony
(left and right panels inside),** *c.* **1501**

Oil on panel • *Museu Nacional de Arte Antiga, Lisbon*

Men and women of holy orders believed that God sent the Devil to confront, tempt or trick them, to make them stronger in their faith. Faced with the worldly temptations proffered him in the guise of the beautiful or grotesque, his steadfast determination to overcome materiality and be closer to God is found in the loneliness of a hermit's life.

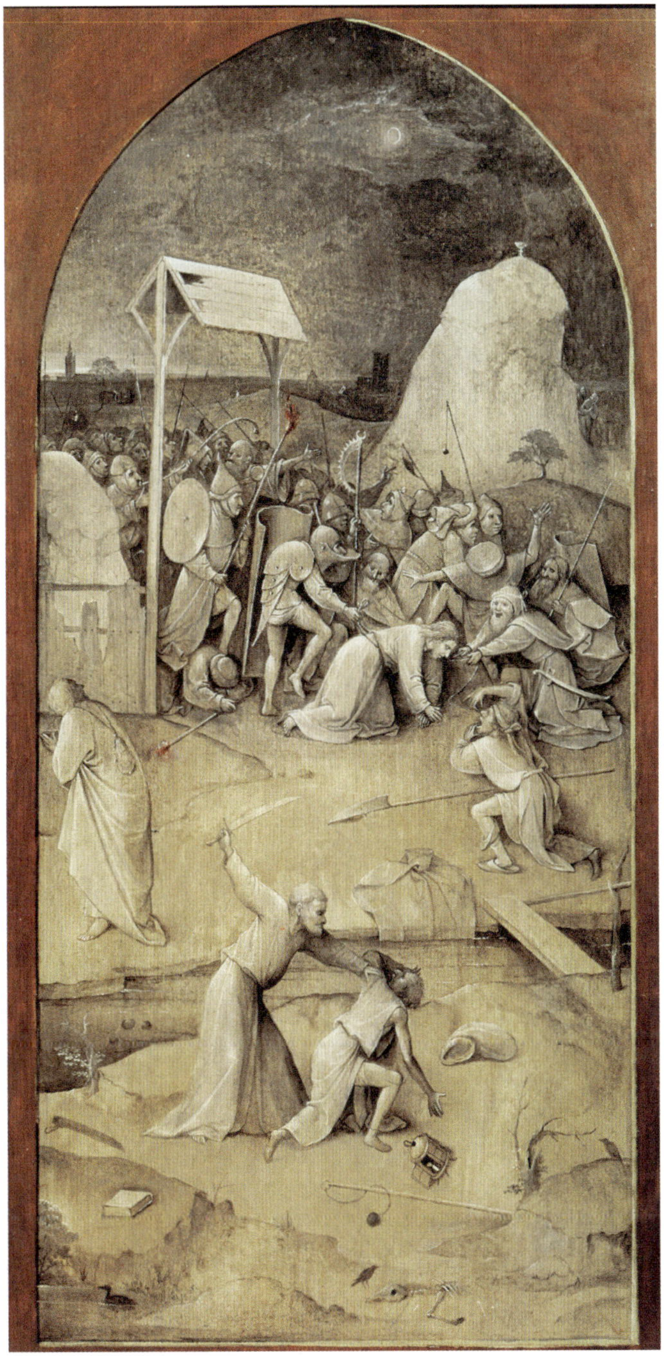

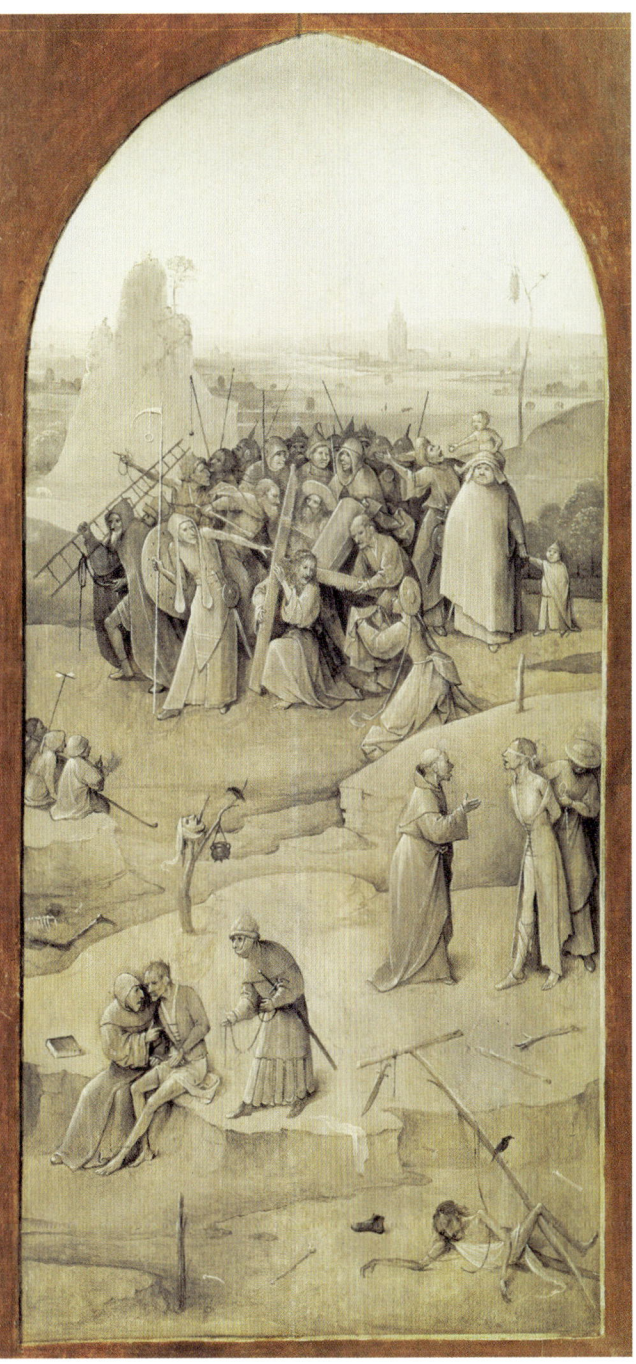

**The Temptation of St Anthony: The Taking of Christ
(outer panel left and right),** *c.* **1501**

Oil on panel • Museu Nacional de Arte Antiga, Lisbon

The outer doors illustrate two scenes from Christ's Passion. On the left panel the artist portrays a disturbing scene as Christ is taken prisoner after his betrayal by Judas. In the centre Christ on his sorrowful path to crucifixion (John 19:17) falters under the weight of the Cross amidst a sea of people. In the foreground, monks converse with condemned thieves about to be crucified.

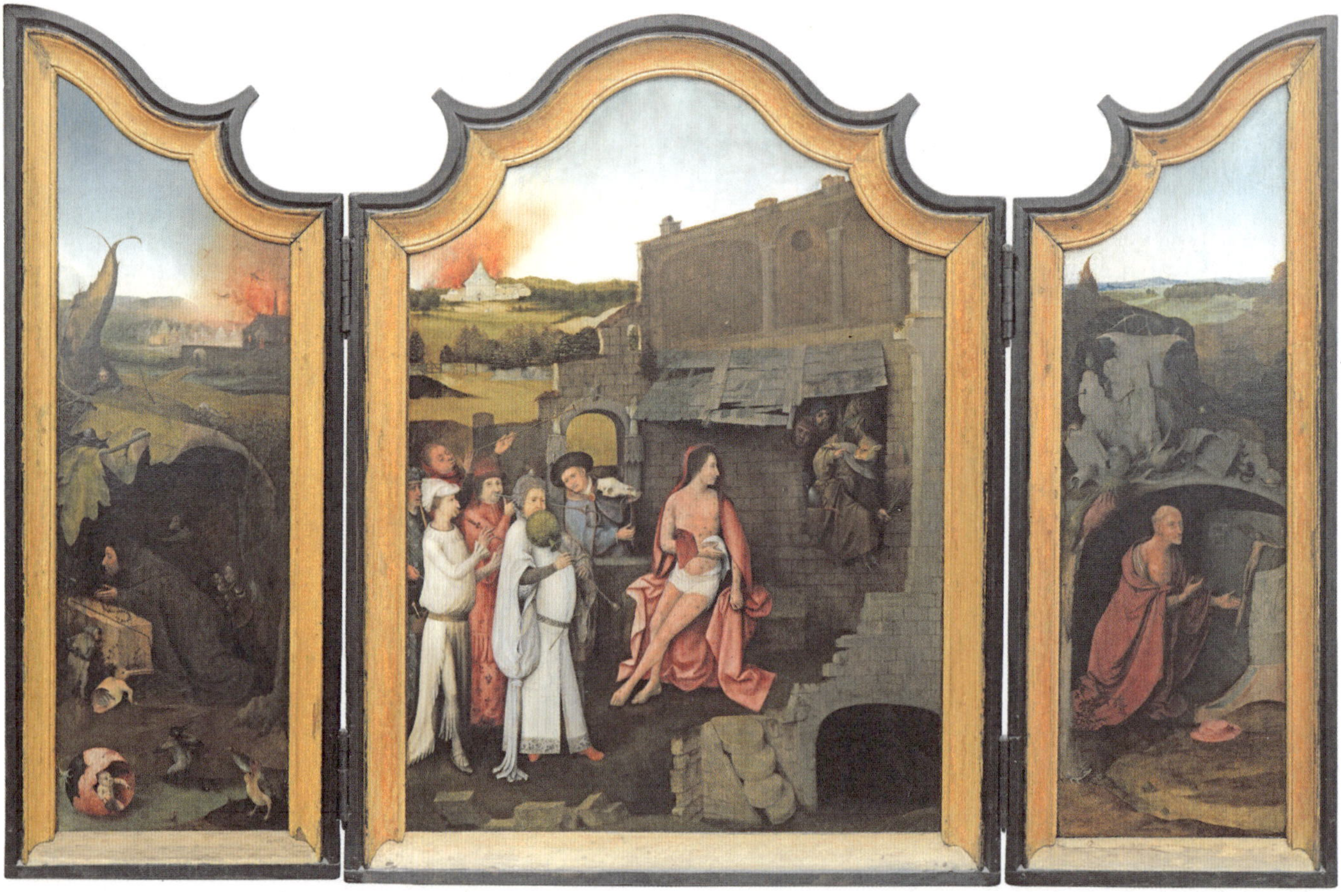

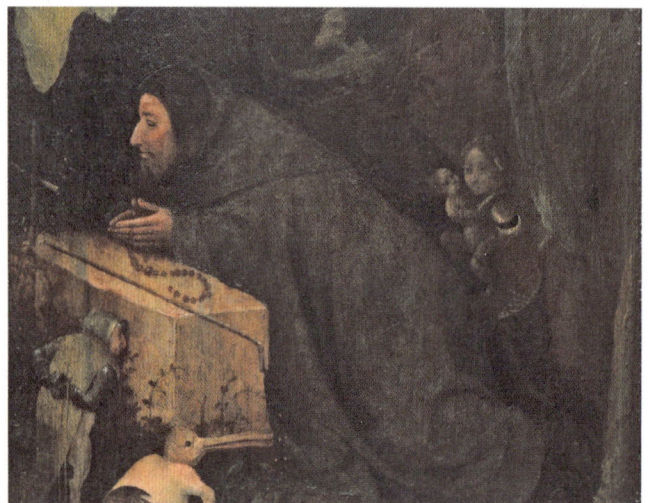

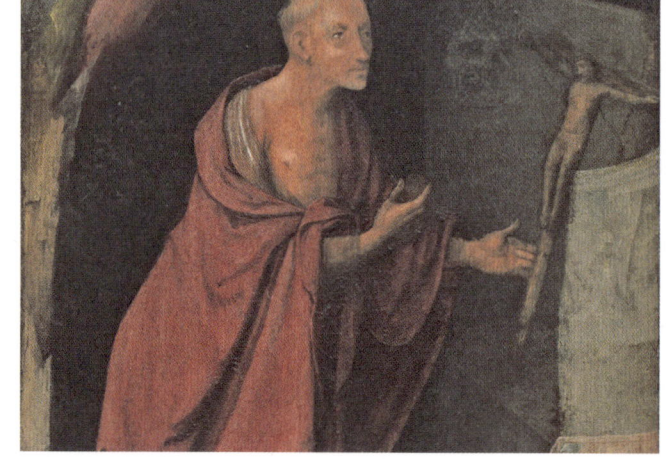

The Story of Job, *c.* 1507–15, Bosch workshop, or follower
Oil on panel, 98.3 x 132.8 cm (38¾ x 52⅓ in)
• Groeninge Museum, Bruges

The Old Testament *Book of Job* relates the progress of Job's life from happiness and prosperity to loss of family, health and wealth. Through God's guidance, he reclaims the wealth of his material and spiritual life. On the left and right respectively, St Anthony and St Jerome are at focused prayer.

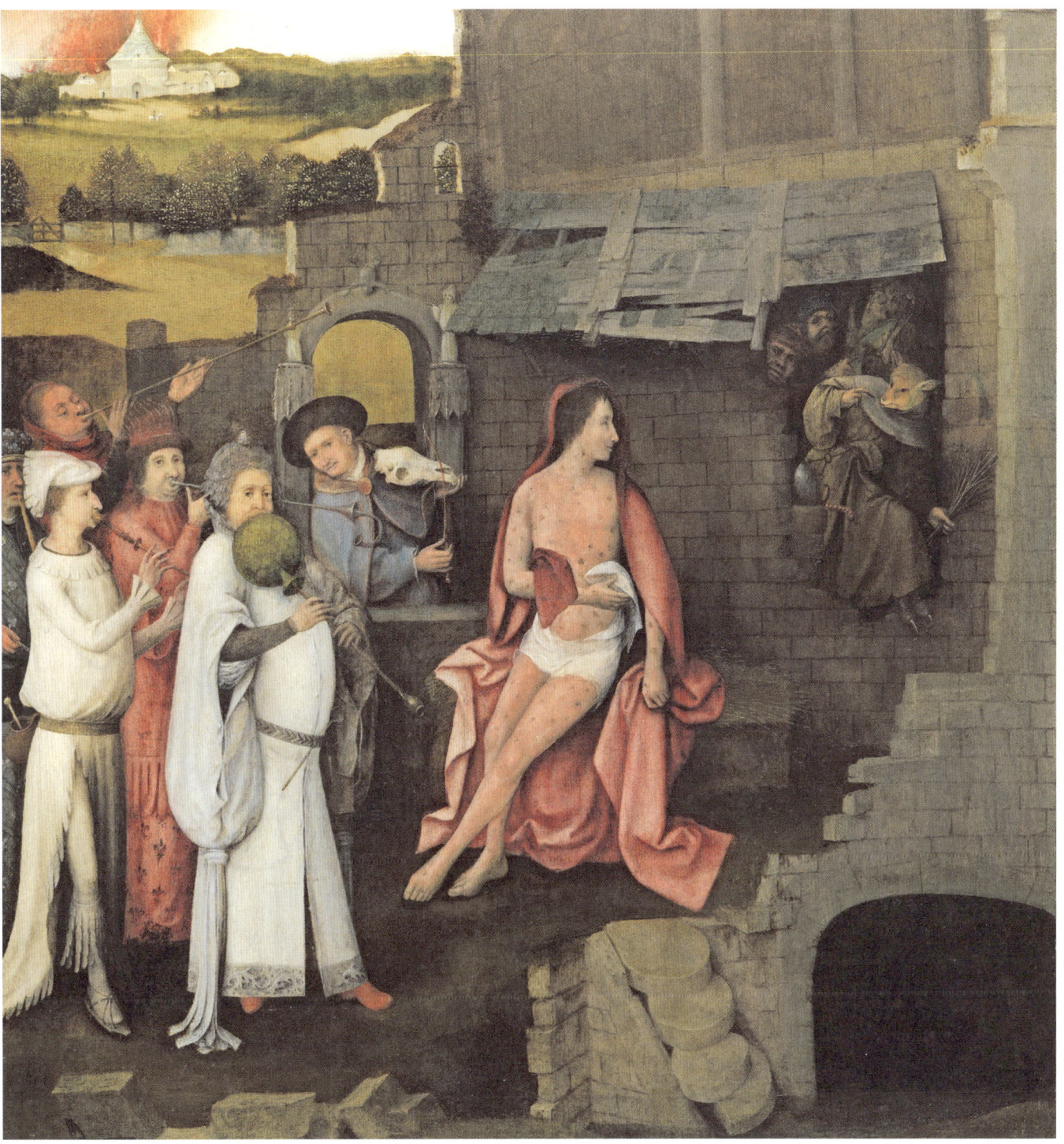

The Story of Job (central panel), *c.* 1507–15
Oil on panel • Groeninge Museum, Bruges

In an architectural setting similar to the central panel of *The Temptation of St Anthony* (*see* pages 92–95), Job sits in a ruined building, where evil is present, suffering from a disease of boils created by the Devil on God's orders (Job 2:7).

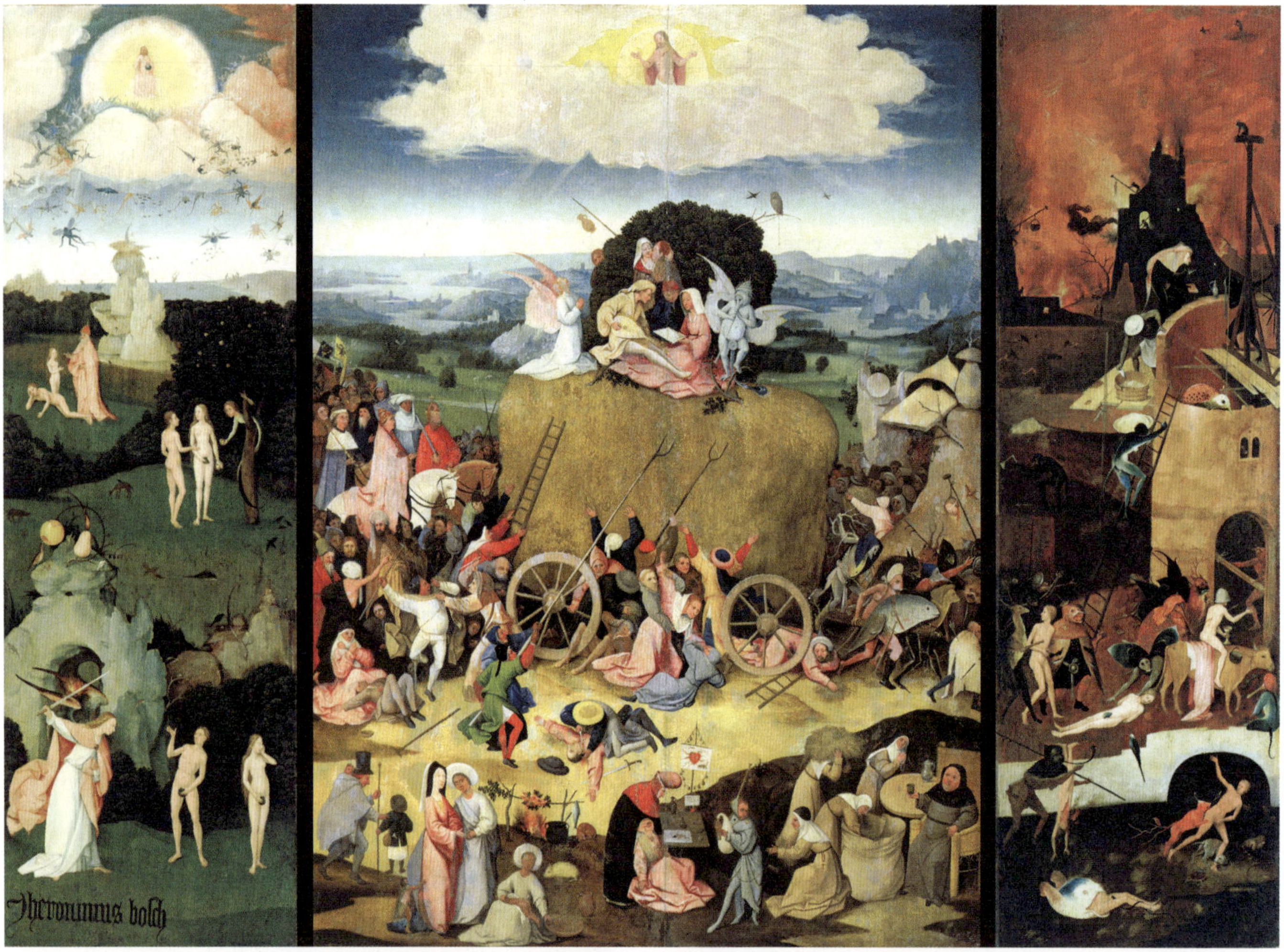

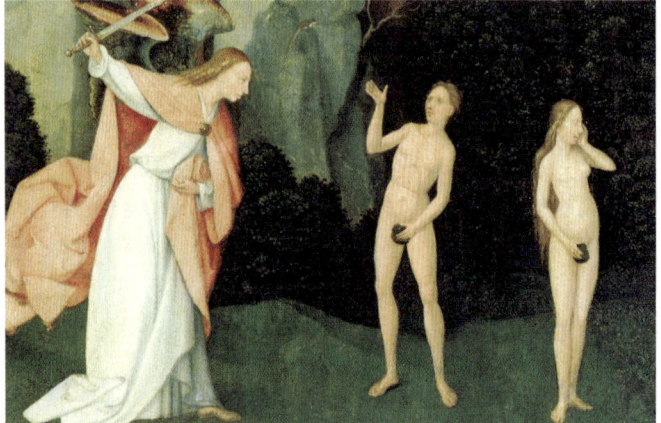
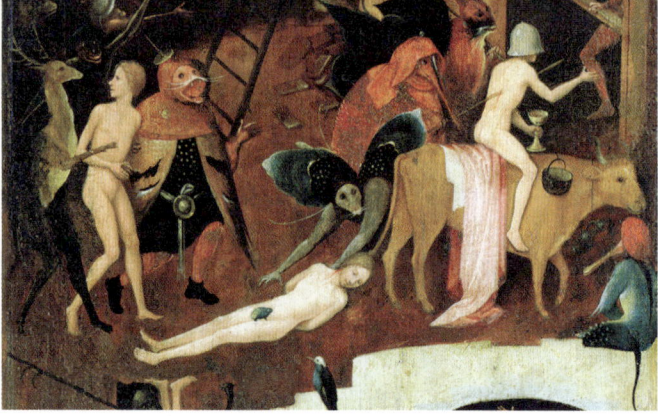

The Haywain, _c._ 1510–16
Oil on panel, 147 x 212 cm (58 x 83½ in)
• Museo Nacional del Prado, Madrid (alternate version at El Escorial)

The Haywain, a comic tragedy of moral symbolism, represents Man's journey from the innocence of the Garden of Eden to the dark spaces of Hell, with the vagaries of earthly life represented around a loaded haywain.

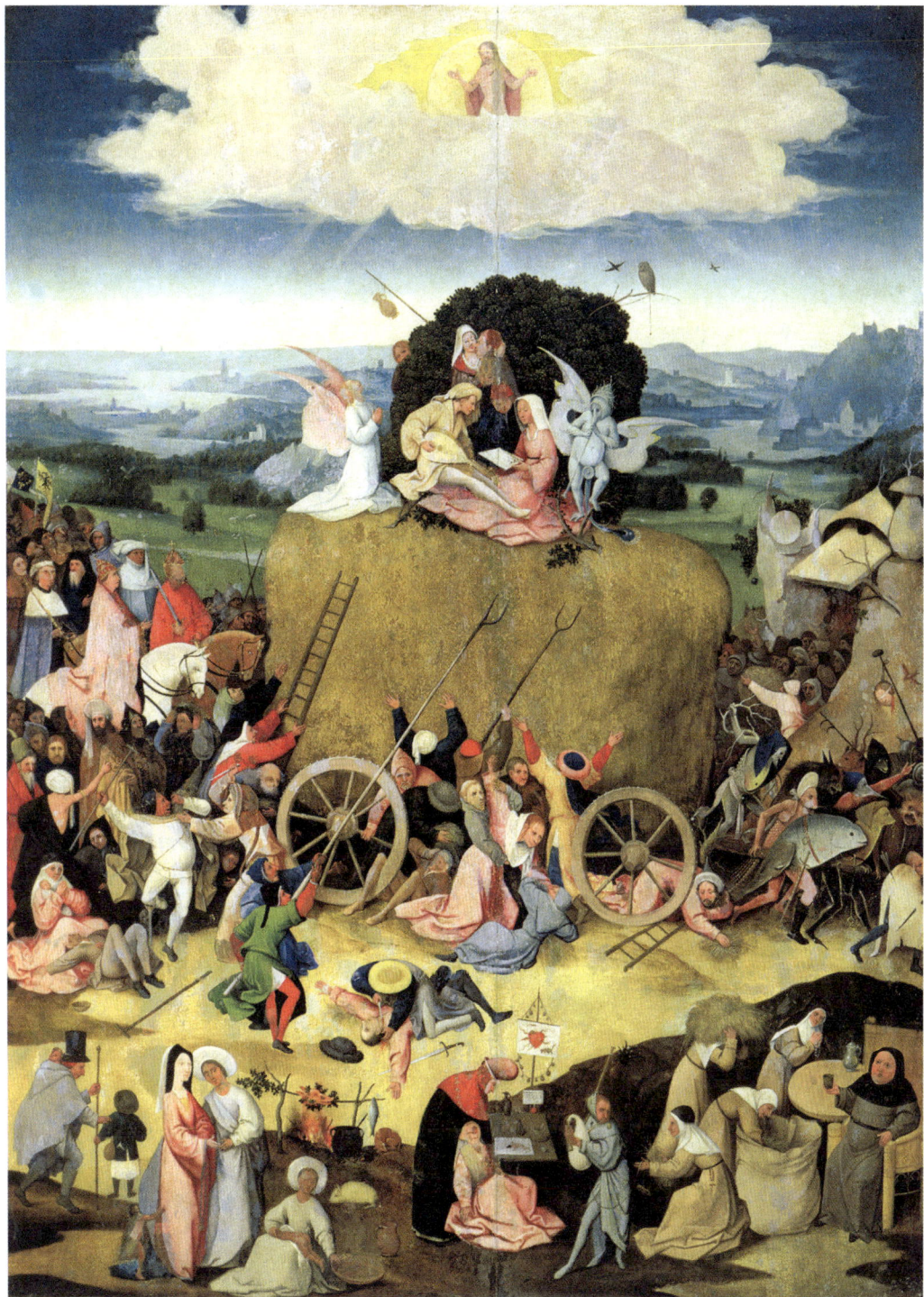

**The Haywain: The Hay Wagon
(central panel),** *c.* **1510–16**

Oil on panel • Museo Nacional del Prado, Madrid
(alternate version at El Escorial)

On top of a hay wagon, two pairs of lovers are serenaded by a lute player (a symbol of lust), unaware that the wagon is travelling towards Hell. On the left an angel prays fervently, as a winged devil and owl look on.

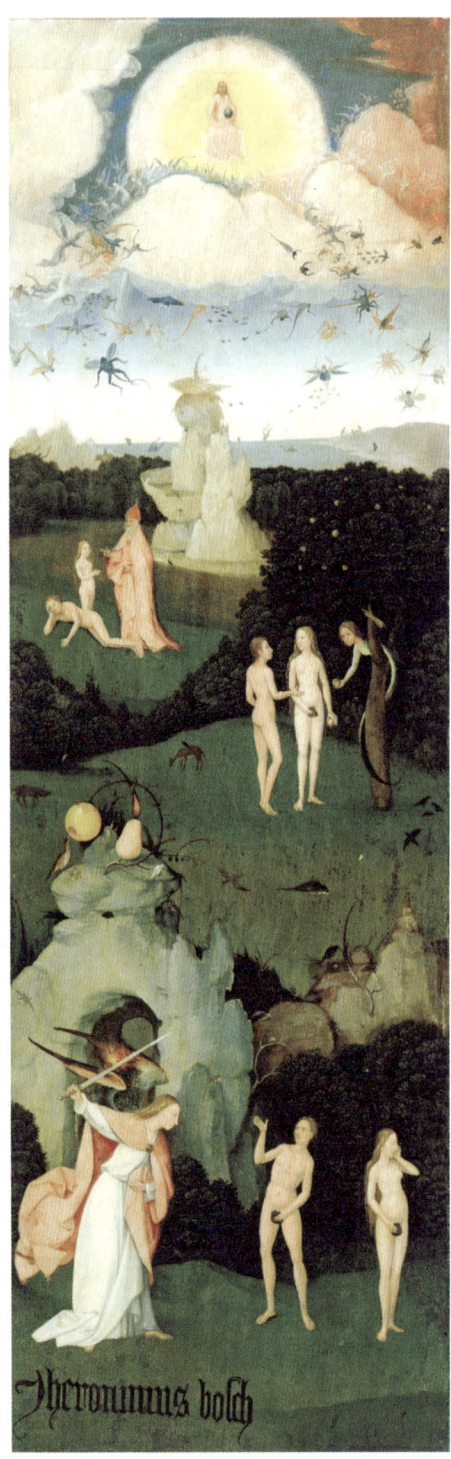

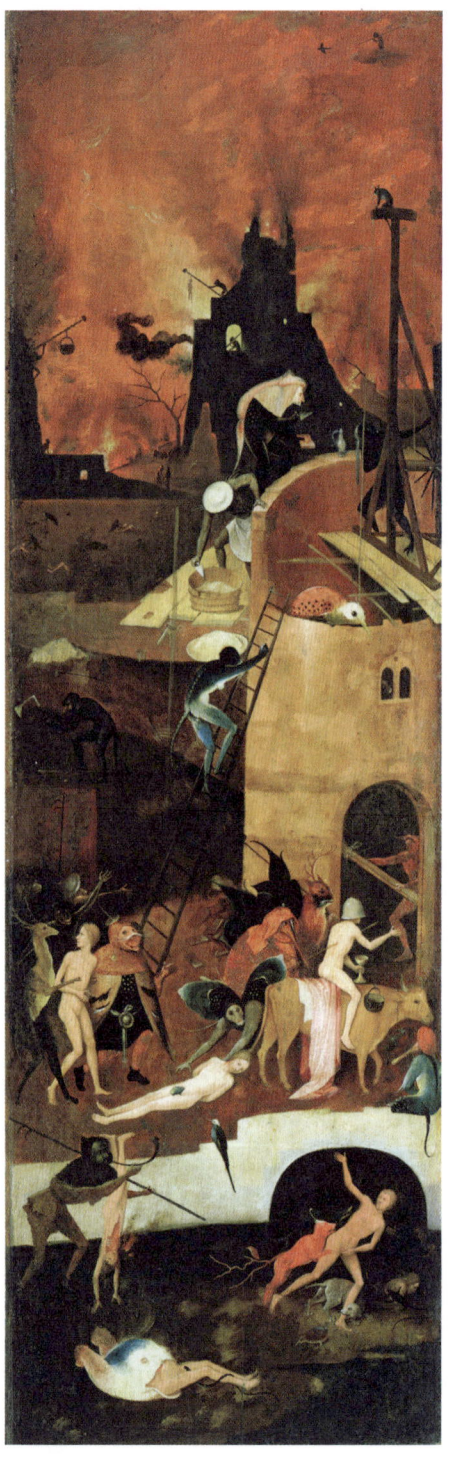

The Haywain: The Fall of Man (left panel), *c.* **1510–16**
Oil on panel • Museo Nacional del Prado, Madrid

A scene of the ejection of the Devil and his rebel angels from Heaven leads the eye downwards to the Creation of Man and Woman in the Garden of Eden, followed by their Fall through disobedience to God and subsequent expulsion by archangel St Michael.

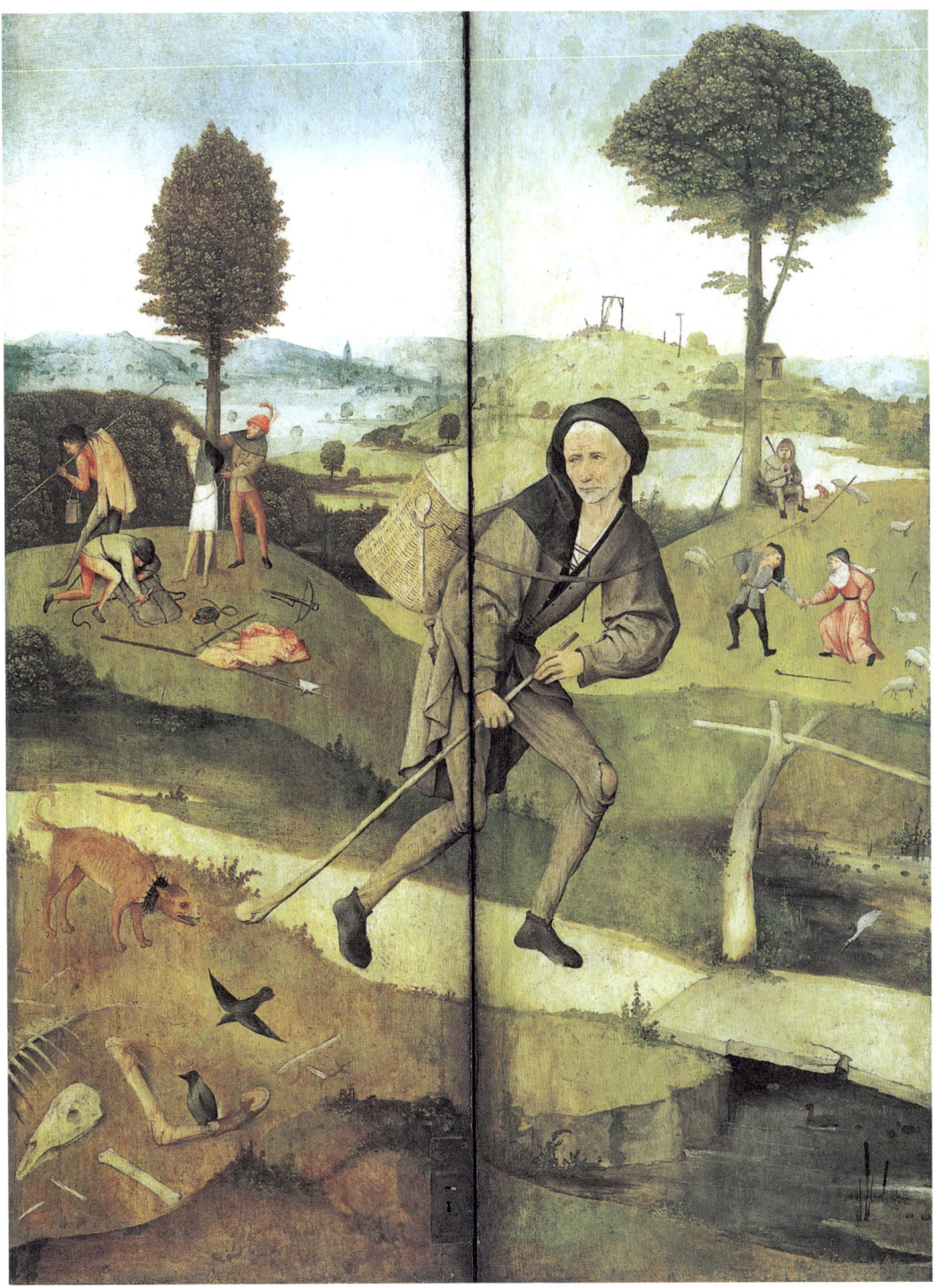

The Haywain: Everyman Walking the Path of Life (closed doors), *c.* **1510–16**

Oil on panel • Museo Nacional del Prado, Madrid

A pedlar walks on a narrow path through a landscape of disorder, from thieves robbing a man of his clothes and possessions, to a distant hill with a hangman's scaffold, a foretaste of the moral tale behind the closed doors.

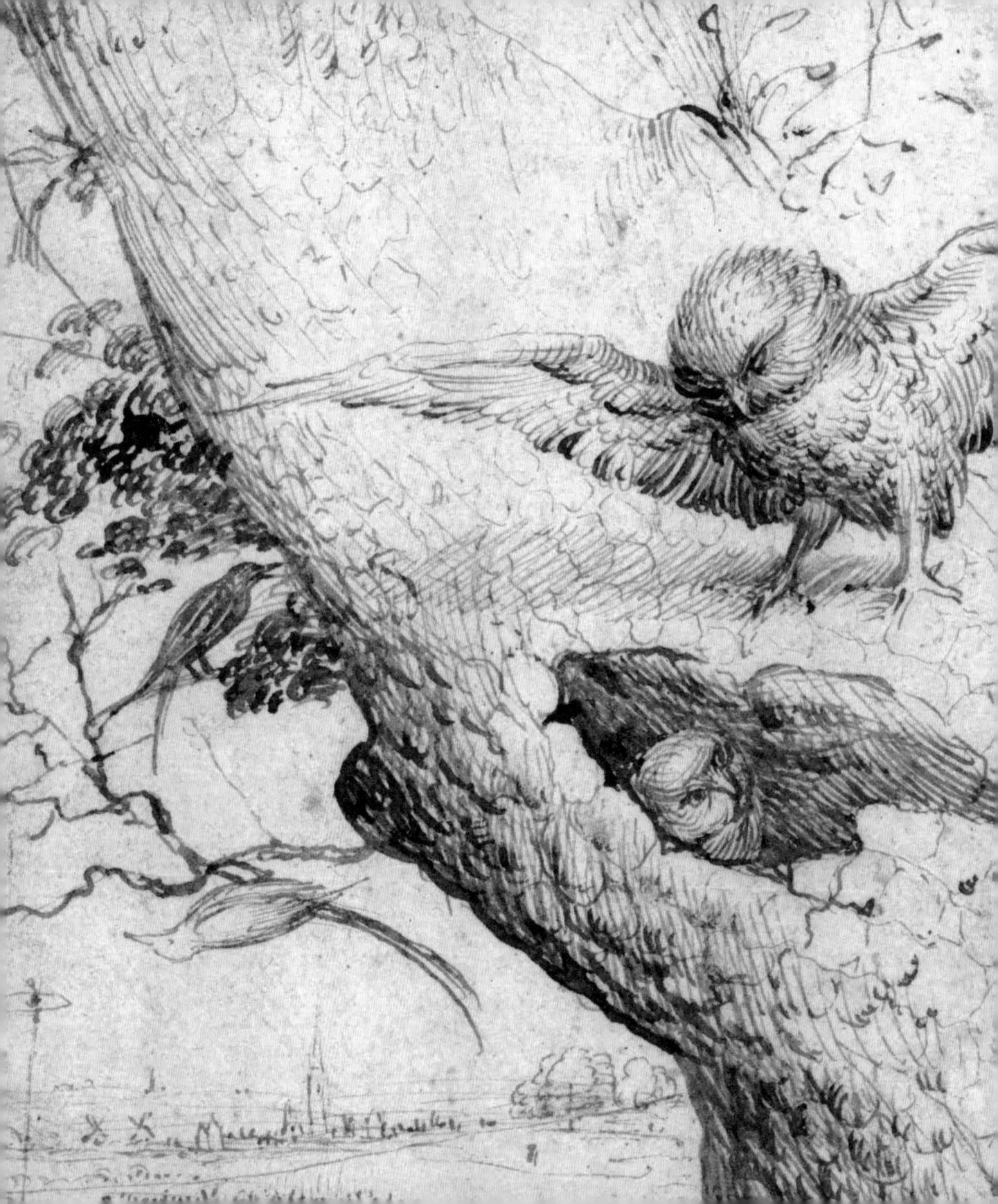

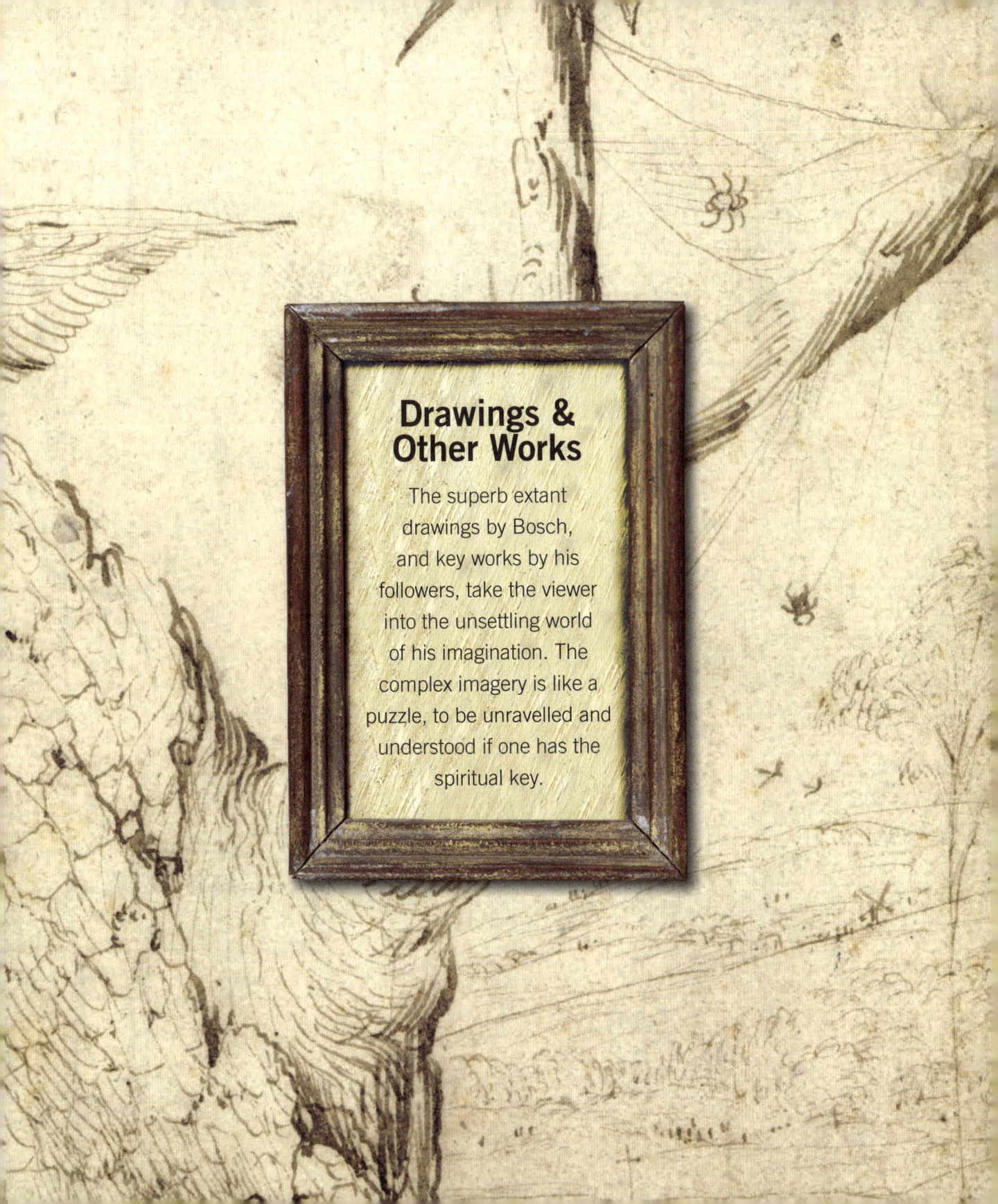

Drawings & Other Works

The superb extant drawings by Bosch, and key works by his followers, take the viewer into the unsettling world of his imagination. The complex imagery is like a puzzle, to be unravelled and understood if one has the spiritual key.

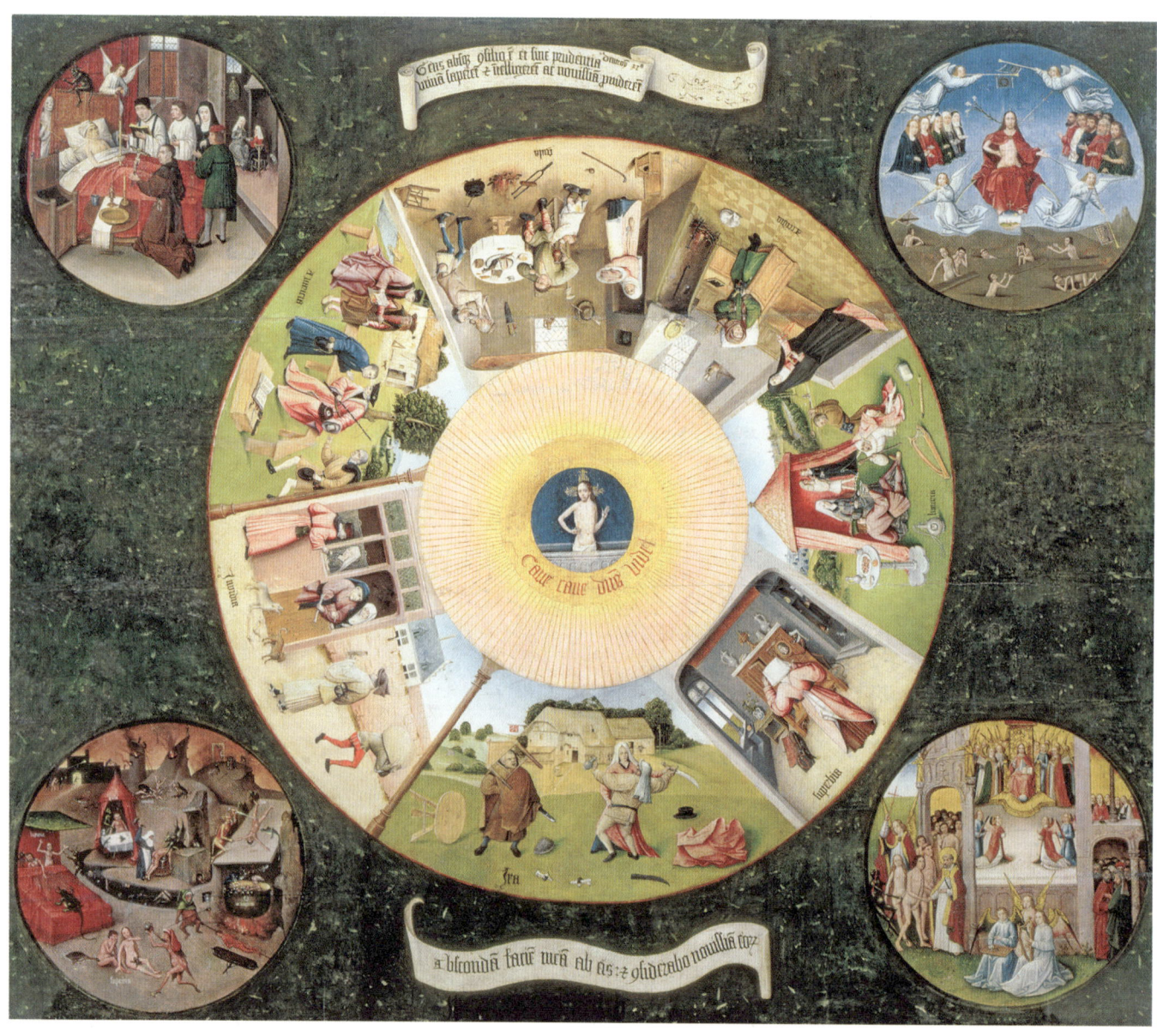

The Seven Deadly Sins and the Four Last Things, *c.* 1480, follower
Oil on panel, 120 x 150 cm (47¼ x 59 in)
• Museo Nacional del Prado, Madrid

Originally part of the Spanish Royal Collection of Philip II, this painting by an unknown artist possibly working in the van Aken/Bosch workshop in 's-Hertogenbosch is considered an exceptional work. Some depictions relate to other works by Bosch such as *Allegory of Intemperance/Gluttony* (*see* page 61), *Death and the Miser* (*see* page 61), and *The Last Judgement* (*see* pages 76–77).

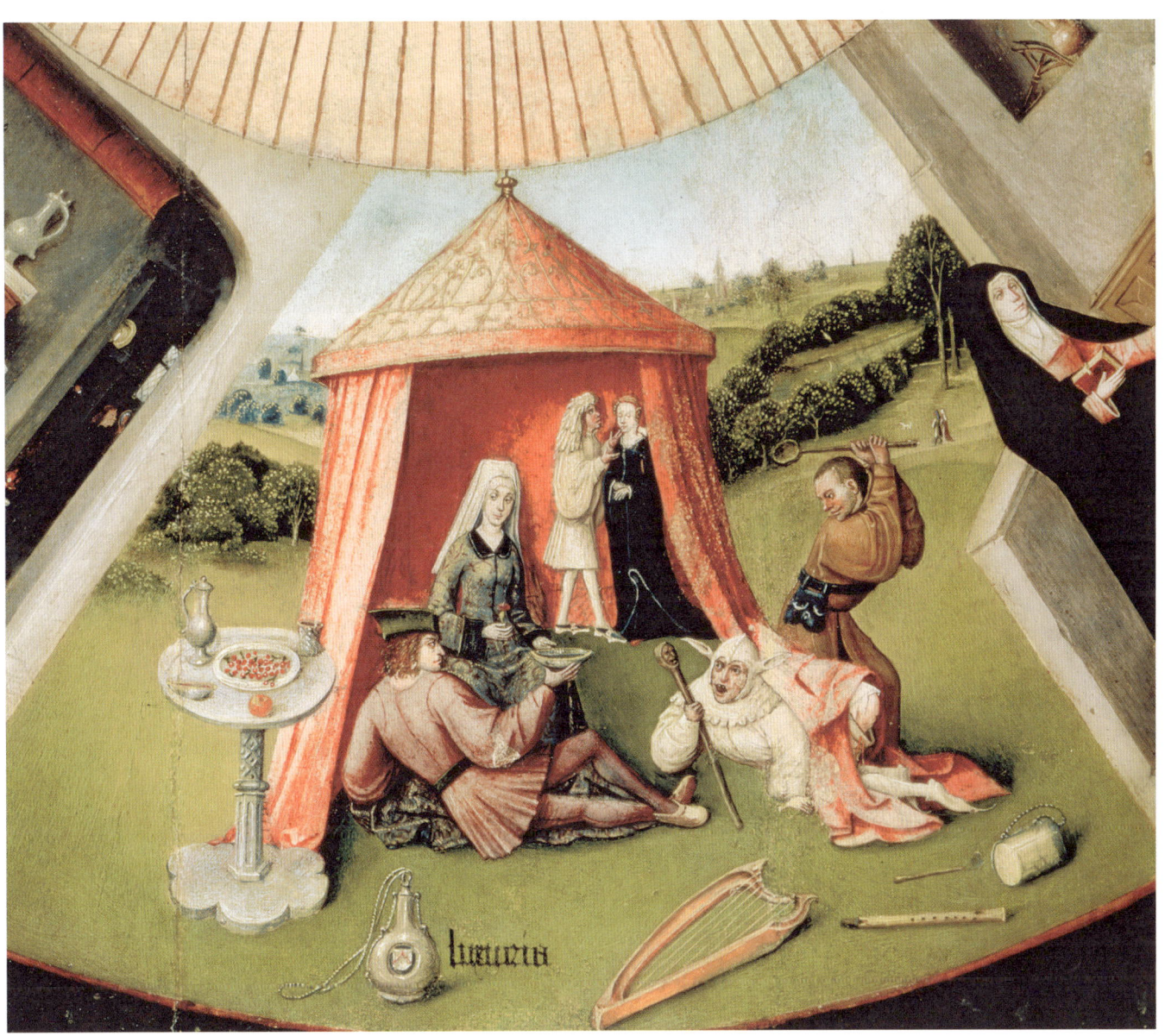

**The Seven Deadly Sins and the Four Last Things:
Lust (Luxury) (detail),** *c.* **1480**
Oil on panel • Museo Nacional del Prado, Madrid

The central roundel symbolizes the Eye of God, where Christ rises up from his earthly sarcophagus.
Around him, each sin is accompanied by its Latin name. Lust (Luxury) depicts two couples relishing
a life of luxury, entertainment, fine food and wine.

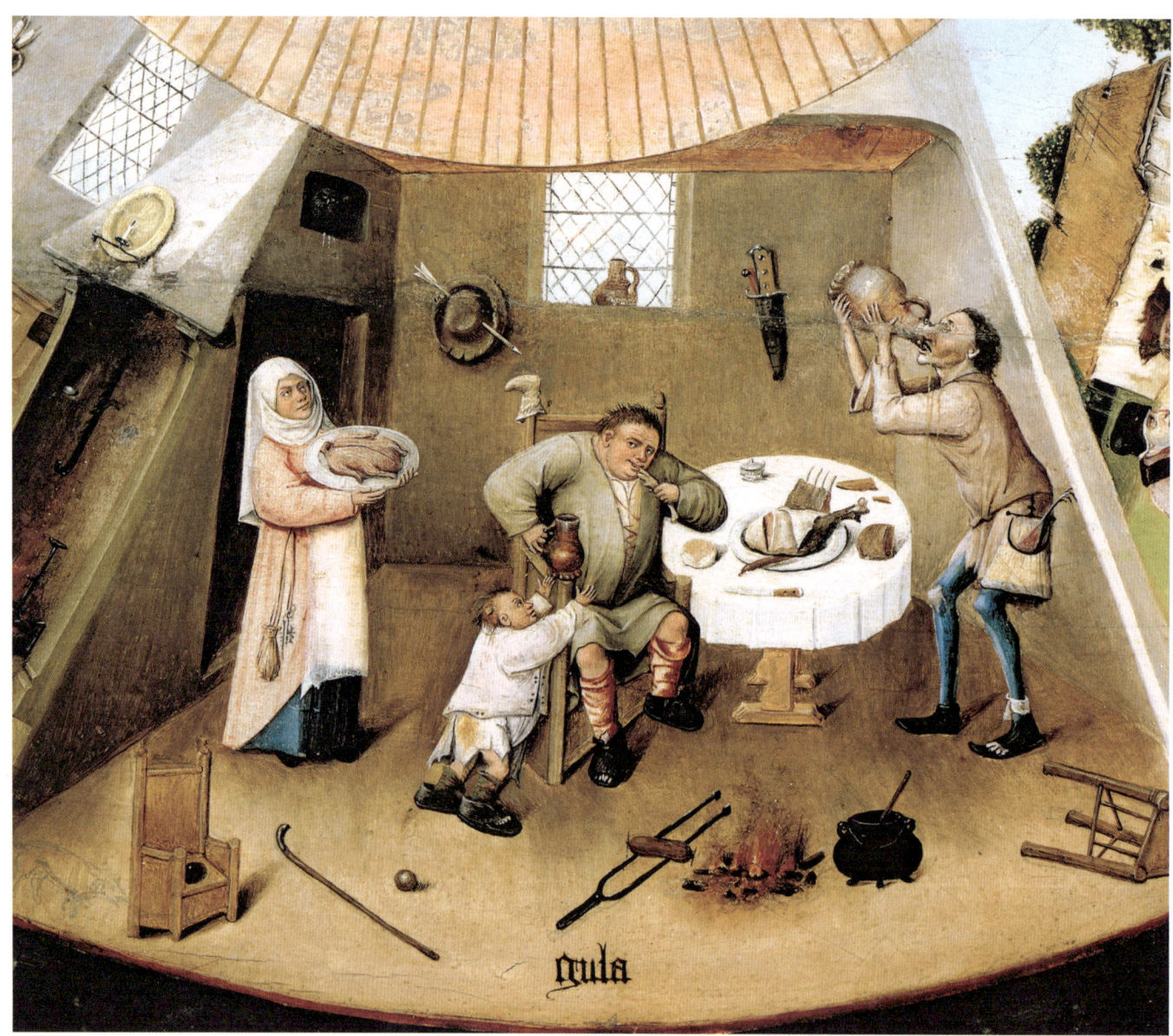

The Seven Deadly Sins and the Four Last Things: Gluttony (detail), *c.* 1480

Oil on panel • Museo Nacional del Prado, Madrid

The habit of overeating is the sin of Gluttony, illustrated in this domestic scene, where a woman proffers a generous plate of food to her large-gutted husband and overweight child. All present seem to relish in their excessive appetites.

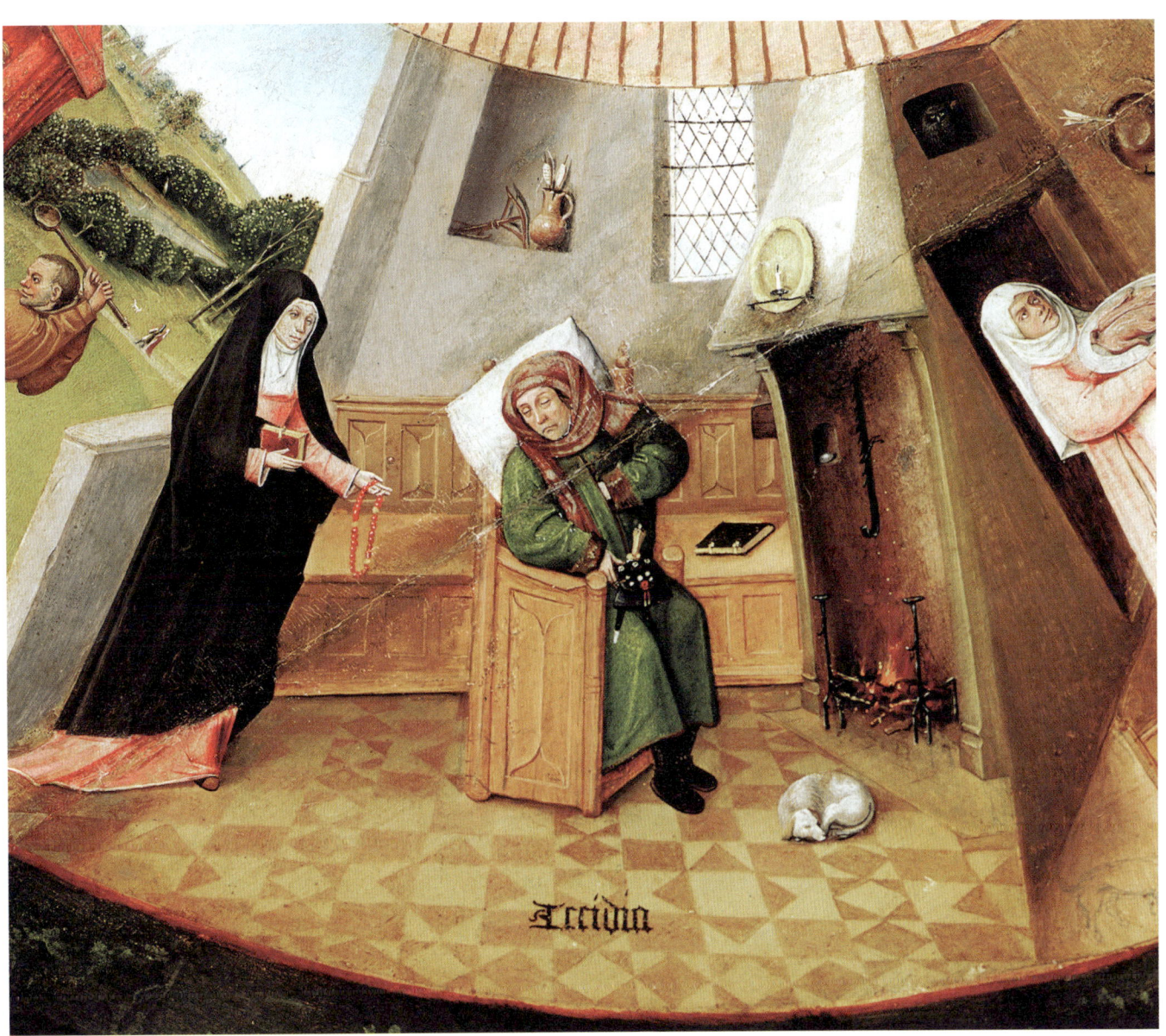

**The Seven Deadly Sins and the Four Last Things:
Sloth (detail), _c._ 1480**

Oil on panel • Museo Nacional del Prado, Madrid

Written on the roundel, around the all-seeing Eye of God, is _cave cave deus videt_
('Beware, Beware, God Sees'). Those who default to sin by idle, slothful behaviour
are represented by the man refusing to undertake his spiritual duties.

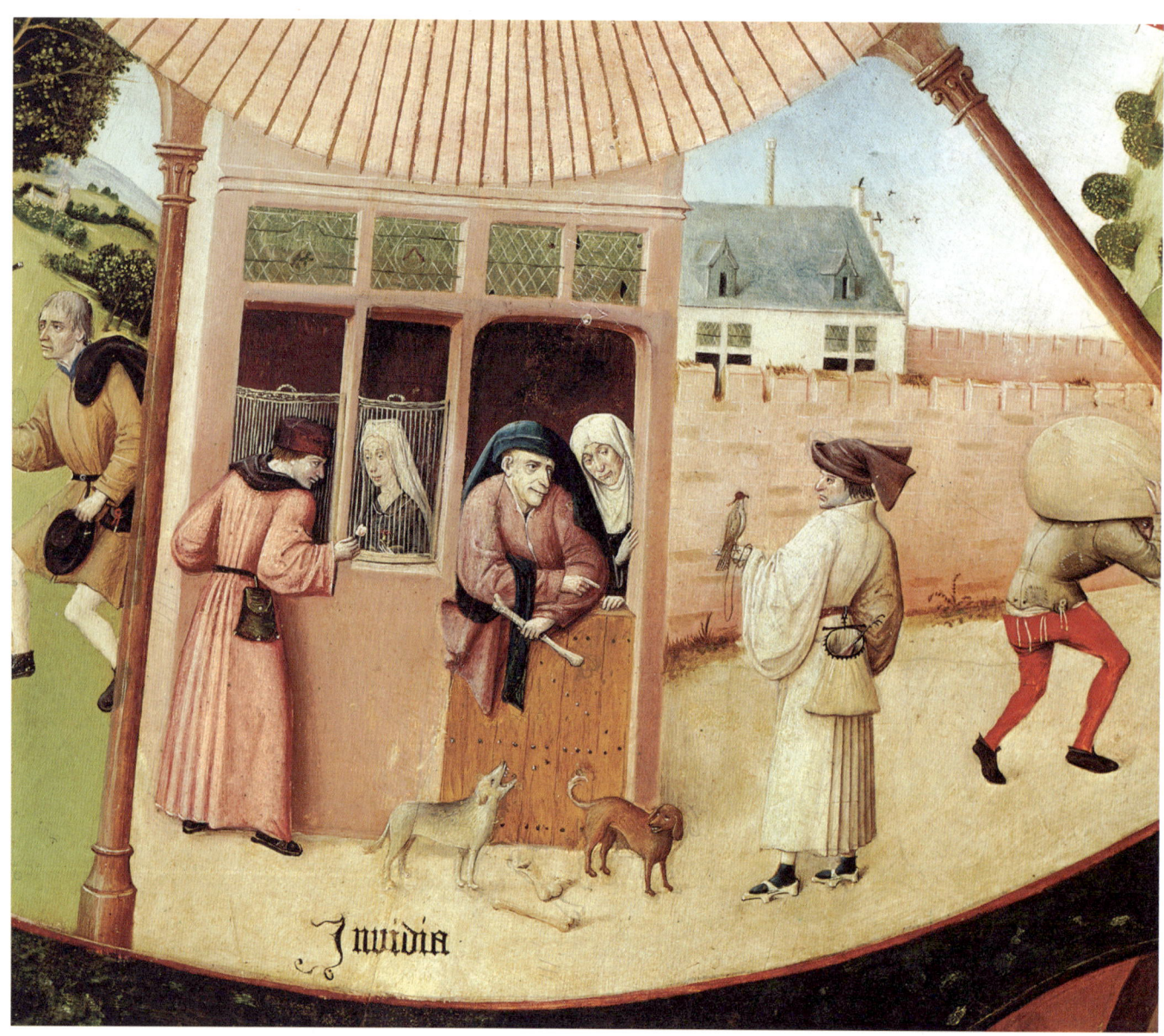

**The Seven Deadly Sins and the Four Last Things:
Envy (detail), *c.* 1480**

Oil on panel • Museo Nacional del Prado, Madrid

Coveting your neighbour's beautiful wife or a friend's falcon can lead to the sin of
Envy. The Seven Deadly Sins were not part of biblical teaching, but were part of the
early Church tradition.

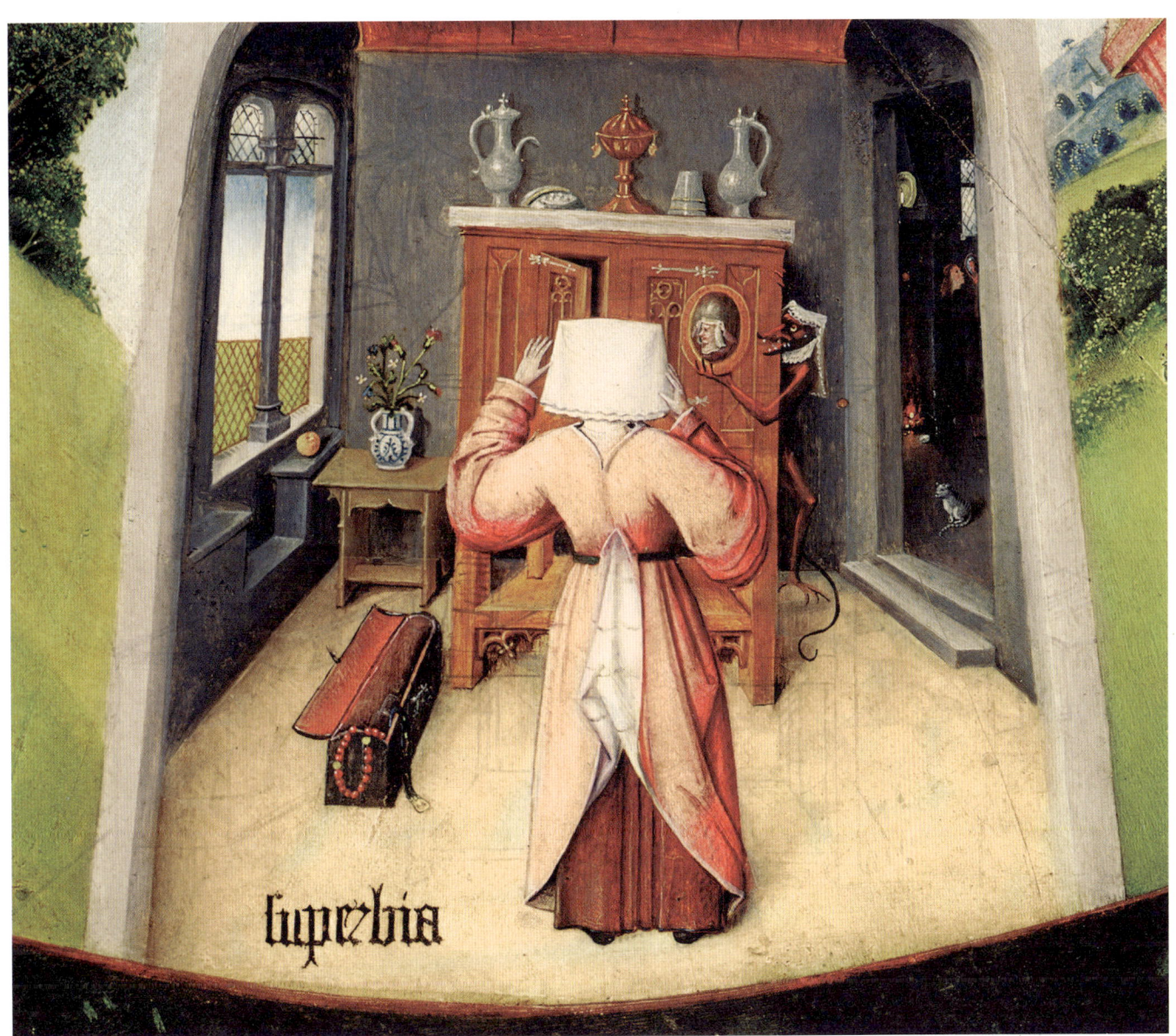

**The Seven Deadly Sins and the Four Last Things:
Pride (detail),** *c.* **1480**

Oil on panel • Museo Nacional del Prado, Madrid

Here, Pride is perhaps the most humorous depiction of all Seven Deadly Sins on this roundel. It reveals a woman gazing at herself in a new hat, unaware that a demon in a woman's headdress is holding up the mirror.

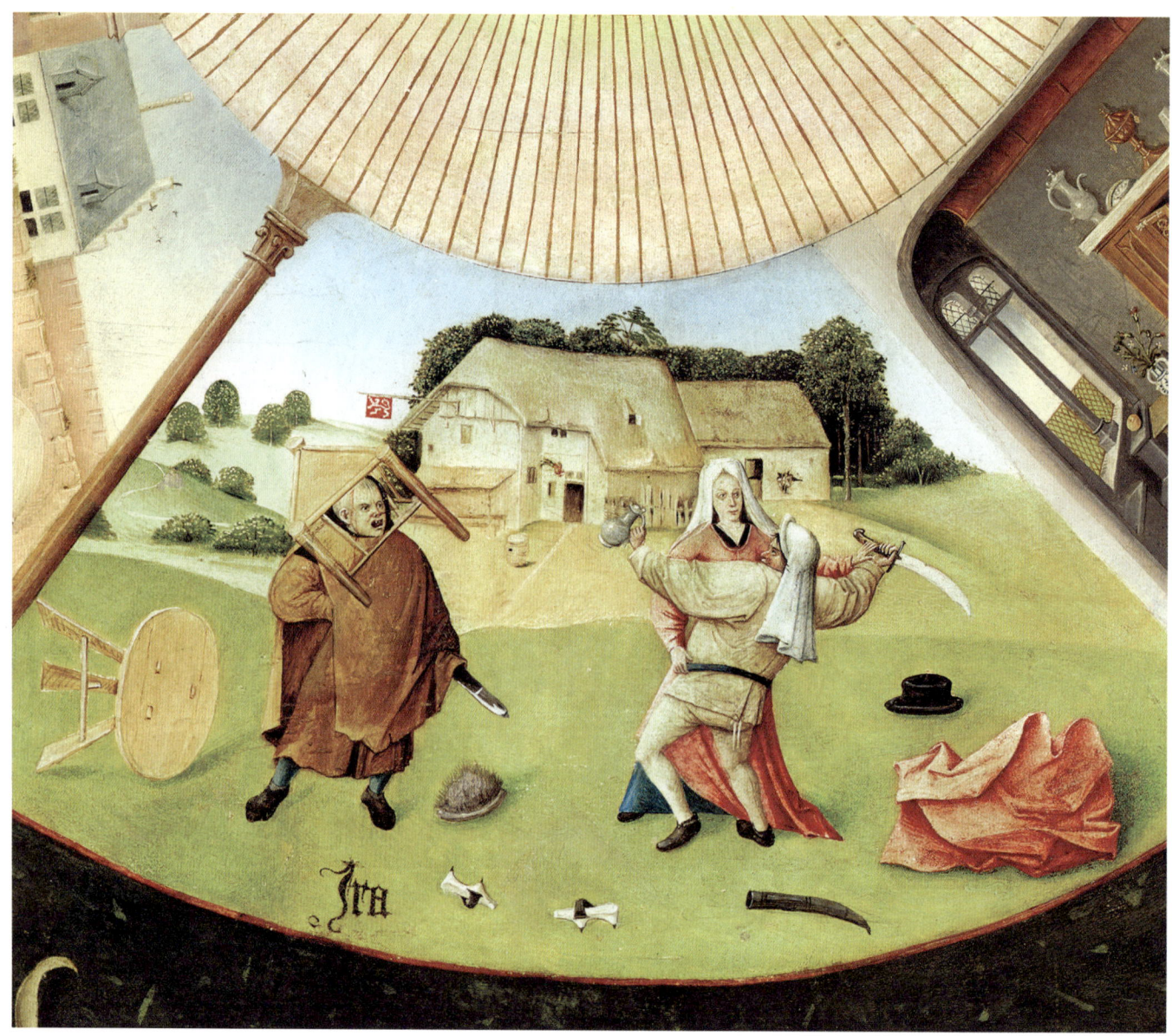

**The Seven Deadly Sins and the Four Last Things:
Wrath (Anger) (detail),** *c.* **1480**

Oil on panel • Museo Nacional del Prado, Madrid

A heated argument, possibly in the grounds of a country tavern, has led to furniture being thrown and Wrath (Anger) vented with a sword drawn, in a spat between two men. A woman tries to intervene without success.

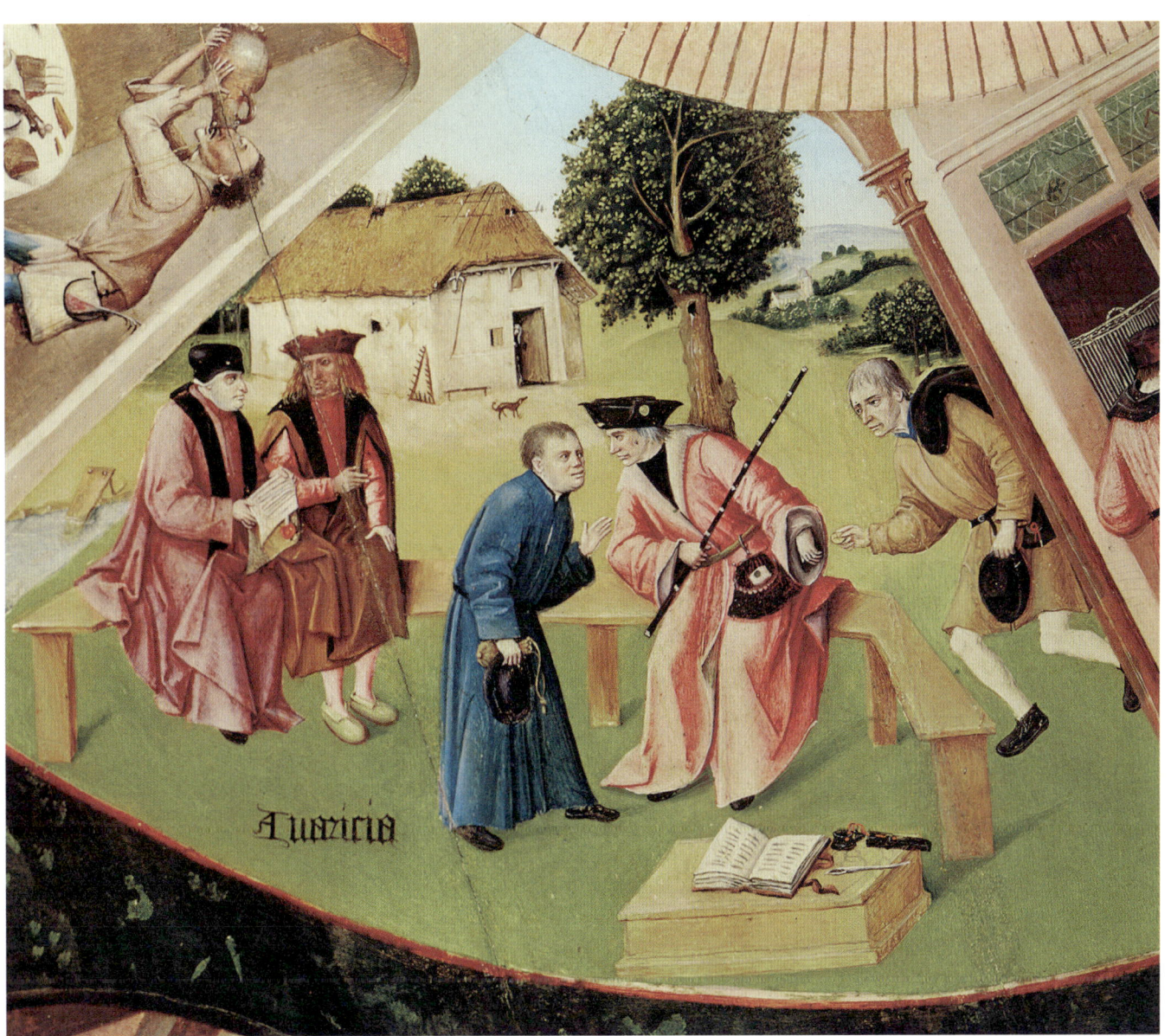

The Seven Deadly Sins and the Four Last Things: Greed (detail), *c.* **1480**

Oil on panel • Museo Nacional del Prado, Madrid

Greed, in a similar setting to Wrath, reveals a judge accepting a bribe, breaking the law of the sin of Avarice. Two quotations from Deuteronomy (32:20, 29) are written on ribbons above and below the roundel as warnings to sinners.

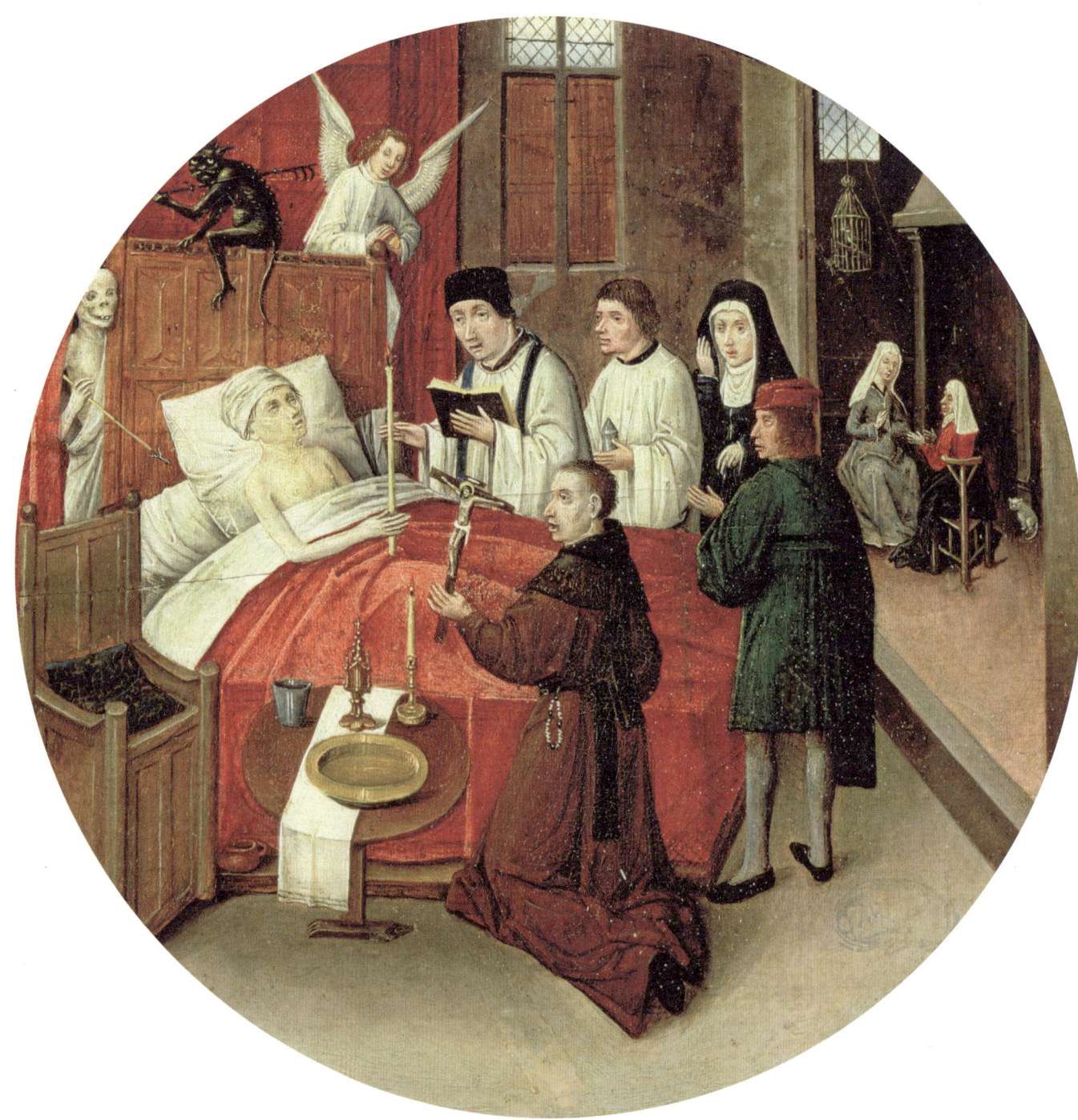

**The Seven Deadly Sins and the
Four Last Things: Death, *c.* 1480**
Oil on panel • Museo Nacional del Prado, Madrid

Depicting the first of the Four Last Things, Death waits to take the departing soul of a dying man who is surrounded by clergy and family. The scene is similar to the portrayal of *Death and the Miser* (*see* page 61).

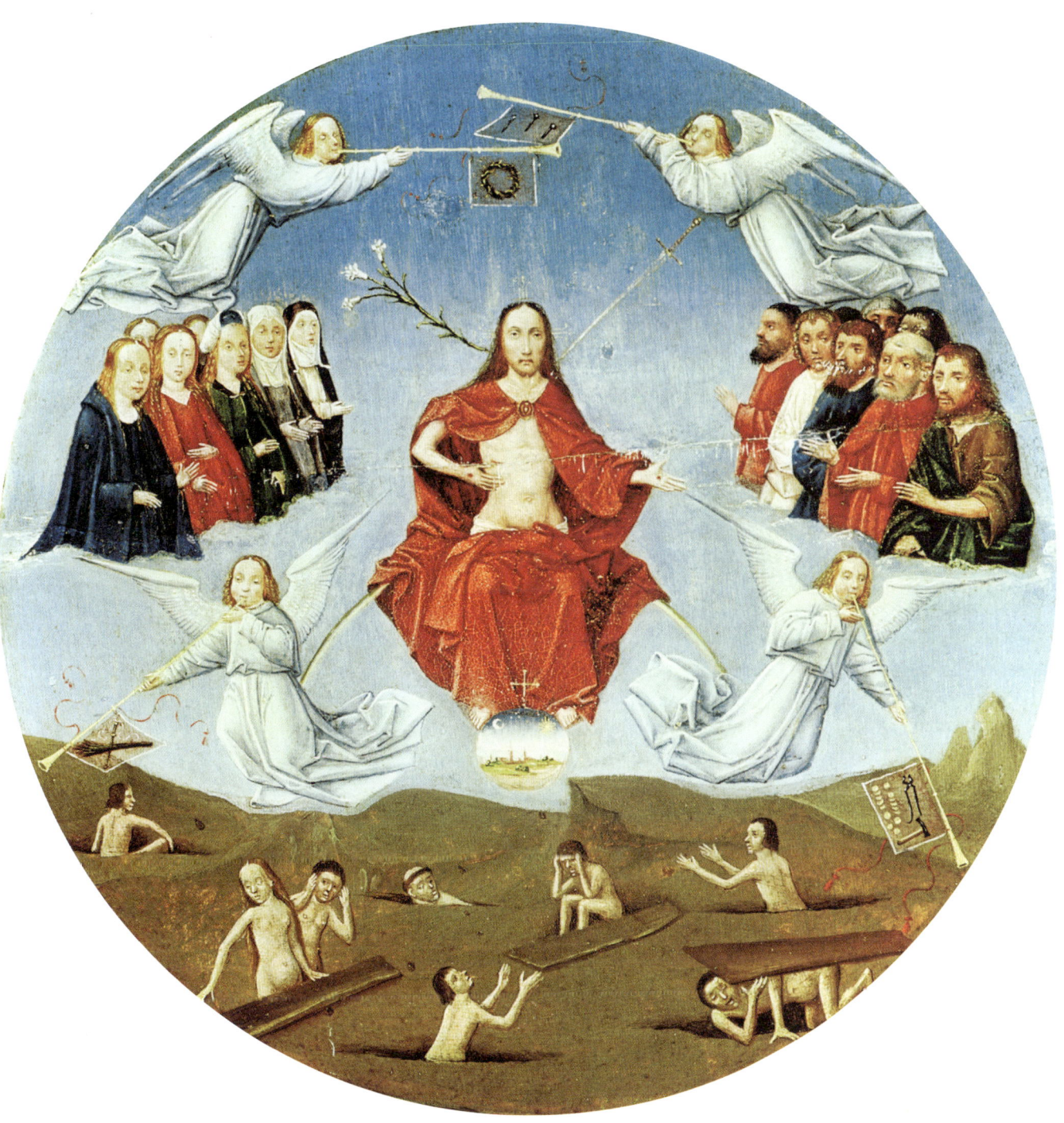

**The Seven Deadly Sins and the
Four Last Things: The Judgement,** *c.* **1480**
Oil on panel • Museo Nacional del Prado, Madrid

The second of the Four Last Things, Judgement finds the souls of men rising from
burial coffins. The depiction of Christ ascended is found in *The Garden of Earthly
Delights* (*see* pages 86–89) and *The Last Judgement* in Bruges (*see* pages 76–77).

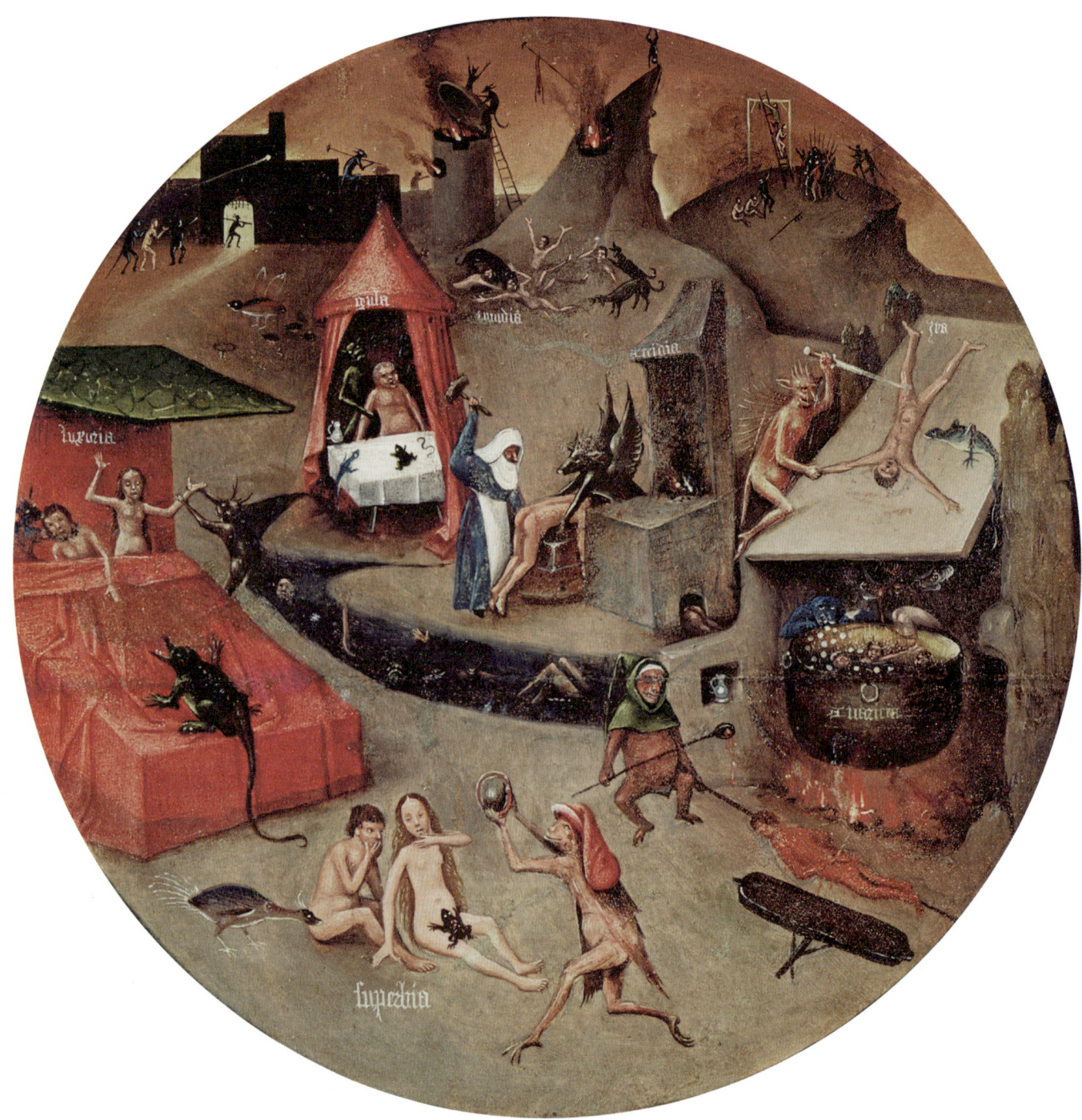

**The Seven Deadly Sins and the
Four Last Things: Hell, *c.* 1480**

Oil on panel • Museo Nacional del Prado, Madrid

Burning, boiling, mutilation, beatings and torture by monstrous otherworldly
creatures await the unfortunate souls who are sent to Hell as punishment for their
participation in the Seven Deadly Sins.

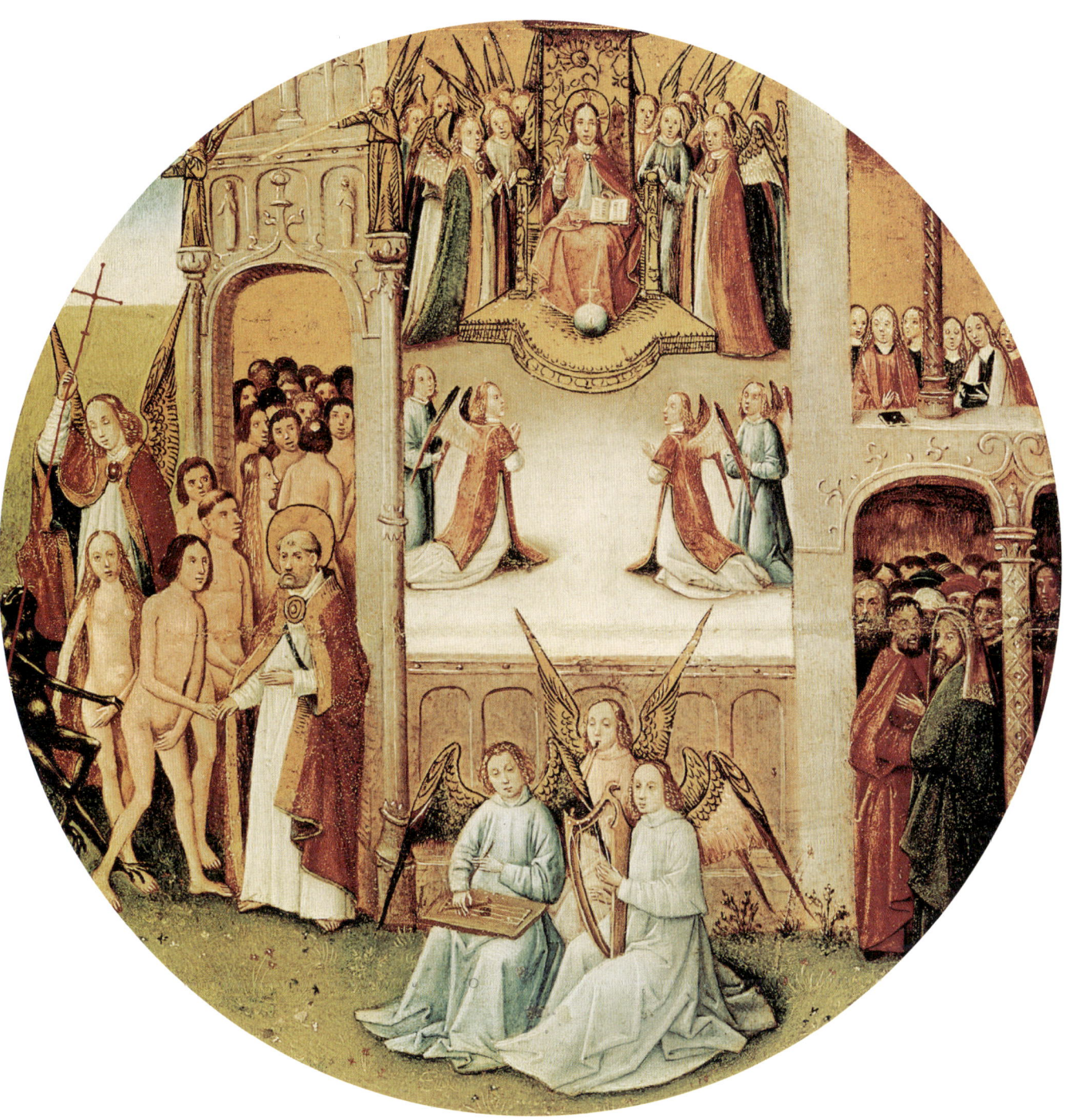

**The Seven Deadly Sins and the
Four Last Things: Paradise,** *c.* **1480**

Oil on panel • Museo Nacional del Prado, Madrid

In an architectural setting, Paradise awaits those who reject the Seven Deadly Sins and the temptation of evil. The artist depicts the hierarchy of Christ and his followers, serenaded by angelic musicians, waiting to receive the godly souls.

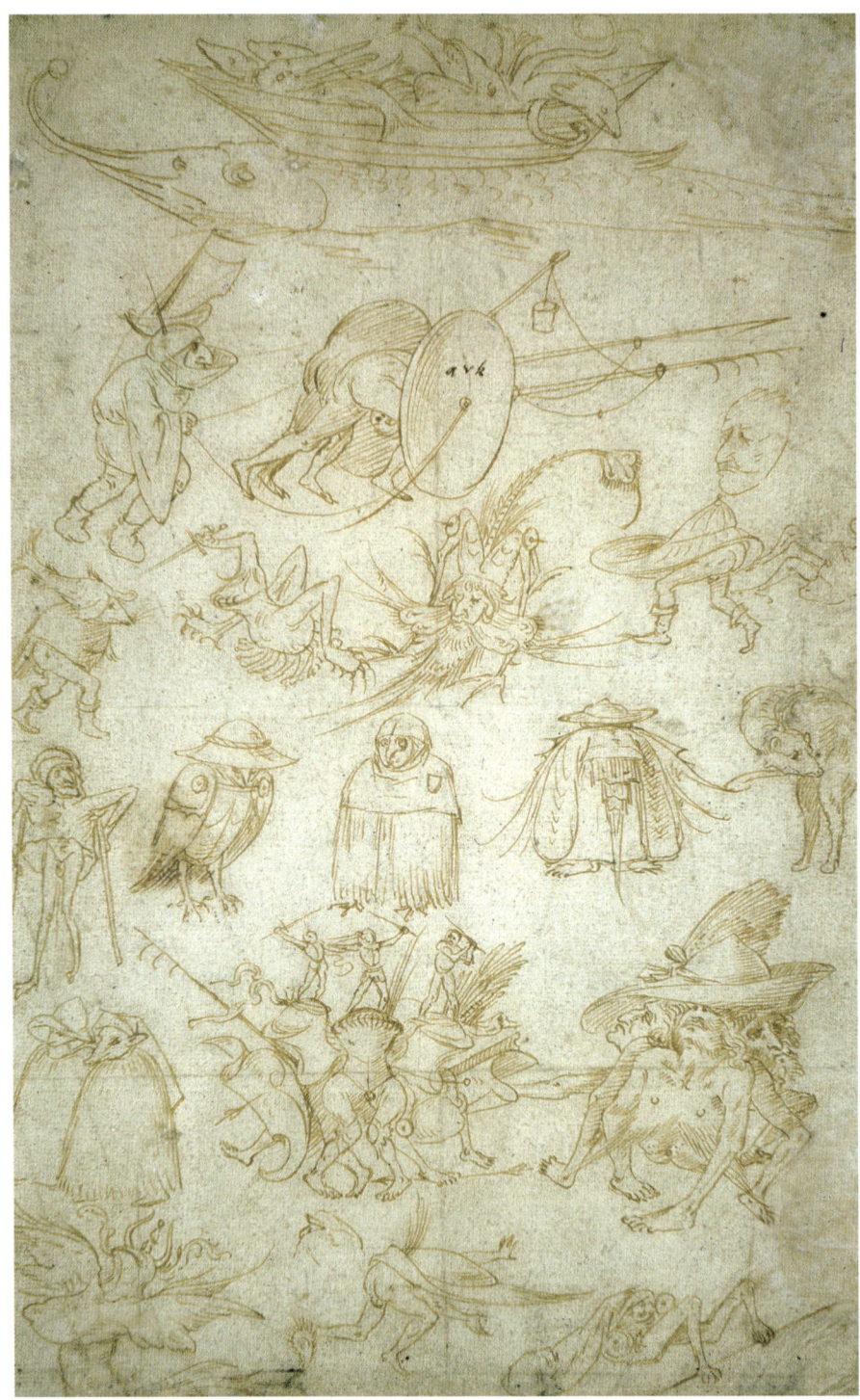

Grotesque Studies, *c.* 1500
Pen and bistre on paper, 31.7 x 20.9 cm (12½ x 8¼ in)
• Ashmolean Museum, University of Oxford, Oxford

A sheet of drawings, grotesque studies of otherworldly birds, animals and insects, plus many-bodied half-men, lethal machines and a hat on legs lead up to a boat carrying sprawling fish. Versions of many of these made it on to the painted panels of Bosch's *oeuvre*.

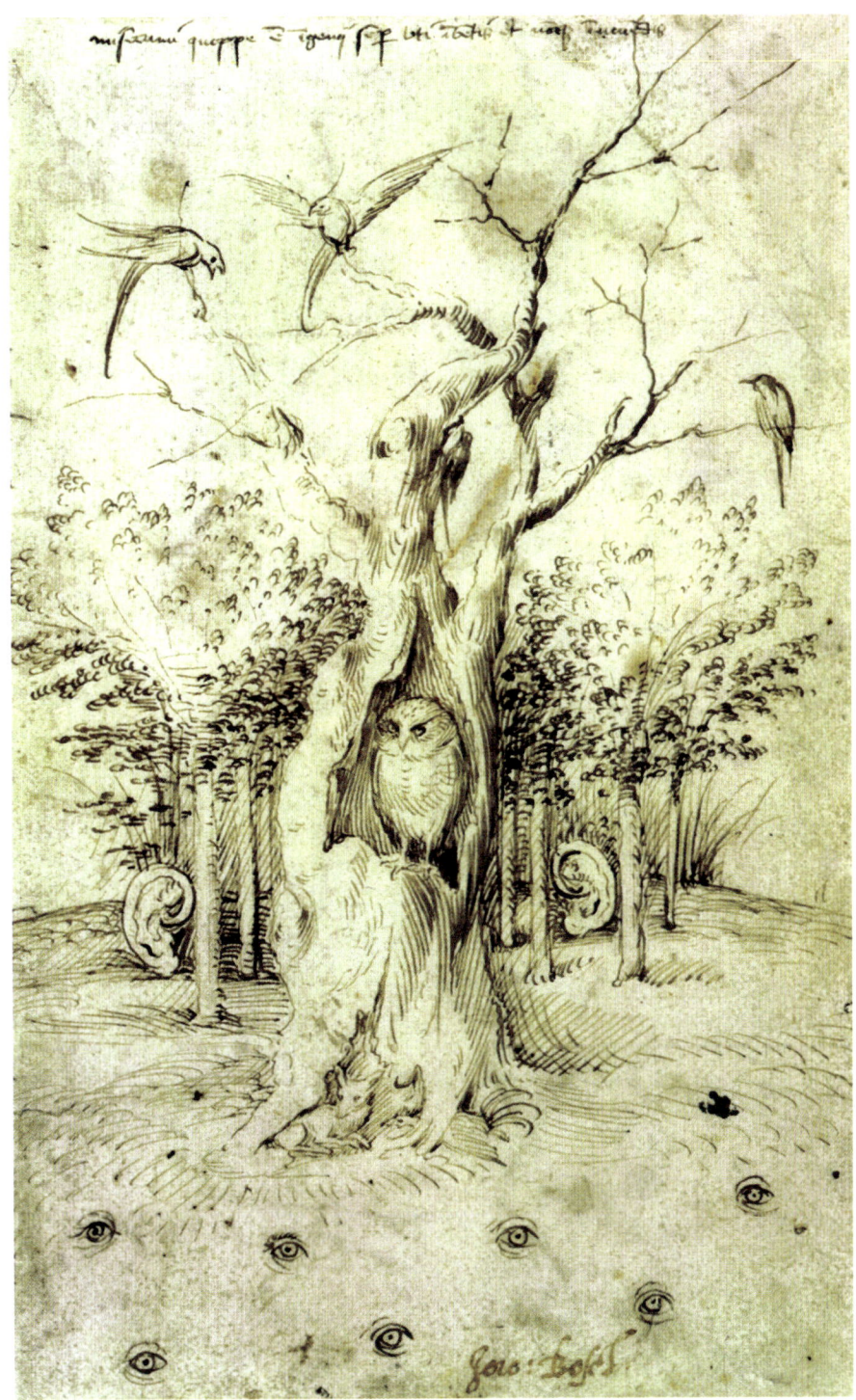

The Wood Has Ears, The Field Has Eyes, *c.* **1500**
Pen and ink on paper, 20.2 x 12.7 cm (8 x 5 in)
• Kupferstichkabinett, Berlin

A watchful owl looks out from a tree hollow surrounded by daytime birds. At the tree's base a fox and a cock sit together. Night and day meet in the forest, where all-seeing eyes watch, and ears listen.

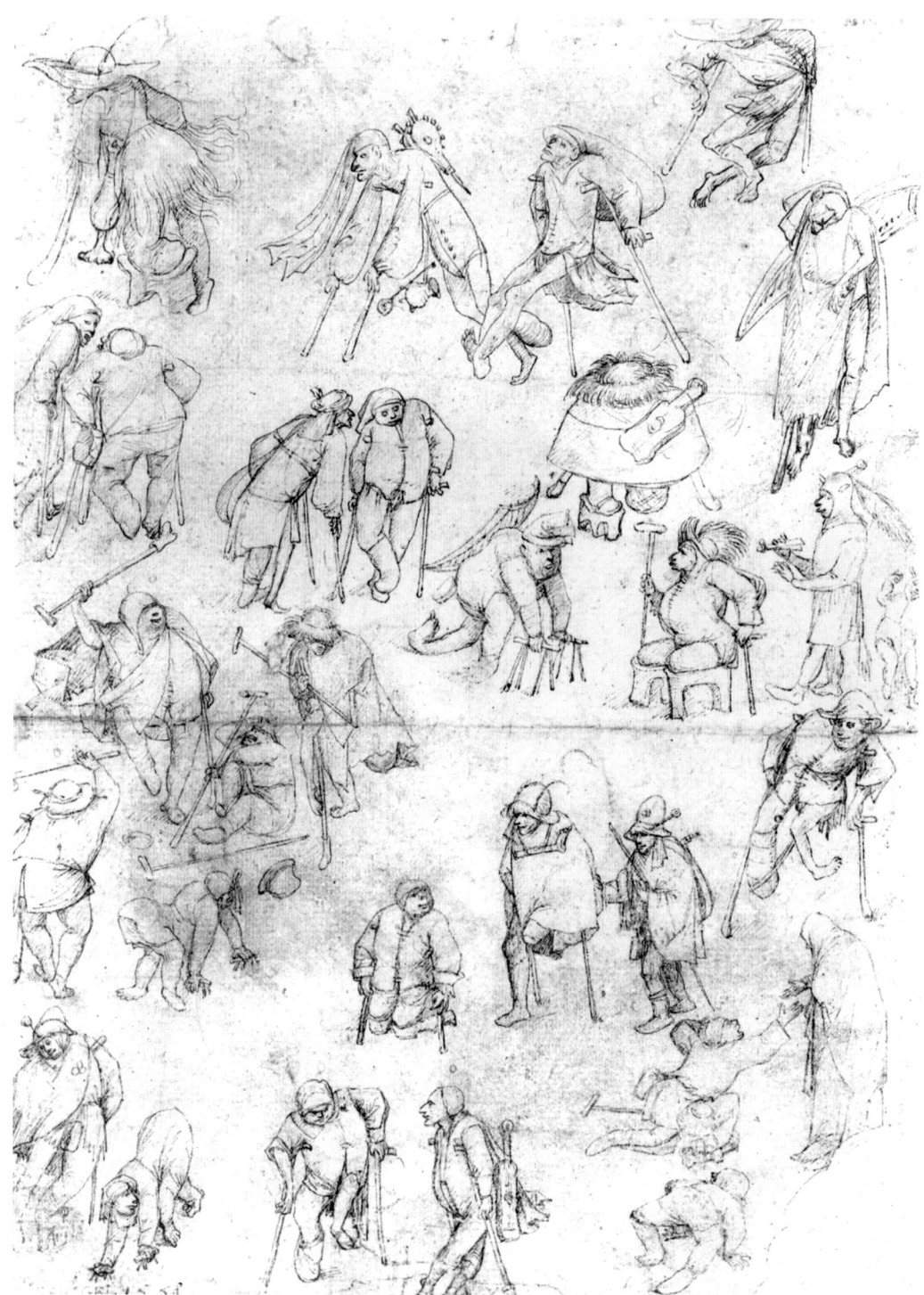

Beggars, *c.* 1500
Pencil on paper, 28.5 x 20.5 cm (11¼ x 8 in)
• Musées Royaux des Beaux-Arts de Belgique, Brussels

A sheet of sketches of beggars, some obviously crippled, inform the myriad of figures, from mendicants to thieves and deceivers, seen in Bosch's paintings. The crush of bodies on the paper, one of several sketch sheets, suggests rapid sketching from life.

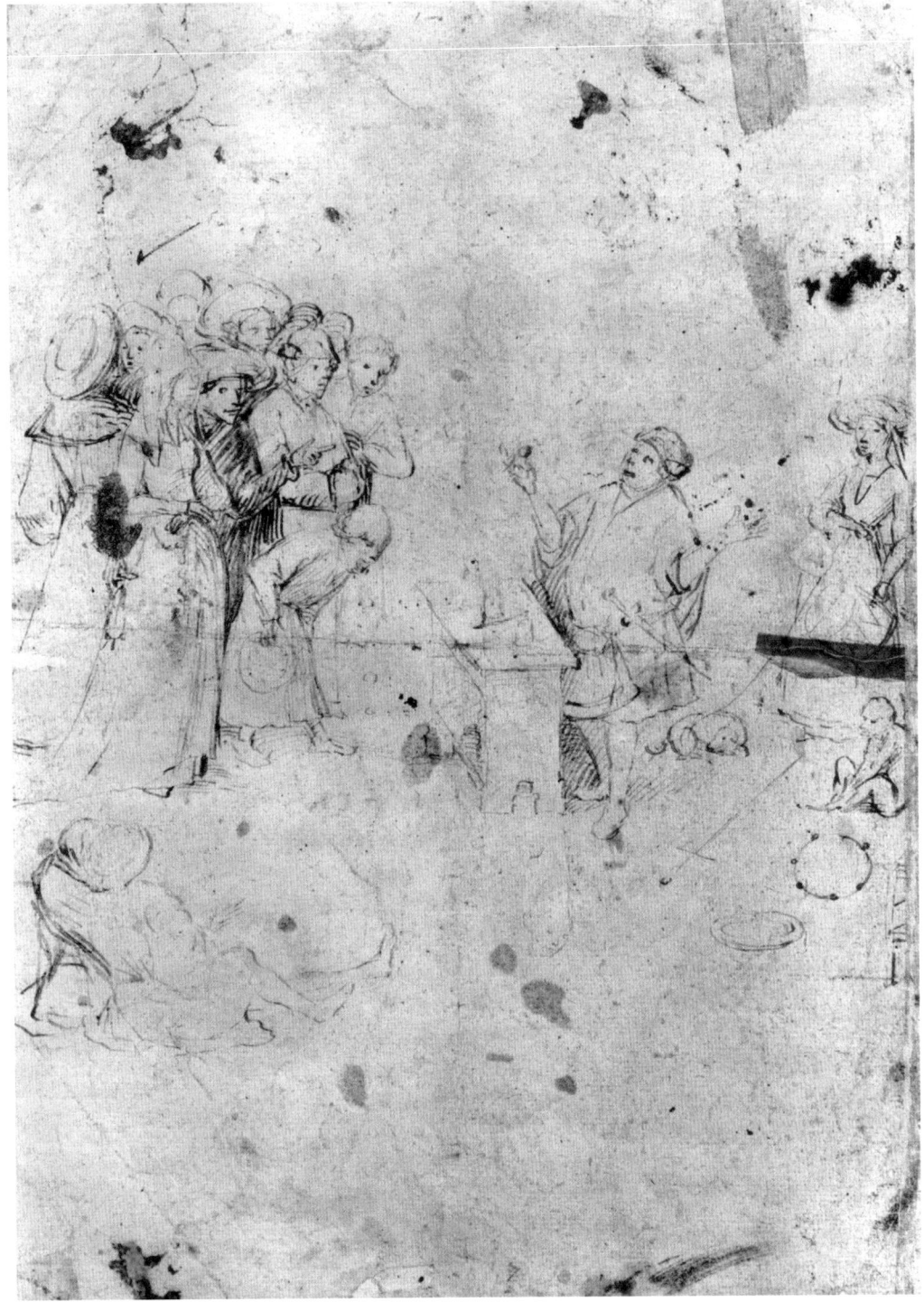

The Conjuror, *c.* 1500
Pen and ink on paper
• Louvre (Cabinet de dessins), Paris

Considered a copy of an original drawing by Bosch, with elements of his lost painting *The Conjuror*. On the left, an animated crowd gathers close to the conjuror, seated on the right and about to trick them.

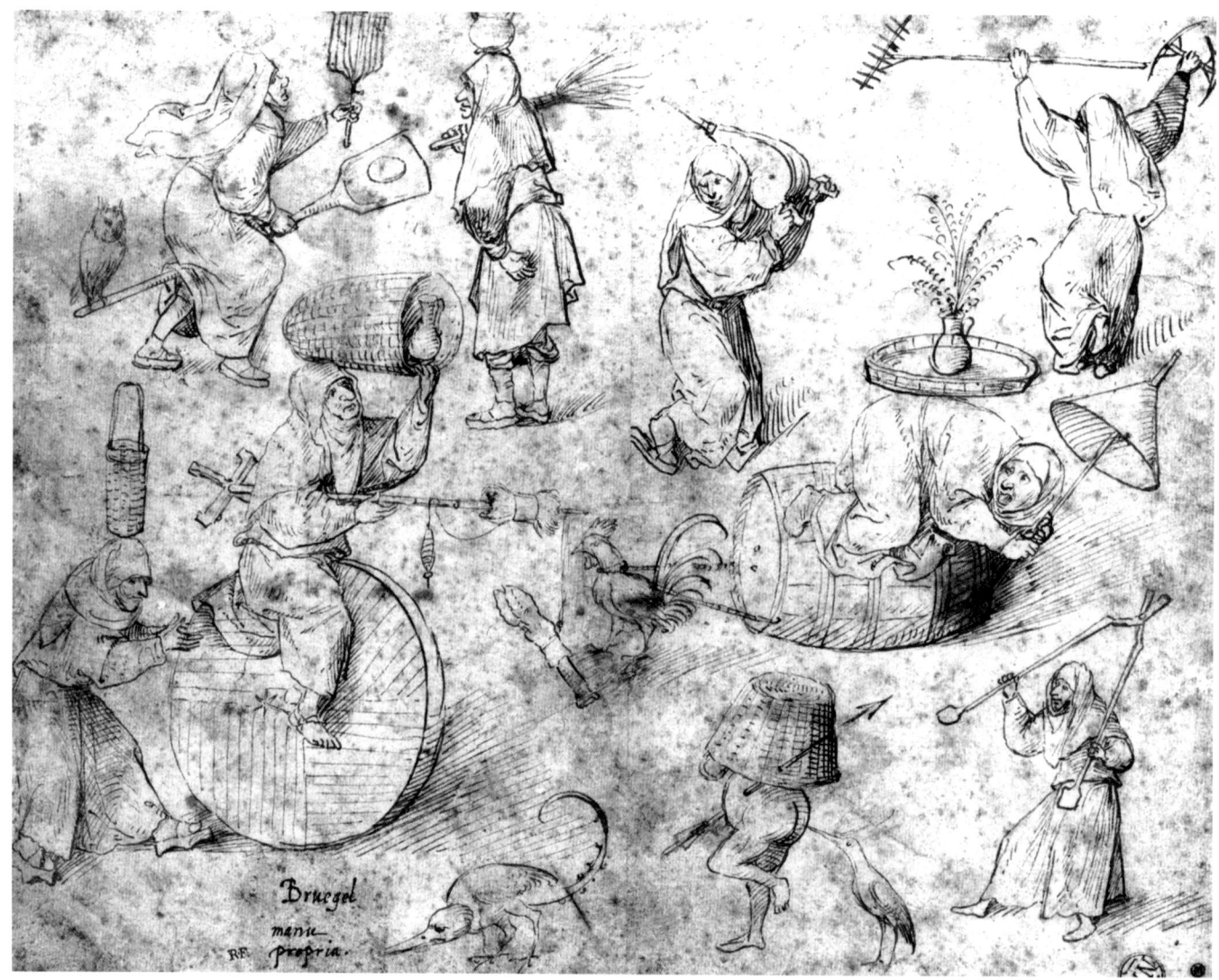

Witches, c. 1500
Pen and ink on paper, 20.3 x 26.4 cm (8 x 10⅓ in)
• Louvre (Cabinet de dessins), Paris

In a riotous page of drawings of women, believed to be witches, the artist depicts them as if they are intoxicated, running amok with agricultural implements, or riding a wheel whilst holding a beehive. Mischievous depictions unfold on the page.

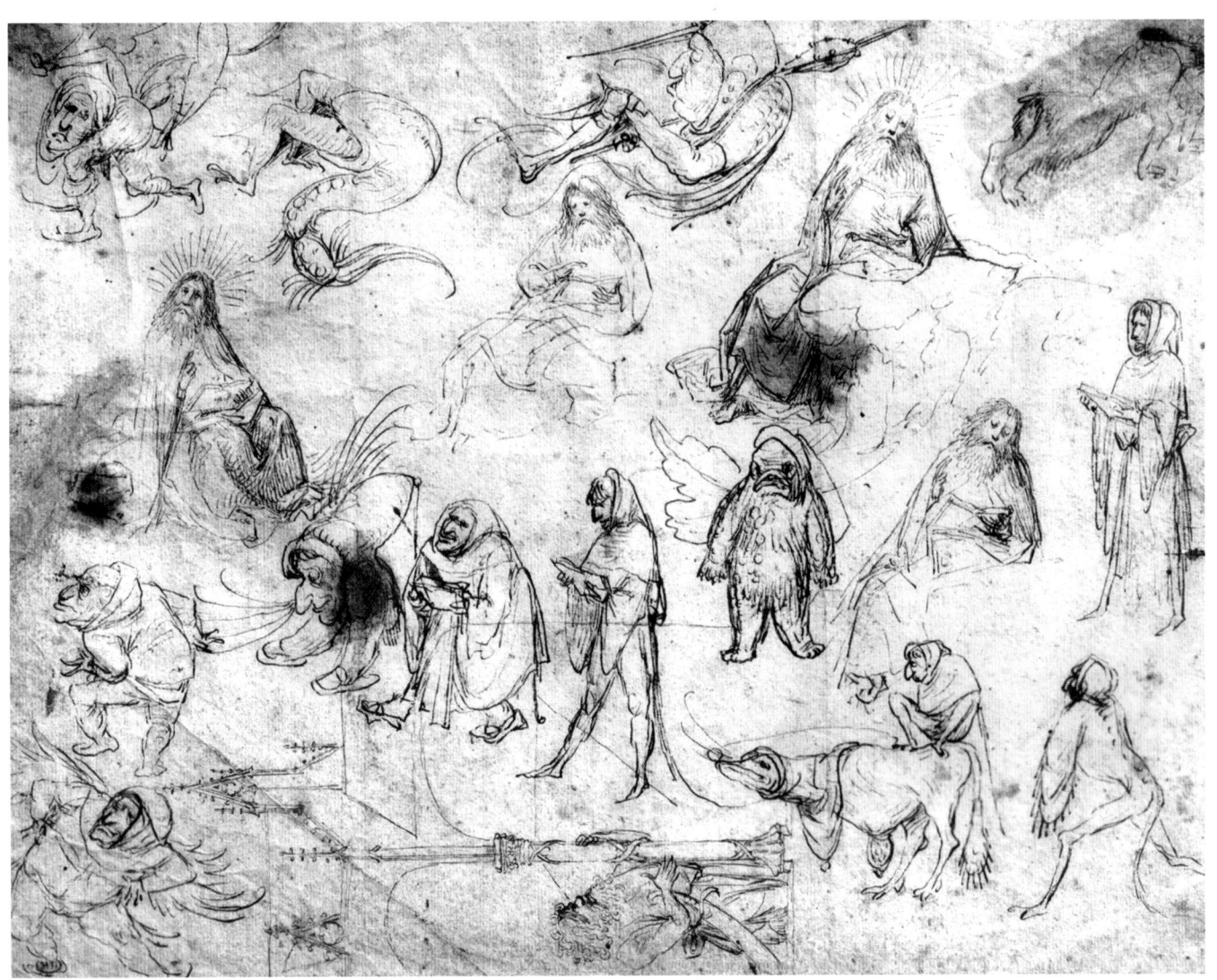

The Temptation of St Anthony, *c.* 1500
Pen and ink on paper • Louvre (Cabinet de dessins), Paris

Bosch frequently depicted the hermit St Anthony, seen refusing the many material temptations that crossed his righteous path. This page of sketches relates to paintings of the saint. On the reverse are sketches of monstrous animals.

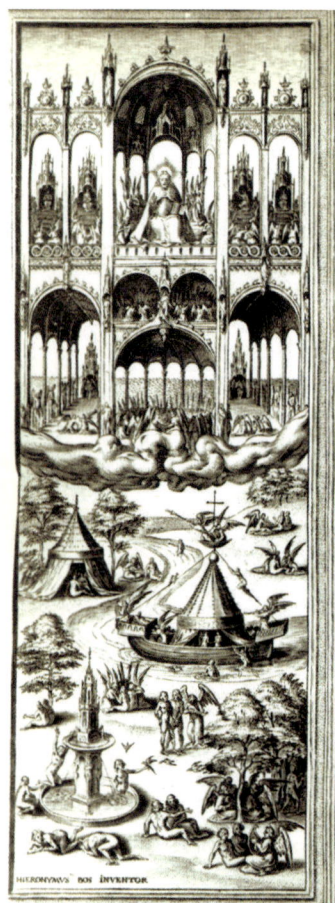
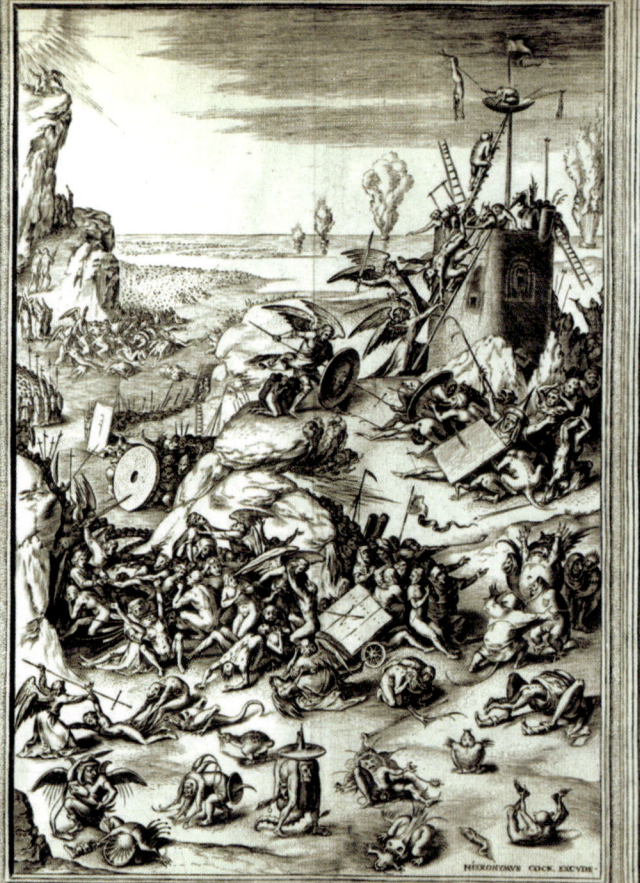
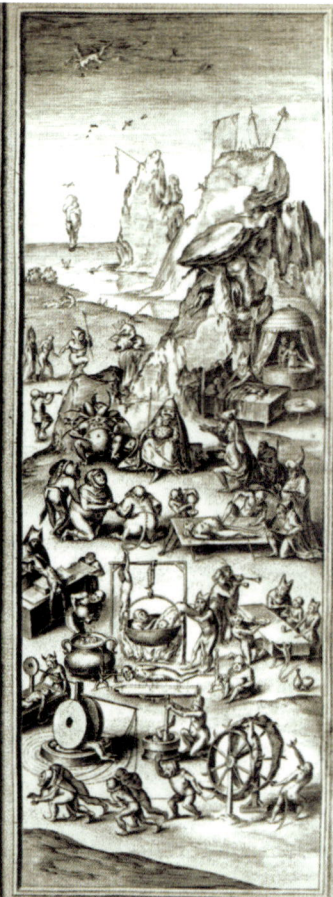

The Last Judgement, *c.* 1500, after Bosch
Engraving and etching, 33 x 48 cm (13 x 19 in)
• The Israel Museum, Jerusalem

The Last Judgement is an engraving and etching after Bosch, by a follower. It was engraved by Cornelis Cort (1533–78) and published by Antwerp-born Hieronymus Cock, who sold commercial prints of works by Netherlandish artists, including Bosch and his followers.

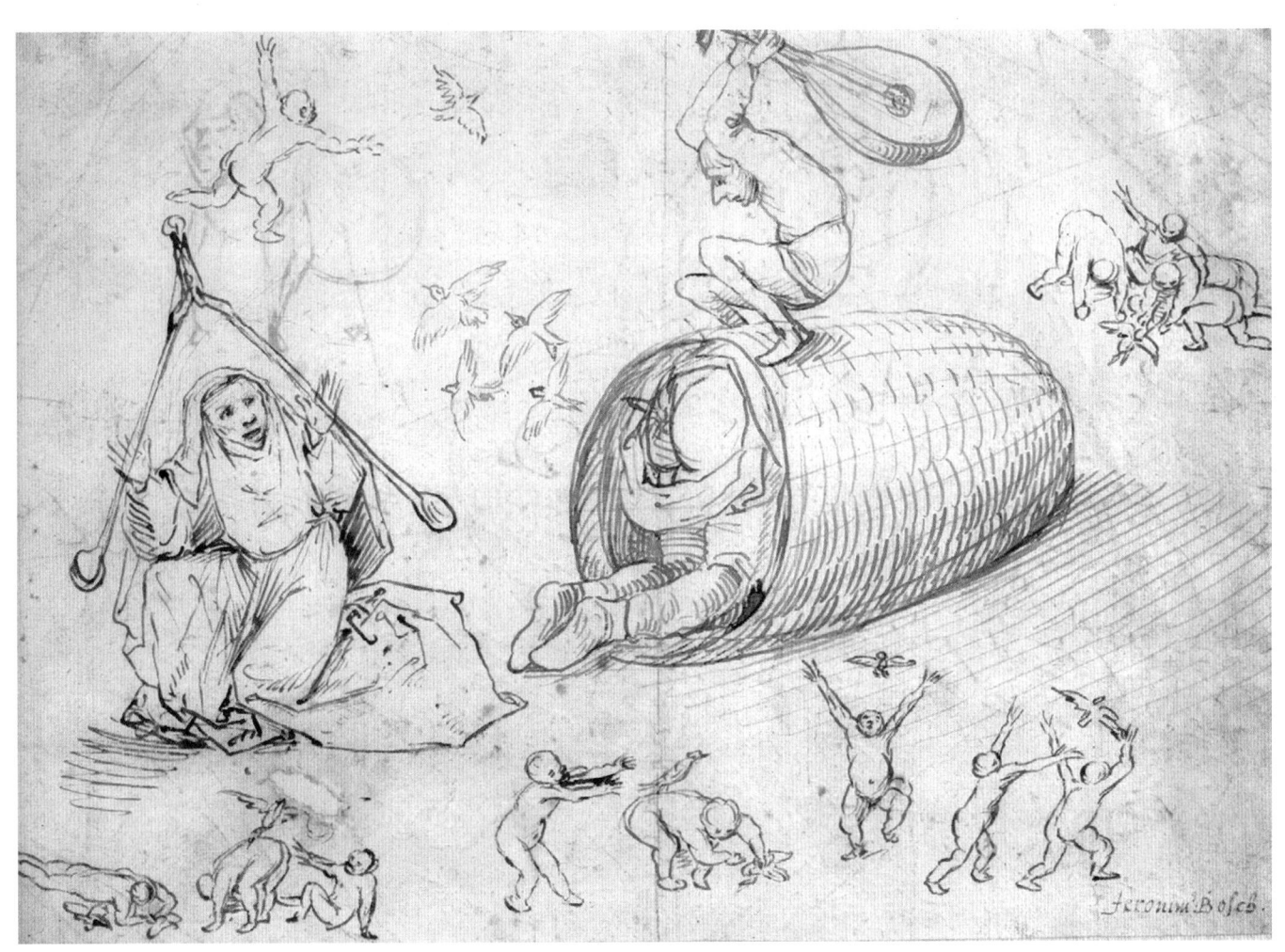

Beehive and Witches, c. 1500
Pen and iron gall ink and wash on paper, 19.2 x 27 cm (7⅔ x 10⅔ in)
• Graphisch Sammlung, Albertina, Vienna

The drawing of *Beehive and Witches* informs a small part of the content of *The Hermit Saints* triptych (*see* pages 78–79). It can be seen as a decorative element of St Jerome's broken throne.

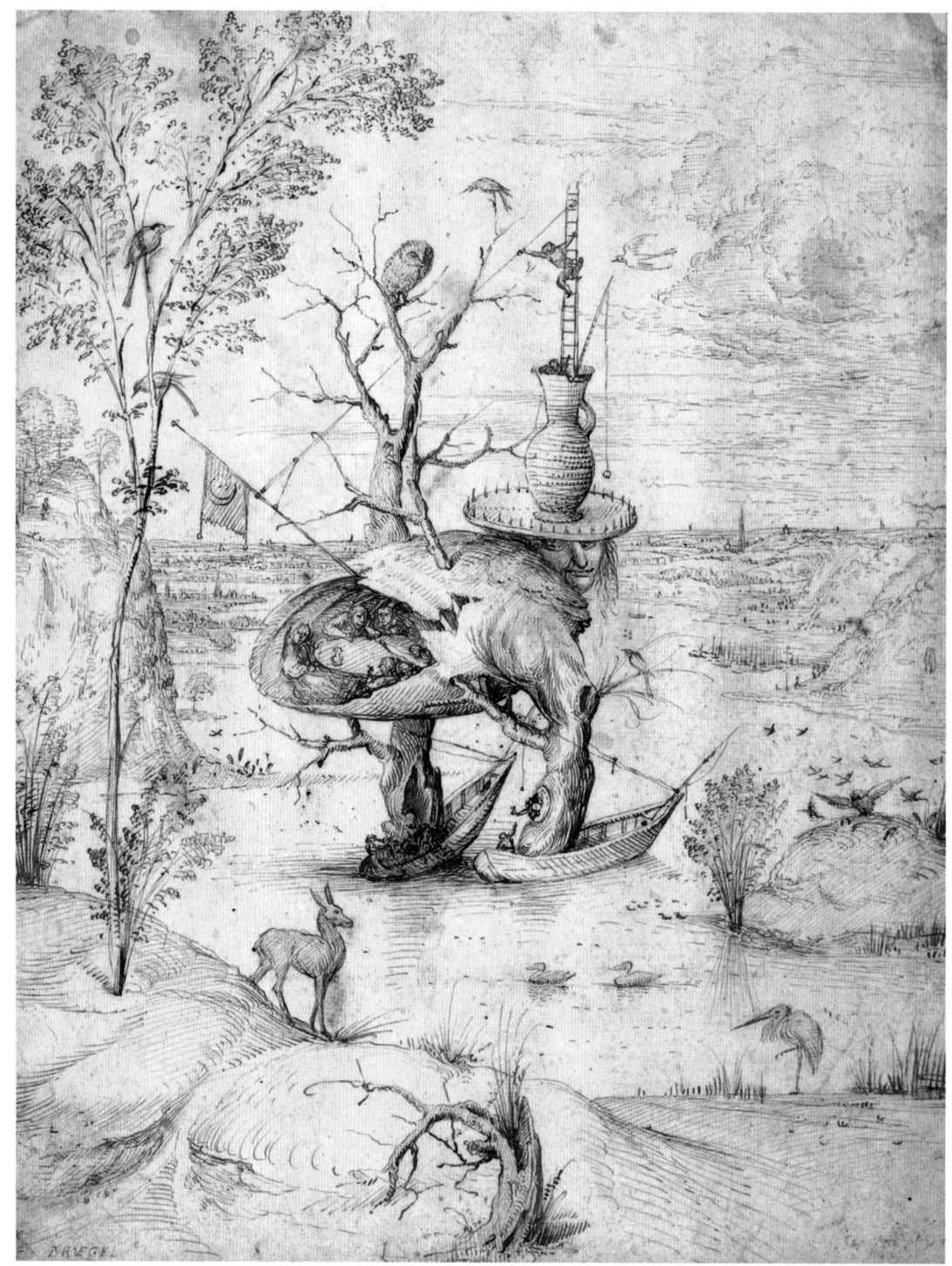

The Tree-Man *c.* **1505**
Pen and brown ink on paper
• Graphisch Sammlung, Albertina, Vienna

The Tree-Man informs the depiction of the ghostly creature in the right panel that demonstrates Hell in *The Garden of Earthly Delights* (*see* pages 86–89). A similar creature appears in Bosch's *Infernal Landscape* drawing (*see* page 30).

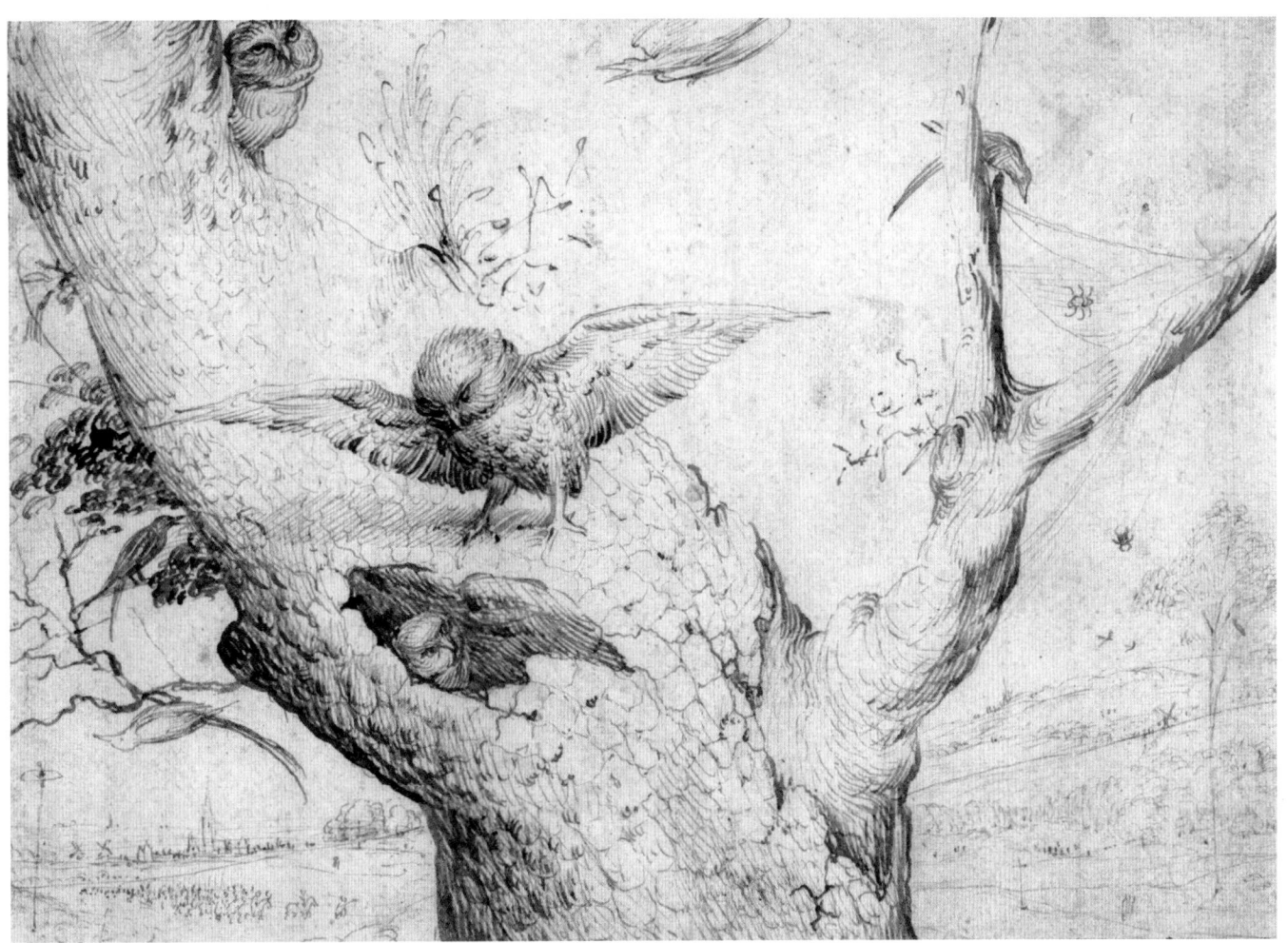

The Owl's Nest, *c.* 1505–16
Pen and brown ink on paper, 14.1 x 19.7 cm (5½ x 7¾ in)
• Museum Boijmans van Beuningen, Rotterdam

Together with *The Wood Has Ears, The Field Has Eyes* (Kupferstichkabinett, Berlin), *The Owl's Nest* reveals Bosch's superb draughtsmanship and close observation of nesting owls. The nocturnal birds appear in many of his paintings.

Indexes

Index of Works

General Index

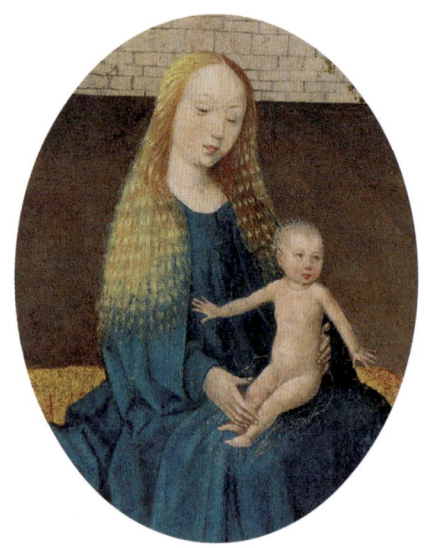

Masterpieces of Art
FLAME TREE PUBLISHING
A new series of carefully curated print and digital books covering the world's greatest art, artists and art movements.